Law and Society
Recent Scholarship

Edited by Melvin I. Urofsky

A Series from LFB Scholarly

Regulatory Takings and the Environment

The Impact of Property Rights Litigation

Darren Botello-Samson

LFB Scholarly Publishing LLC
El Paso 2010

Library of Congress Cataloging-in-Publication Data

Botello-Samson, Darren.
Regulatory takings and the environment : the impact of property rights litigation / Darren Botello-Samson.
p. cm. -- (Law & society : recent scholarship)
Includes bibliographical references and index.
ISBN 978-1-59332-400-1 (hardcover : alk. paper)
1. Eminent domain--United States. 2. Right of property--United States. 3.
Environmental law--United States. I. Title.
KF5599.B68 2010
343.73'0252--dc22
2010014570

ISBN 978-1-59332-400-1

Printed on acid-free 250-year-life paper.

Manufactured in the United States of America.

Table of Contents

Acknowledgements

I am indebted to several individuals, who have contributed in a number of ways to the completion of this book. First, I would like to thank those people that have contributed comments and advice on the overall content of this book. In particular, I would like to thank Susan Lawrence, Milton Heumann, Bonnie McCay, and Lisa Miller, all from Rutgers University, for their valuable advice and direction.

Additionally, I would like to thank those who have made more specific, but equally valuable contributions to this book. Special thanks go to Jing Chen, who provided helpful assistance with STATA software and whose knowledge of cross-sectional time-series research proved invaluable. I would also like to thank Laura Hatcher of Southern Illinois University – Carbondale and Wayne McIntosh of the University of Maryland, who provided insightful comments on sections of this book, which were included in an additional project. I also extend thanks to Anil Lal of Pittsburg State University for his assistance with budget data. Of course, a great deal of thanks are also extended to the personnel in the U.S. Fish and Wildlife Service, the U.S. Office of Surface Mining, and various state environmental and natural resources agencies, who made time in their busy schedules to provide insightful and candid interviews.

Finally, special thanks go to my wife, Anita, whose love and support made this book possible.

Some components of this book have been published as articles in the *Journal of Natural Resources and Environmental Law* and the *Duke Environmental Law and Policy Forum*, and as chapters in two forthcoming books: *Property Rights and Neoliberalism: Cultural Demands and Legal Actions* and *Perspectives on Evil, Law and the State*.

Commonly Used Acronyms

AMD	Acid Mine Drainage
AML	Abandoned Mine Lands
AVF	Alluvial Valley Floor
CO	Cessation Order
DOI	Department of the Interior
DWR	Department of Water Resources
ESA	Endangered Species Act
ESC	Endangered Species Committee
FWS	Fish and Wildlife Service
HCP	Habitat Conservation Plan
ITP	Incidental Take Permit
OSM	Office of Surface Mining
NMFS	National Marine Fisheries Service
NOV	Notice of Violation
PCSE	Panel Corrected Standard Error
RPA	Reasonable and Prudent Alternative
SMCRA	Surface Mining Control and Reclamation Act
SWRCB	State Water Resources Control Board
TDL	Technical Deficiency Letter
TSCS	Time-Series Cross-Sectional
TVA	Tennessee Valley Authority
TWQCA	Tennessee Water Quality Control Act
UFM	Unsuitable for Mining
VER	Valid Existing Rights

CHAPTER 1

Introduction

The courtroom dramas of television and film have acquainted numerous Americans with the content of the Fifth Amendment. Beyond the individual protections from self-incrimination and double jeopardy, however, the Fifth Amendment contains a provision seldom, if ever, the subject of entertaining portrayals of courtroom procedures. The last line of this amendment, the Takings Clause, states, "nor shall private property be taken for public use, without just compensation."[1] When the Takings Clause rises to occupy a position within the collective public consciousness, it is generally through a controversy arising from the government's use of its power of eminent domain.

In 2005, the U.S. Supreme Court's decision in *Kelo v. City of New London*[2] accomplished this feat and, in the process, produced a short-lived yet highly vitriolic backlash to the power of eminent domain.

> As expected, property rights groups and Libertarian organizations excoriated the majority opinion and celebrated the dissents. More interesting is the reaction of the rest of the population. Americans of most political persuasions, and education and income levels found the outcome counterintuitive at best, or more often, simply repulsive.[3]

Part of this general reaction to the *Kelo* decision could be found at the state level, as property rights interest groups mobilized around the public reaction to *Kelo* and sponsored ballot initiatives to define "public use" within the states' laws on eminent domain to curtail, what were seen as, *Kelo*-style abuses. In the 2006 elections, eleven state ballots contained such initiatives,[4] and those initiatives succeeding in all but three states.[5] In general, *Kelo* was used by property rights interest groups as one part of a larger effort to shape eminent domain law.[6]

In addition to state initiatives which redefined "public use" to restrict the state's power of eminent domain, four state initiatives contained additional language related to property value diminution and just compensation.[7] Arizona's Proposition 207, for example, requires that the state or municipality compensate for any loss in property owners' rights to use, divide, sell, or possess property caused by the enactment or applicability of regulations, excepting a list of regulations aimed at the following, non-exhaustive list: nuisance, health, safety, pollution control, traffic control, sex offenders, illegal drugs, pornography, and topless dancing.[8] Such initiatives not only limit the degree to which the state can physically confiscate property, they also require compensation for property use restrictions that may decrease the value of the property but leave it in the hands of the owner.

The sort of action such initiative clauses focus upon is called a regulatory taking, which, like eminent domain, is rooted in the language of the Fifth Amendment. The lesser-known regulatory takings law, however, differs significantly from the law of eminent domain. The plaintiff in an eminent domain case has had his or her property physically confiscated, has received compensation, but is arguing that the state had no right to take the property, as the state's proposed use for that property was not properly public. A regulatory takings plaintiff, however, still maintains possession of the property but his or her use is restricted, the public nature of that restriction is accepted, but the owner demands compensation for the indices of property which were "taken." Whereas the purpose of eminent domain reform is the explicit restriction of the state's ability to take property, the explicit purpose of just compensation clauses within such reform and the litigation of plaintiffs seeking such compensation is the idea of a more equitable distribution of the costs and benefits of regulation.

Or, as the Supreme Court has put it, "The Fifth Amendment's guarantee that private property shall not be taken for a public use without just compensation was designed to bar Government from forcing some people alone to bear public burdens which, in all fairness and justice, should be borne by the public as a whole."[9]

It is the implicit purpose of regulatory takings litigation that concerns environmentalists and advocates for smart development. Absent an expressed requirement within the laws and regulations of the state, a property owner seeking compensation for regulation might seek it through litigation. If courts rule in such cases in a manner which develops a strong precedent for compensation, i.e. if "the burden of proof in takings cases [starts] falling on the government, considerable litigation is inevitable."[10] The feared end result is that regulatory agencies responsible for the enforcement of environmental and other such laws that protect the public from noxious private uses will begin reducing their regulatory activities, either due to diminished resources caused by litigation or the fear of such diminishment. This chilling effect of regulatory takings litigation is the focus of this book.

COMMON STORIES AND LEGAL INSTITUTIONS

The classical story of regulatory takings focuses on an inborn desire on the part of governmental agencies to maximize the amount of regulatory activity in which they can engage, a natural fact of finite budgetary resources which those agencies can access, and a strategic response by those agencies which is characterized by the achievement of public goods through private cost, when possible. As property owners find the enjoyment and use of their property hampered by regulatory restriction, i.e., as public good is provided through private loss, they may choose to react litigiously, seeking compensation, not for property physically confiscated by the state, but for restrictions which are felt to have the same effect. Through successful, or potentially even numerous unsuccessful, lawsuits, the governmental regulatory regime learns a lesson: they cannot rely on such a strategy to provide public services at low cost.

The power of such a narrative may rest on its facial neutrality. Whether one judges such an outcome positively or negatively, as worthy of derision or celebration, agreement is still possible over the general plot of the story. From a neoliberal position, in which cooperative, free negotiations over property use are preferable to a coercive model of state authority,[11] solace can be found in evidence that "greater compensation does deter government action."[12] A more public perspective might see the unadulterated private use of property as the problem, as the source of many public "bads" and, therefore, view the situation differently. "As such, local governments will have to do more individualized analysis of the expected impacts of land use changes and the conditions they impose on them. Not only will this be more costly but it will likely have a chilling effect on regulatory activity at that level."[13] Whether seen positively or negatively, the central theme of the classical regulatory takings story remains the same: regulatory takings litigation has a chilling effect on regulatory output.

Despite the warnings issued by organizations concerned with the potential weakening of environmental land-use regulations, as well as the premature celebration of organizations long aiming at such declinations, some have questioned the existence of such chilling impacts. Cornell law professor Gregory Alexander, in an excellent comparative assessment of takings jurisprudence, declared "the takings clause dead as a tool for conservative judges to end the expansion of the regulatory state."[14] While Alexander notes that continued property rights conflicts with and challenges against regulation will occur, and future confrontations will likely occur in legislative arenas, the Supreme Court is portrayed as an institution that, while occasionally deferential to property owners' takings claims, has substantially upheld land use regulation against constitutional challenges.[15] Alexander's assessment of the historical and current state of takings jurisprudence is accurate, but it also raises a different sort of question. Does the potential for a chilling effect-style impact related to regulatory takings litigation exist, even in the light of a jurisprudence that is deferential to regulation?

A problem arises in the attempt to answer this question. Most of the existing literature on regulatory takings relies predominantly upon either a legal focus or an economic focus. Approaching the question of regulatory takings through a legal lens is not without its advantages. Law review articles on the current state of takings jurisprudence are of great assistance to those with a fundamental interest in the way in which courts have actually ruled on such cases. Potential litigants, regulatory decision-makers, property and/or environmental lawyers, and academics focusing on judicial decision-making all benefit from knowledge of the manner in which actual judges have decided actual disputes. Furthermore, normative assessments of how regulatory takings cases *should* be decided are broadened beyond inquiries into costs and benefits through a focus on the ethical and communitarian obligations that accompany property rights, a question that is legal in nature. The contributions to an understanding of regulatory takings provided by legal scholarship, however, should not blind one to the incomplete nature of those contributions. Ultimately, full inquiries into the phenomenon must realize that the questions raised by regulatory takings are questions that extend outside the courtroom and law offices and into other arenas of political activity.

More in depth contributions have been made by the field of economics and, in particular, the field of law and economics. Operating at the analytical level of the rational individual strategically working to maximize his or her own benefits, economic disciplines seem better poised to answer the distributive questions of regulatory takings, especially those questions focused on the impact of such litigation on regulatory regimes. Not only might "economic analysis of government behavior…illuminate the instances in which compensation will have a desired result and when it may be redundant or undesirable,"[16] but it may also demonstrate the unwillingness of government actors to pursue regulation when facing such compensation. Questions surrounding individuals' propensities to pursue takings litigations against the regulatory state are also pared down, with more attention paid to the costs and benefits attributed to all choices of action; a population's desire to avoid pollution and/or secure jobs, the pressure of economic competition from other jurisdictions, and the mobility of the regulated interest may all affect the willingness to sue and/or regulate.[17] Finally, the discipline of law and economics can lay claim to the ability to decipher not only the results of takings law, but also its purposes, origins, and meanings. "By uncovering its latent order—concealed beneath the law's chaotic surface and inexpressible in its own terms—they seek to show that the law has a greater intelligibility than it appears to, and that the historical accidents to which it seems to owe its shape are in reality the product of actions that conform to certain timeless laws of human behavior."[18]

Economic analyses of regulatory takings certainly add a dimension of understanding beyond the letter of the law and into the realm of observable human behavior. However, in the attempt to clarify and simplify the chaotic mass of takings jurisprudence, an oversimplification has been forged. In the process of narrowing the level of analysis down to the rational individual, institutional factors have been omitted, factors which greatly shape the practices of litigation and regulation, altering both the strategies of participants and the social contexts of meaning in which such actions occur.

The law and economics school associated with Richard Posner frequently answers questions about the proper direction of law by focusing upon efficiency and equating the most efficient distribution of goods with the moral purpose of the law.[19] This position not only prescribes the end of law, but also claims to describe the law, in practice, as essentially an obfuscation of embedded, underlying economic principles.[20] The application of such an idea to regulatory takings results in a focus upon who is bearing what costs and whether such costs could be, and therefore should be, distributed more efficiently. This conclusion is made by analyzing the amount which individuals will pay or forego to receive a benefit or avoid a cost. "In a world of private bads, external costs that affect, and are confined to, easily defined economic agents are seen as a private matter by the common law. Economic theory sees the problem as a matter that may be resolved by bargaining."[21] The problem for economic analysis occurs when the subject being studied moves beyond the more predictable individual situations and finds itself wrapped in a complex set of social institutions which would force each actor to adopt coping strategies.

The economic analysis of public bads calls for a different theoretical approach than that required for private bads. Indeed, the economic theory of public goods and bads inevitably includes such things as collective decisionmaking, free-rider problems, government coercion, and strategic behavior. Because of the level of decision-making costs, the world of public bads is not as neat as the world of private bads. In the private world, the small numbers of agents and clearly defined property rights enable bargaining to emerge as a low-cost way to eliminate relevant private bads. The problem is more costly to resolve in the world of public goods and bads.[22]

Since regulatory takings claims arise in the face of regulation aimed at the control of private property for the purpose of prevention of a public harm or the securing of a public good, an understanding of such litigation must incorporate political and social institutions and avoid the hegemonic role that economic factors have historically played in such studies.

In addition to the strategic elements added to regulatory takings litigation by political institutions, the realm of politics also adds values beyond those stressed by economics. Adherents of natural law would disagree here, arguing that normative values attached to property are *a priori* values, not values that come out of politics. Some of the staunchest advocates of strong private property rights and near-universal compensatory rules argue so partially in thanks to such Lockean assumptions that posit property as prior to the state.[23] Others point out the historical inaccuracies involved in giving priority to property over the state, arguing that property could not exist without the state and "the history of property regimes shows a strong streak of top-down features."[24] The creation of property under a body of law imposes upon it certain obligations that inherently limit one's property rights.[25] What both sides of this argument agree upon is that the debates surrounding regulatory takings have as much to do with normative values as economic values. The decision to take or not to take, to compensate or not to compensate is frequently about much more that distributing costs and benefits in an efficient manner. Regulatory takings are inherently political, touching upon issues of right and obligation, and any analysis of takings must consider that political dimension.

Considerations have already been made about how institutions may shape the value systems surrounding similar property situations by contributors to the commons literature. Most contributors to the commons literature describe their discipline as historically being rooted in Garrett Hardin's 1968 "The Tragedy of the Commons,"[26] which painted a bleak, inescapable, predictable outcome for situations in which individuals rely on access to resources held in common. The tragedy plays itself out in the following paraphrasing:

> There is a resource—usually referred to as a common-pool resource—to which a large number of people have access.... Overuse of the resource creates problems, often destroying its sustainability.... If all users restrain themselves, then the resource can be sustained. But there is a dilemma. If you limit your use of the resources and your neighbors do not, then the resource still collapses and you have lost the short-term benefits of taking your share.[27]

Central to this dilemma are the following two conditions: (1) every benefit drawn from the common pool is enjoyed solely by the individual that does the extraction, but (2) the burdens of that extraction are shared by all who share the pool.[28] The only ways foreseeable by Hardin to avoid such an event would be allocate common resources into private property[29] or to directly prevent such behavior through "mutual coercion mutually agreed upon."[30]

While not identical, the commons situation shares many similarities with a situation under a takings claim. In both, common ownership results in use conflict. Although the commons situation involves the more traditional conflict between users, each seeking to maximize their use of the common pool, the takings situation involves a conflict between the ownership claims of a single user and the "ownership" claims of the state to the same property, but for a different purpose. The American legal tradition has long recognized the common nature of certain resources, such as wildlife, and roots that nature in its historical ownership by the Crown (and eventually the state).[31] So at least in some circumstances, a situation that has historically resulted in a "tragedy of the commons" is quite similar to one ending up in a courtroom under a regulatory takings challenge.

The inability of the takings literature to address institutional constraints is mirrored, historically, by the same problem in the commons literature. Early approaches which dominated the commons literature had as their primary focus the efficient distribution of commonly held resources. This focus came from an early reliance upon Gordon-Schaefer economic models, which "drew attention to the economic factors in the management of ...common-pool resources."[32] In these models, initial levels of extraction effort by multiple users from a common resource result in high rates of return, but returns diminish at higher levels of effort, despite a constant increase in the level of costs, until a point is reached when the resource can no longer fully replenish itself, and additional extractive efforts result in a decrease of total revenues. This decrease can continue until the costs associated with high levels of effort exceed the total revenues received from that effort. It is this point in the model that indicates the level of resource extraction that would occur in a pure condition of open access; this level exceeds both the maximum sustainable yield (the highest level of effort at which the resource can still fully replenish itself) and maximum economic yield (the level of effort at which the total revenues most exceed the total costs).[33] The question the Gordon-Schaefer model poses for commons researchers is as follows: What sort of "rules regulating access and harvesting practices limit effort to the economically optimal strategy"?[34] The important question of sustainability was central; of little-to-no concern were questions of the justness of distribution. "That one individual ends up with a bigger share is not socially costly in itself (the gain to that individual perfectly offsets the loss imposed on other members of the pool), but the way in which the individual makes that appropriations is likely to involve actions that are on net costly in the linked commons of the resource-gathering environment."[35]

The practical benefits of the Gordon-Schaefer model and other economic accounts of commons problems are clear; however, their analysis of the phenomenon is limited. While the logic of the model is cohesive, "that logic depends on a set of assumptions about human motivation, about the rules governing the use of the commons, and about the character of the common resource."[36] Out of a concern over the limits of these assumptions and the model they produce, a substantial body of research has emerged from the commons literature that offers more nuanced and complex explanations of common resource management. Central to these approaches is the realization that, historically, examples exist of communities' successful collaborative management practices over communally held resources.[37] The lesson learned from these observations is that "(i)nstead of presuming that the individuals sharing a commons are inevitably caught in a trap from which they cannot escape,...(one might observe that) the capacity of individuals to extricate themselves from various types of dilemma situations *varies* from situation to situation."[38]

The explanation of such variance shifted focus within the commons discipline from the rational individual level of analysis to institutions which confine and affect the individuals acting within commons dilemmas. Some of these approaches maintain a strong reliance on the individual level of analysis, but frame their motivations differently; considering the individuals not simply to be single-mindedly motivated by benefit maximization, but strategically acting to satisfice those goals in the contexts of the actions of others to create suboptimal results which, from a "tragedy of the commons" perspective, could only be seen as irrational.[39] However, while institutions do clearly establish "the rules of the game" which confine and limit the choices of individual actors, they do more.[40] "Accordingly, the emergence of institutions for the commons should include not only rules and governance systems but also new and changed patterns of behavior and norms and values."[41] The introduction of institutional analysis to the commons literature does more than demonstrate the limits which particular resource users confront; the commons literature now has the tools to understand more than the choices available to a user, but also how the user might understand those choices. "Rather than focus on ostensibly universal motivations such as rationality or selfishness..., interpretivists try to reconstruct intentional states of mind and cultural or political contexts in the hope that [they] can induce with some confidence the reasons that led a particular person to adopt a particular course of conduct."[42]

Concerns over the perceptions that potential resource users have of their situation, the significance of the resource, and the ethical questions involved in accessing or limiting access to the resource are far from mere esoteric inquiries. Research indicates that how resource users have perceived the economic, political, cultural, and ecological contexts in which they find themselves may affect the ultimate resource distribution.

> In a number of important commons contexts, resource users have vehemently denied that there is a problem (despite relatively substantial evidence that a serious problem exists), argued that intervention by the government or other outside institutions is unnecessary (despite repeated failures by the community of resource users themselves to voluntarily or

collectively limit resource use), and opposed suggested solutions as unfair and unwise.[43]

Contextual factors like (perceived) scientific uncertainty and the discounting of future losses can dramatically affect whether resources users even believe there is a problem, much less consider acting to solve it.[44] Furthermore, "(w)hen common-pool resource users are faced with the need to invest time, energy, money, and other resources in developing or changing self-governing institutions, the rational choice of free-rider strategies can overwhelm the effort.... Small steps have low initial costs and the prospect of early successes, which can change the decision-making environment."[45]

The aforementioned developments with the commons literature posit that the perceptions of actors behaving in economic situations affect their behavior in a manner that is distinguishable and theoretically prior to their rational calculations. These perceptions are shaped by factors external to the individual, as they are formed by the cultural and definitional contexts surrounding them. One of the crucial institutions affecting common property regimes is the law itself, as it not only situates the strategic economic behavior of actors through the creation of rules of exchange and behavior, but it also acts as a source of norms and values that mold perceptions.[46] This understanding of the role of law in human behavior is a more advanced understanding of law than under traditional economic modes of thought for two reasons. First, while such an approach does not reject the idea that laws may coercively confine strategic behavior, it adds an additional explanation, one focused on social context and perception, giving a more rounded explanation. Second, by focusing on the manner in which law shapes perception, the explanation moves closer to an understanding of how law works, including in the aforementioned strategic situations.

This development within the commons literature has inspired this current inquiry into regulatory takings. The classical story of regulatory takings impact uses a simple understanding of law: the involved court renders a decision or a set of decisions and regulators modify their behavior in anticipation of facing a similar lawsuit or in reaction to encouraged litigants. A more nuanced story does not have to ignore the possibility of this scenario. However, by understanding law and litigation in a more fully institutionalized manner, new avenues of possible impact on regulatory policies present themselves, and explanations for observed cases of "non-impact" become more evident. Engagement in such an analysis requires a more thorough understanding of the nature of law, litigation, and regulation.

NEW STORIES AND LEGAL PLURALISM

The central argument of Mary Ann Glendon's oft cited book, *Rights Talk*, is that American "rights talk, in its absoluteness, promotes unrealistic expectations, heightens social conflict, and inhibits dialogue that might lead toward consensus, accommodation, or at least the discovery of common ground."[47] Despite the focus on the general discourse on rights, Glendon is particularly critical of the role courts play in the development of such discourse. Courts are the loci of rights discourse development and litigation its modus operandi and the opinions of the Supreme Court, in particular, allow one rights claim to trump another, oversimplify modern moral discourse, and obfuscate the process through the illusion of legal inevitability.[48] The public responds by continuing to understand issues of political and moral significance through this overly-simplistic rights rubric.

This critical portrayal of the judicial aspect of rights discourse portrays the American judiciary in a manner synonymous with the image of the court behind classic stories of regulatory takings. When property owners sue the state for compensation for regulatory restrictions placed upon his or her property, the court must decide whose property claim trumps and whose property claim is trumped, the private owner or the public common. After the decision is made, similarly situated regulators perceive the court's attitude (i.e. see which party did the trumping) and, in the event of a finding of a taking, restrict regulatory activity to avoid a similar outcome. The assumption behind this behavior is that the court is perceived by the public, including the regulatory part of that public, as a "moral arbiter"[49] which has established an absolute boundary between property rights and permissible regulation.

Of course, this may happen. Much of the story told during my own analysis of regulatory takings focuses on the possibility that court decisions, and the law in general, act as an institution that shapes the expectations of regulators and property owners alike. This observation is made in response to the analyses of regulatory takings undertaken in the field of economics; the simple response is that the law does matter as it shapes the way economic actors perceive their world. However, this book also highlights the presence of other institutions which shape the decision-making environment surrounding regulatory takings litigation. The end result is a model of regulatory takings impact that is more complex than that admitted to by economic analysis. Too many factors are part of the reality of regulatory takings for any impact to be explained solely through a focus upon the isolated individual of economic modeling.

Insights into this institutional complexity can be found in Glendon's *Rights Talk*, for although the general purpose of the book is a criticism of an absolutist understanding of rights in contemporary American political discourse, her discussion on property rights paints a picture that demonstrates the discourse and compromise for which she calls. Consider the following excerpt:

> The exaggerated absoluteness of our American rights dialect is all the more remarkable when we consider how little relation it bears to reality. There is a striking discrepancy...between our tendency to state rights in a stark unlimited fashion and the common sense restrictions that have to be placed on one person's rights when they collide with those of another person. On any given day, in courtrooms all over the nation, at all seasons of the year, when harried judges handle garden-variety disputes, they use a chastened, domesticated, concept of rights.[50]

Although a discourse which perceives of property rights as absolute exists, the actual practice of property law in the U.S. is better characterized as emphasizing the rights AND responsibilities of property owners and an effort to balance those rights with the needs of the society as a whole. Later, a discussion of regulatory takings jurisprudence will demonstrate that these are the essential tenets in this specific body of property law, as well. At the moment, it should suffice to point out that, although the U.S. Supreme Court has issued takings rulings that, in effect, understand property rights as absolute, such rulings are the exception, not the rule.

These observations demonstrate that legal property rights are far more fluid than rigid. This leads to two conclusions. First, the fluidity of property rights under the law diminish their predictability, making economic and rational choice models less useful and making the classic story of regulatory reaction less probable. If, after all, the idea of property rights is in flux, then a key regulatory decision-maker is going to be less likely to predict their application to specific regulations, and is less likely to reduce regulatory outputs, at least for the reason generally attributed. Second, if property rights are fluid, they are better understood not as pre-existing rights but as the products of external institutions. Any attempt to understand why a key regulatory decision-maker may reduce regulatory outputs to avoid a conflict with property rights should inquire into what those rights mean at that place and time and why.

Thinking About the Law

The classical story of regulatory takings invokes an understanding of law that is most consistent with the jurisprudential position of legalism, the key features of which are

> (1) the separation of law from other varieties of social control, (2) the existence of law in the form of rules that both define the proper sphere of their own application and (3) that are presented as the objective and legitimate normative mechanism whilst other normative types are partial or subjective, and (4) yield determinant and predictable results in their application in the juridical process.[51]

Taken together, these tenets of legalism comprise a self-referential theory of law, in which law exists a priori and independent of human institutions. An assumption that an invocation by one or a number of judges that a particular regulatory action requires compensation will result in an avoidance of such actions rests upon the belief of law as objective and replicable.

Even the school of law and economics, itself a product of legal realism and its rejection of legalistic explanations of legal behavior as naïve, ultimately relies on a legalistic understanding of law when considering regulatory takings. Although law and economics rejects the first assumption of legalism, that law is independent of other forms of social control, its reliance upon the economic foundations of law produces remarkable predictability and objectivity by arguing "that the law has a greater intelligibility than it appears to, and that the historical accidents to which it seems to owe its shape are in reality the product of actions that conform to certain timeless laws of human behavior."[52] It is the characterization of law as predetermined and scientific that is the focus of the former Dean of Yale Law School, Anthony Kronman's, *The Lost Lawyer*, in which he laments the pedagogical focus on technique in the law school education at the loss of a more appropriate focus on fostering prudentialism, an innate characteristic indicative of the wise judgment of Abraham Lincoln and Earl Warren and anathema to expertise.[53] Kronman associates prudentialism with the common law tradition and its focus on judge-made law, as opposed to efforts to achieve "scientific respectability" in the law through codification.[54]

In addition to the law and economics school, Kronman also criticizes the critical legal studies (CLS) movement, which due to "their belief that only a theory of the highest possible abstraction can describe" the law, has "encouraged an outlook hostile to the prudentialism on which the lawyer-statesman ideal is based."[55] Despite such criticism, CLS also portrays the law as currently existing is a split state of conflict similar to the conflict between prudentialism and scientific realism described by Kronman (a point which Kronman acknowledges).[56] Duncan Kennedy, long a leading figure in the CLS movement, has stated that the law currently exists in a state of conflict between a focus on rules and a focus on standards. Advocates of a rule-based legal order advocate recognition of "formal realizability" and a strict adherence to "a list of easily distinguishable factual aspects of a situation by intervening in a determinate way."[57] Conversely, a "standard refers directly to one of the substantive objectives of the legal order," and requires that a judge "discover the facts of a particular situation and...assess them in terms of the purposes or social values embodied in the standard."[58]

For Kennedy, the choice between rules and standard-based applications of the law is no mere choice between neutral processes which exist independent of the value-laden choices of politics. "They are also an invitation to choose between sets of values and visions of the universe."[59] Therefore, the observed conflict within the law between rules and standards indicates a parallel conflict between opposed political goals and values, namely, between the values of individualism, which Kennedy associates with a rules-focus, and altruism, associated with standard-based law.[60] Kennedy claims that these conflicts are irresolvable and, therefore, the essence of the law is dialectical and inherently contradictory.[61] While Kennedy acknowledges that both rules and standards within the law may end up serving liberating or oppressive ends,[62] his ultimate advocacy is toward the use by judges of standards, altruism, and informality to throw out unconscionable contracts over the claims of rules-based determinism.[63] Kronman advocates a more "conservative view of politics," under which "human beings pursue a variety of worthwhile but incommensurable ends, and...that in many cases neither reason nor intuition can rank their competing claims."[64] Both advocate a role for judges beyond the simple interpretation of rules set in stone. More significantly, both are describing a situation in which the law is better characterized as an evolving relationship between conflicting ideas (prudentialism vs. scientific realism, individualism vs. altruism, formal rules vs. informal standards) instead of settled and single uniformity.

What both Kronman and Kennedy point to is a characteristic of the law antithetical to the law as constructed by advocates of the school of law and economics. This characterization of the law as "a collage of obligatory practices and norms emanating both from governmental and non-governmental sources alike"[65] is commonly utilized in the field of legal anthropology, and is referred to as legal pluralism. Originating in discussions of "the legacy of colonial pluralism" surrounding the transition of African nations from colonial rule,[66] and evolving more recently to a focus on the dialectic, hermeneutic, and symbolic interactions of various structural legal components,[67] legal pluralism generally refers to any situation in which "in which two or more legal systems coexist in the same social field."[68] It is this characteristic of law that informs the analysis of regulatory takings litigation in the following chapters. Attention to the multiple systemic origins of law is important in the general field of regulatory takings for two reasons.

First, legal pluralism, as an idea, highlights the multiple avenues of action available to key regulatory decision-makers confronting potential regulatory takings challenges and facing courts ruling for compensation in similar situations. The classical story of regulatory takings, that heightened compensatory rulings in the courts produce a chilling effect in enforcement, presents a possible reaction of key regulatory decision-makers to litigious activity, but it ignores other possibilities. While budgetary concerns are likely to be high among key regulatory decision-makers, one cannot automatically assume that takings cases and compensation-threats are going to overpower every other variable affecting those concerns. Furthermore, concerns other than budgetary ones shape regulatory behavior. This will be discussed in greater detail below, in the section of regulatory agencies. Presently, it is important to remember that regulatory agencies are enforcement agencies,[69] and are likely motivated by a corresponding organizational culture, sometimes referred to as the "gotcha syndrome,"[70] which provides motivations counter to those central to the idea of a takings chilling effect. The second advantage that legal pluralism brings to the study of regulatory takings provides insight into the possible origin of this enforcement culture.

Second, and more significantly, legal pluralism provides a far more realistic conceptual foundation for regulatory takings law than that provided by law and economics. At the heart of regulatory takings jurisprudence is a conflict of law, a conflict implicitly recognized by the Supreme Court throughout its articulation of that jurisprudence. The conflict is between codified constitutionalism and common law tradition. Private property rights, sanctified by the literal word of the Constitution, have, nevertheless, always been understood within a common law context that limits those rights in the interest of the common good. Plaintiffs and their counsel in regulatory takings cases often, looking to the Founders' vision of property as "integral to the Constitution" and "as part of our very ideals of justice, liberty, and democracy,"[71] argue that the enjoyment of their property is sacrosanct and advocate a level of judicial intervention capable of insulating those rights from public intrusion.[72] Yet America's inheritance of the common law tradition from England, an inheritance demonstrated by an advocacy of the writings of Blackstone even after their decline in use in England,[73] has always been a source of public rights over and against total private appropriation of property.[74]

Yet even in the face of a clear constitutional statement insulating private property rights, it is necessary to fit that statement within an "altruistic mold. The rules against violence, for example, have the *effect* of changing the balance of power that would exist in the state of nature in that of civil society.... The thief is a very paragon of self-reliance, and the property owning victim has failed to act effectively in his [sic] own defense."[75] Despite the rhetoric of individualism, the idea of private property rights cannot be fully separated from the public protections found in the U.S. common law. Even at times when American property law drifted toward doctrines that advocate the individual over the collective, the spirit of common law public protections was still present. When riparian rights were abrogated in favor of the appropriation doctrine in Western mining law, a key concern driving that decision was the prevention of monopolization and a favoring of those that actually use the land.[76]

The significance of legal pluralism for the study of regulatory takings litigation is that the law, by its nature, is the product of two conflicting yet coexisting legal traditions. Actors within the law are no longer seen as attempting to unveil a single systematic and logically cohesive set of rules governing takings and compensation; that cohesiveness does not exist. Instead, the law is a site of conflict. At one point in time, the influence may be greater from constitutionalism; during others, it may be the common law. The purpose for studying regulatory takings moves from a search for a single calculus to an inquiry into the current balance of the two legal traditions and the factors that determine that balance. Furthermore, the actors lose their passive natures. Litigants are now seen as working to solidify the predominance of one legal tradition over the other. This is particularly true for advocates of strong private property rights. By advocating a judicial adherence to the constitutional codification of property rights, Kennedy's rule form of the law is being advocated. This form of the law "shores up the legitimacy of judicial action" by "obscur[ing]...the process of justification" and then "disguis[ing] the discretionary element involved in applying it to the cases."[77]

Thinking About Courts

If the progression is made from an understanding of regulatory takings as a unified, logically-cohesive body of law to an understanding of that law as a dialectical conflict between constitutionalism and the common law, then the perceived role of the judiciary within the law must, likewise, progress. Advocates of a constitutionalist interpretation of takings law, such as Richard Epstein, see the right in property as paramount; the role of the state is limited, in a Lockean sense, to the assurance of "individuals to escape the uncertainty and risks of social disorder without having to surrender to the sovereign the full complement of individual rights."[78] The protection for the individual from an overreaching state takes the form of the court, which must have strong powers of judicial intervention over the state to protect the rights of the property-owning individual.[79]

Scholars from the field of law and economics generally see a weaker version of the judicial role as it relates to property. Like property constitutionalists, the law and economics field understands takings law as singular and cohesive; unlike constitutionalists, that law is a calculus aimed at the most efficient distribution of property. The clearest example is William Fischel's prescription for the proper judicial role in regulatory takings cases. An advocate of the process theory of judicial review, Fischel seeks to limit judicial intervention into property takings to cases in which the decision to restrict property use was made through undemocratic processes.[80] When the process is fair, Pareto optimal solutions result. When a property owner lacks voice in the political process or the ability to remove that property from a political jurisdiction, conditions Fischel associates primarily with municipal governments, the judiciary can justify intervention in the redistribution of property.[81]

While both the high level of judicial intervention justified by property constitutionalists and the process theory of law and economics are opposite judicial role prescriptions, both modes of thinking share one important aspect in common: both see the courts as having a fundamentally limited role in shaping regulatory takings law. For both, the law itself is either a constitutionally protected right or a set of objective economic variables; the court is only called upon to be a neutral enforcer of the rules, and the role of "courts to define and formalize the boundaries of rulemaking" by executive agencies is diminished.[82]. Once having done so, the only question left to ask is whether or not those commanded by the courts and those similarly situated comply with that decision.

Ever since Jerome Frank argued that the idea of the predictability and cohesiveness of law was an illusion backed by "the childish desire to have a fixed father-controlled universe, free of chance and error due to human fallibility,"[83] contemporary legal scholarship has been hard-pressed to find any justification for a theory that posits no role for the judge in the actual construction of law. The idea of legal realism is more consistent with the spirit of contemporary legal studies than either a simple constitutionalist position or the school of law and economics. Furthermore, evidence is strong that judges have been involved in the development of regulatory takings law.

Unlike the constitutions of some other countries, the U.S. Constitution makes no mention of a social obligation norm in its handling of property, which would form "as a fundamental aspect of the constitutional right of property…an integral aspect of the vision of property as the material basis for promoting the common social good."[84] If judges were not an integral part in the shaping of regulatory takings law, the subsequent cases would not present the idea of social obligation in property rights. A reading of the Supreme Court's decisions on regulatory takings, however, demonstrates a consistent awareness and/or implementation of an implicit social obligation norm.[85] Even the Supreme Court decisions most aligned with a strong interpretation of property rights acknowledge, with caveat upon caveat, that a "property owner necessarily expects the uses of his [sic] property to be restricted, from time to time, by various measures newly enacted by the State in legitimate exercise of its police powers."[86] In the process of tempering the words of the Constitution's Fifth Amendment with the nuisance-based traditions of our common law history, judges are doing more than "discovering" the balancing point between constitutionalism and the common law, they are creating that balancing point.

While this observation may conjure images of judges legislating from the bench, or making law not interpreting law, it is a necessary and unavoidable feature of the American judiciary.[87] In recent decades, the increased demand from the American populace that its government do more and more to provide for the social welfare has confronted a distrust of that government to do so, resulting in an increased public use of the courts as a traditional tool of governance.[88] As social legislation programs expanded in the 1960's and 1970's, courts became necessary enforcement tools to spur recalcitrant agencies to act, a plan intended by Congress, evidenced through the frequent inclusion of citizen suit provisions within social legislation.[89]

In addition to the ingrained nature of judicial activity in the implementation of regulatory law, judges are also involved in the formation, maintenance, and shaping of legal norms and values. "Indeed, for some researchers the real interest lies in the impact and influence of general principles, or the legal values and norms enunciated or implied in judicial decisions."[90] Studying the ways in which judicial decisions may shape public values and expectations is difficult, and it lends itself more nicely to interpretive, as opposed to positivistic, methodologies.[91] Nevertheless, such research is important, especially considering the presence of legally pluralistic characteristics within regulatory takings law. As much of the law is based upon the reasonable expectations of property owners, societal shifts in terms like "reasonableness" affect the level to which property owners and regulators alike assume property use may be restricted without compensation. Within the common law tradition, courts have been seen as engaging in experiments. "Courts modified legal rules that appeared not to be working and adapted rules to new factual situations or changing societal circumstances."[92] As that process continues, courts play a frequently necessary role in legitimizing a balancing point between the Constitution and the common law.

Thinking About Regulatory Agencies

Frequently ignored in discussions of judicial impact, and in discussions of American governance in general, are the regulatory agencies that implement and enforce the laws passed by legislatures. Too often, these agencies are treated as the proverbial "black box" within interpretive models. The classical story of regulatory takings and the chilling effect is guilty of this action as well, assuming a monolithic response from bureaucratic automatons governed only by an organizational script found in enabling legislation. However, "one cannot properly understand the nature of the impact of judicial review on administrative procedures without first understanding the nature of administrative procedures."[93] At a minimum, one should acknowledge the possibility that, when reacting to a judicial stimulus, key regulatory decision-makers must interpret the decision, search for a way to implement the change without fundamentally altering the "*ésprit de corps*" of the agency, and then choose an implementation strategy.[94] Each of these steps is a point in time in which the regulator has discretion in the manner in which a judicial decision will be implemented, or if it will actually be implemented at all.

Acknowledging the discretion exercised by regulators is an important step in understanding the regulatory process, which is a precondition to understanding the potential for judicial impact on regulatory behavior. First, simply acknowledging the discretion used by regulators provides a more realistic and detail description of their existences. "(T)he idea of regulators devoid of discretion is just that: an idea. In reality, they have always exercised their discretion, and they always will. They do so partly out of necessity, because there are far too many regulations and far too many instances of noncompliance and insufficient resources to tackle more than a fraction."[95] It is an important fact to keep in mind while assessing regulatory behavior, for fears of appearing lazy or overzealous, biased or unreasonable, corrupt or draconian, seldom give way enough to allow a regulator to admit that he or she uses discretion.[96]

Second, by acknowledging the discretion inherent in enforcement, different avenues of regulatory reactions to judicial decisions become more apparent. Regulators do not regulate in a vacuum; just as regulators are living, breathing people, so too are the individuals being regulated. The extent to which individuals involved in regulatory practices interact and are involved with one another, and the degree to which they trust one another, can shape the type of regulatory relationship that exists,[97] which may affect how the agency reacts to judicial decisions affecting that relationship. One possible consequence is that a takings ruling that has the potential to be applied to a large number of regulatory activities may be rendered moot by the ability of the regulator and the regulated to work out an alternative solution. In other words, understanding the process of regulation may lead to insights of judicial impact invisible through a focus on the ends of regulation.[98]

Likewise, the particular characteristics of those being regulated will likely shape such interactions, and must be considered when assessing the possibility of agency wide impact caused by a takings decision. A key focus of much research on regulator/regulated interactions has been on the probability of agency capture, in which the executive agency becomes nothing more than a representative for the particular industry it is charged with regulating. A focus on the bargaining nature of agencies certainly allows for that possibility, but a focus on the processes and interactions of regulation is ultimately ambivalent to the question of capture. The real concern is the degree to which takings decisions shape regulatory behavior. Whether an agency is captured or not is not important for this inquiry; their behavior after a case is. However, the degree and nature of interactions between the agency and the regulated industry may still shape the manner in which impact is possible or occurs.

Acknowledgement of discretion in regulation should not be taken to a point in which the internal and external institutions which shape regulatory behavior are ignored. One can realize that regulators have choice in their behavior, and this may shape the degree to which that individual reacts to a takings case. However, the structures that confine the ability of that regulator to act discretionarily are of theoretical primacy. This approach seeks a middle ground between an exclusive focus on individual decisions, which too frequently operate under unrealistic assumptions of individual motivation, and an overly deterministic Marxist/Weberian approach, which ignores the possibility of agency altogether.[99] Beyond shaping the degree to which a regulator may exercise discretion, structures shape the very way regulators perceive their role as regulators. Key among such structures is the organizational culture of the particular agency, which will likely contain characteristics unique to that agency, others which are common throughout agencies, and others still which are associated with a particular geographic region or body of regulation, such as environmental or economic.

Of key interest in the following chapters is the organizational culture within regulatory agencies as enforcement agencies. Contemporary prescriptions for regulatory reform frequently seek private sector solutions to problems in the areas of agency service and customer satisfaction.[100] Such prescriptions frequently run into a contrary agency culture, one which is an essential component of agencies' nature. It is important to remember that regulatory agencies are, first and foremost, enforcement agencies. "When people are arrested or fined or have their license revoked or their property seized, most often they are not pleased. Government does not seek to serve them in that instant. In many cases government creates an experience for them that is by design unpleasant."[101]

In situations involving a regulator facing a regulatory takings precedent that could be interpreted as likely to require that particular agency to provide compensation for a large amount of their regulatory practices, the regulator is faced with conflicting demands. One demand is to the constitutional requirement for compensation, the other is to the language of the statute empowering the agency to act. When the regulatory takings law is precedential in nature, i.e. not applying directly to a particular regulator, more discretion is left to the agency to evaluate the likelihood that those whom are being regulated will seek compensation or the degree to which the ruling applies to their actions. More significantly, any such interpretations must confront the agency enforcement culture, under which agency personnel understand their roles and responsibilities as being statutorily defined. "Statutory obligations on regulators are often demanding because the public wants high levels of protection, particularly if someone else is paying for it."[102] Furthermore, this agency enforcement culture is a product of the historical development which has shaped the interactions between executive agencies and the courts. After the passage of social legislation in the 1960's and 1970's by a Congress untrusting of executive commitment,

> federal judges have shown themselves to be increasingly suspicious of regulators who stray very far from a narrow interpretation of their statutory authority.... Increasingly, administrators must justify such policy choices to generalist judges in an adversary proceeding. The safer and easier path, both legally and politically, is thus often a narrow and mechanistic application of the authorizing statute.[103]

The end result is an enforcement culture, defined by statute, which must be "overcome" if regulatory takings decisions are to have a chilling effect on regulatory output.

CONCLUSION

As stated above, the ability of regulatory takings cases in which compensation is granted to have a chilling effect on the regulatory output of agencies regulating land use is contingent upon overcoming the enforcement culture of regulatory agencies. Although the following chapters demonstrate that regulatory personnel primarily define their roles through the requirements of the statutes which they are charged with enforcing, it is still possible to conceptualize such a chilling effect. Ultimately, the feature of takings litigation that could prove successful in causing a chilling effect is the ability of that litigation to alter perceived roles and expectations.

One manner of changing the role perception of key regulatory decision-makers is to reshape the statutory framework which shapes the basis of an enforcement culture to be more conducive to the interest of private property holders. Statutes may be written to require analysis of property impacts or to require compensation for all property value diminishment above a certain threshold percentage. Governments may choose to institutionalize property rights within the decision-making apparatuses of governance; the state of Utah, for example, operates an Office of the Property Rights Ombudsman to "investigate and recommend solutions if a government action may violate private property rights."[104] The creation of such political institutions requires a mobilization of property rights interests through the political process and litigation, win or lose, may serve that purpose.

Such mobilization may also serve to shape the cultural expectations surrounding the institution of property itself. A key dimension of regulatory takings jurisprudence deals with the reasonableness of private property owners' economic and use expectations. The Courts have not attempted to establish a mathematical formula to quantify those expectations; such quantification may be impossible and/or undesirable. The spirit of the Takings Clause is the protection of only the most vulnerable of society, those unlikely to be fairly represented in the political process.[105] A rule-oriented takings-determination would likely produce perverse results in multiple situations. A reliance on "reasonable" expectations, however, is tremendously fluid and changes as a society's notion of reasonable property uses changes. Agency personnel deciding whether or not to regulate, and property owners and developers deciding whether or not to litigate, may find their expectations altered by the amount of prominent property rights litigation within a present political climate.

The following chapters do not seek to demonstrate how these social expectations and norms concerning property use have shifted through time, nor do they provide any discussion about what such expectations should be. The following chapters present an analysis of the institutions surrounding the regulatory environment in which regulatory takings litigation occurs with an eye toward identifying structures which hold the potential to increase or decrease an agency's likelihood of experiencing a chilling effect in reaction to such litigation. The research involved in this analysis is quantitative, qualitative, theoretical, and legal in nature. This multi-methodological approach is justified by the complex and interstitial nature of the subject matter and the selected case studies. The overall spirit of the research is deeply descriptive; greater attention is given to the complex structure of regulatory takings litigation and its subject regulation than the parsimonious identification of select variables at the expense of real-world depth. Finally, the focus of this research is on the chilling effect at the federal level. Regulatory takings litigation occurs at every level of government, from federal agencies to local zoning boards. The conclusions drawn from this research may contain inferences that are applicable to the local level, but such inferences should be made with extreme caution. The variances in conditions and the localized natures of pressure and influence may meet significantly less resistance from an enforcement culture at the local level.

Chapter Two provides an historical overview of the development of the U.S. Supreme Court's regulatory takings jurisprudence. "Conventional wisdom teaches that the Supreme Court's takings doctrine is a muddle. And the Supreme Court's opinions have given conventional wisdom considerable ammunition."[106] Despite the chaotic nature of this jurisprudence, this step is a necessary one. An institutional analysis of the regulatory takings chilling effect must remain within touching distance of shifts in the jurisprudence to know where and when one is more or less likely to discover such an impact. If the Court's doctrine were historically homogeneous, analysis of its impact would be less interesting. That the jurisprudence does change, and does develop new issues of focus, makes the inquiry of this book more vibrant and alive.

Chapter Three looks at the theories of regulatory takings. This involves an overview of some of the more prominent efforts to understand this tricky body of law. Such attempts have been both descriptive and normative in nature. The primary focus of this research is along the descriptive, analytical vein, but that does not reduce normative inquiries to the status of interesting side note. A normative inquiry into the proper application of the Takings Clause, answering such questions as when to compensate, must always begin, although perhaps implicitly, with an inquiry into the nature of the law itself. Frequently, the prescriptions offered by these writers say just as much about how they understand the law as what they want the law to be. Attempts to theorize regulatory takings generally fall into one of two categories: economic and legal analyses. While neither body of work can be fully disregarded, this research steps out of this dyad and proposes the utilization of legal pluralism to create a more dynamic and fluid understanding of the law of regulatory takings.

Chapter Four focuses on the question of judicial impact. Generally, within the field of public law, the questions of judicial impact and decision-making are treated separately. The institutional focus of this research highlights the degree to which decision-making processes, not just of judges but of litigants and regulators as well, is a question which must be asked before the question of impact can be answered. This chapter works to bring these two inquiries together in ways that should be of general interest to the field of public law, but also in ways specific to the regulatory takings inquiry at hand.

Chapters Five and Six deal with regulatory takings cases involving two U.S. environmental statues, the Surface Mining Control and Reclamation Act (SMCRA)[107] and the Endangered Species Act (ESA),[108] respectively. Enacted in 1977, SMCRA's permitting process requires that all surface coal mining, as well as the surface effects of underground mining, be prohibited unless a permit is acquired which guarantees that all mining will minimize environmental impact and that all land be returned to its approximate original contour (AOC).[109] Enacted in 1973, ESA is likely best known as a law which regulates the treatment of individual species of animals; however, the focus within this book will be on the Habitat Conservation Plan (HCP) component of ESA, which involves the regulation of land use for the purposes of protecting species, allowing acceptable levels of economic activity, and insulating responsible land owners from liability.[110]

SMCRA and ESA were selected as case studies for this book due to their similarities, their differences, and their relationships to the questions inherent in regulatory takings law. Each statute involves the direct regulation of land use. Both statutes are federal environmental laws which have a case history involving regulatory takings challenges to their implementation. However, implementation of ESA is a federal matter, with primary enforcement coming from regional federal Fish and Wildlife Service (FWS) offices. Although SMCRA is a federal law, most implementation and enforcement is performed by states. A unique aspect of ESA is that it is a federal environmental statute that regulates across industries, and while most Americans will not come under its enforcement reach in any practical way, everyone from an individual walking through a forest to a multi-national logging corporation is beholden to the law. SMCRA, on the other hand, is only enforceable against a relatively small segment of society, coal miners and the coal mining industry. Perhaps most significantly, ESA is an incredibly well-known statute, inspiring some sort of response, either positive or negative, from most that hear its name spoken, whether or not one knows the first thing about the content of the law. SMCRA, on the other hand, is a rather unknown law, rarely spoken of in public forums.

In both chapters, the relationship of the environmental statute with regulatory takings litigation is discussed, and for both statutes, two different methods are used to assess the effect that such litigation has on the implementation and enforcement of that statute. The first such approach is quasi-experimental in nature and is referred to as an interrupted time-series analysis. This approach measures policy output trends before and after an interruption, in this case, the presence of a regulatory takings decision for compensation. Simply observing the number of policy outputs before and after a judicial decision may lack internal validity, however, due to "the possibility of a maturation alternative interpretation, ... [in which a] self-improvement trend [could be] visible before the treatment which we assume could have continued even without the change...."[111] Therefore, through the use of time-series regression, the trend, or slope, of policy outputs is measured, helping to control for maturation. Furthermore, policy output trends can be measured within subgroups, or panels, enabling the use of time-series cross-sectional (TSCS) analysis. Not only does this provide more observations, so that variance can more accurately be explained, but it also provides the opportunity to control for various variable which may affect policy outputs differently in different subgroups of the regulatory regime, such as states or regions.

While this quantitative approach is, conceptually, the most direct way to measure the impact of a regulatory takings case on the implementation of environmental statutes, the approach is not without its problems. A problem unique to time-series analyses is stationarity. If the observations of data in a TSCS analysis are not stationary, the estimates will likely be inefficient. "[A] stochastic process is said to be stationary if its mean and variance are constant over time and the value of covariance between two time periods depends only on the distance or lag between the two time periods and not on the actual time at which the covariance is computed."[112] To test for stationarity, Dickey-Fuller and correlogram testing was conducted for the dependent variable for each panel over time. Dickey-Fuller testing produces a tau-statistic [Z(t)], and if the absolute value of that statistic exceeds the absolute value of the critical values, then the hypothesis of stationary data is not rejected.[113] Likewise, correlogram testing produces a Q statistic which, if significant, indicates that the null hypothesis of stationarity should be rejected. In general, a lack of stationarity in the available data make the conclusions of these analyses suspect. All analyses were conducted using STATA version 10.

In addition to cross-sectional time-series regression analyses, interviews were conducted with key decision-making personnel within state and federal agencies charged with the implementation of SMCRA and ESA. The interviews provide a more in depth picture of regulatory processes, illuminating the possibility of awareness of litigation, the possibility of reaction, and the presence of countering forces that make up the day-to-day life of regulatory personnel.

Such elite interviews go directly to the source of regulatory behavior; the strength of such interviews is that the responses come directly from the individuals who may or may not be reacting to regulatory takings litigation. However, one must always remain aware that any observations made through such a process will invariably contain a degree of uncertainty.[114] Therefore, efforts were made to prevent leading the subjects, and the interviews were conducted in a manner that focused on general decision-making processes, narrowing down to various perceived threats to those processes, and eventually narrowing further, if needed, to regulatory takings challenges. In general, the structural forms unearthed by the interviews reveal decision-making processes which reduce the likelihood of regulatory takings litigation directly producing a behavioral adjustment characterized as a chilling effect.

A final note on the presentation and summarization of conclusions made through the elite interviews: It is customary in the presentation of interview-based research to provide direct quotations from interview subjects, while maintaining the subject's confidentiality. However, research interviews of elites require that extra precautions be taken to insure this confidentiality.[115] I observed quickly during these interviews that, not only was I interviewing a relatively small and determinable population, but I was also interviewing a population that was rather familiar with the identities of other members of the group. For this reason, I decided early on in the research process for this book to exercise caution in safeguarding confidentiality by not only refusing to directly identify participants, but to also forego any direct quotations of the respondents.

Finally, Chapter Seven reviews the conclusions of the case studies. In particular, factors present in ESA and/or SMCRA that help or inhibit a regulatory takings chilling effect are highlighted, and additional sources of potential impact are discussed.

NOTES

[1] U.S. CONST. amend. V.
[2] 545 U.S. 469 (2005).
[3] Mihaly, MB. 2007. "Living in the Past: The *Kelo* Court and Public-Private Economic Redevelopment." 34 Ecology L.Q. 1, 3.
[4] Arizona, California, Florida, Georgia, Idaho, North Dakota, New Hampshire, Nevada, Oregon, South Carolina, and Washington.
[5] California, Idaho, and Washington.
[6] Schultz, D. 2010. "Courts Matter: The Supreme Court, Social Change, and the Mobilization of Property Rights Interests," in *Property Rights and Neo-Liberalism: Cultural Demands and Legal Actions*. Ashgate Publishing. Forthcoming.

[7] Arizona (passed), Idaho (failed), Nevada (passed), Washington (failed)
[8] Arizona Secretary of State. "Arizona 2006 Ballot Propositions; General Election, November 7, 2006." p. 178.
[9] *Armstrong v. United States*, 364 U.S. 40, 49 (1960).
[10] O'Leary, R. 2006. "Environmental Policy in the Courts." *Environmental Policy: New Directions for the Twenty-First Century*, 6th ed. Norman J. Vig and Michael E. Kraft, eds. Washington, D.C.: CQ Press. p. 162.
[11] Harrington, CB and Turem, ZU. 2006. "Accounting for Accountability in Neoliberal Regimes," in *Public Accountability: Designs, Dilemmas and Experiences*. MW Dowdle, ed. New York: Cambridge University Press. p. 202.
[12] Fischel, WA. 1995. *Regulatory Takings: Law, Economics, and Politics*. Cambridge: Harvard University Press. p. 96.
[13] O'Leary, at 162.
[14] Alexander, GS. 2006. *The Global Debate over Constitutional Property: Lessons for American Takings Jurisprudence*. Chicago: University of Chicago Press. p. 63; For additional information on regulatory takings in an international context, see Ratner, SR. 2008. "Regulatory Takings in Institutional Context: Beyond the Fear of Fragmented International Law." *The American Journal of International Law*, Vol. 102, No. 3 (July). pp. 475-528.
[15] *Id.*, at 95.
[16] Fischel, at 217.
[17] Butler, HN and Macey, JR. 1996. "Externalities and the Matching Principle: The Case for Reallocating Environmental Regulatory Authority." 14 Yale J. on Reg. 23, 31-33.
[18] Kronman, AT. 1993. *The Lost Lawyer: Failing Ideals of the Legal Profession*. Cambridge: The Belknap Press of Harvard University Press. pp. 226-27.
[19] *Id.*, at 233.
[20] Posner, RA. 1986. *Economic Analysis of Law*, 3rd ed. Boston: Little, Brown and Company. p. 21.
[21] Boudreaux, K and Yandle, B. 2002. "Public Bads and Public Nuisance: Common Law Remedies for Environmental Decline." 14 Fordham Envtl. Law. J. 55, 58.
[22] *Id.*, at 60.
[23] Epstein, RA. 1985. *Takings: Private Property and the Power of Eminent Domain*. Cambridge: Harvard University Press. pp. 216-217.
[24] Rose, CM. 1996. "Propter Honoris Respectum: Property as the Keystone Right?" 71 Notre Dame L. Rev. 329, 339.
[25] Singer, JW. 2000. *Entitlement: The Paradoxes of Property*. New Haven: Yale University Press. pp. 16-17.
[26] Hardin, G. 1968. "The Tragedy of the Commons." *Science* 162:1243-1248.

[27] Dietz, T, et al. 2002. "The Drama of the Commons," in *The Drama of the Commons*. E Ostrom, et al., eds. Washington, D.C.: National Academy Press. p. 3.
[28] Hardin, at p. 1244.
[29] *Id.*, 1245.
[30] *Id.*, 1247.
[31] See *Martin v. Waddell*, 41 U.S. 367 (1842); *McCready v. Virginia*, 94 U.S. 391 (1877); *Geer v. Connecticut*, 161 U.S. 519 (1896)
[32] Dietz, at 9.
[33] *Id.*, at 9-10; See also Townsend, R., and Wilson, JA. 1987. "An Economic View of the Commons." *The Question of the Commons*. BJ McCay and JM Acheson, eds. Tucson: University of Arizona Press. p. 317.
[34] *Id.*, 9.
[35] Fennell, LA. 2004. "Common Interest Tragedies." 98 Nw. U.L. Rev. 907, 923.
[36] *Id.*, 3.
[37] McCay, BJ. 1998. *Oyster Wars and the Public Trust: Property, Law, and Ecology in New Jersey History*. Tucson: University of Arizona Press. p. xxiv; Agrawal, A. 2002. "Common Resources and Institutional Sustainability." *The Drama of the Commons*. E Ostrom, et al., eds. Washington, D.C.: National Academy Press. p. 42; Rose, CM. 2002. "Common Property, Regulatory Property, and Environmental Protection: Comparing Community-Based Management to Tradable Environmental Allowances." *The Drama of the Commons*. E Ostrom, et al., eds. Washington, D.C.: National Academy Press. p. 234; Fennell, at 912.
[38] Ostrom, E. 1990. *Governing the Commons: The Evolution of Institutions for Collective Action*. New York: Cambridge University Press. p. 14.
[39] Engel, KH and Saleska, SR. 2005. "Subglobal Regulation of the Global Commons: The Case of Climate Change." 32 Ecology L.Q. 183.
[40] McCay, BJ. 2002. "Emergence of Institutions for the Commons: Contexts, Situations, and Events." *The Drama of the Commons*. E Ostrom, et al., eds. Washington, D.C.: National Academy Press. pp. 361-362.
[41] *Id.*, 362.
[42] Gillman, H. 1999. "The Court as an Idea, Not a Building (or a Game): Interpretive Institutionalism and the Analysis of Supreme Court Decision-Making." *Supreme Court Decision-Making*. Chicago: University of Chicago Press. p. 78.
[43] Thompson, BH. 2000. "Tragically Difficult: The Obstacles to Governing the Commons." 30 Envtl. L. 241, 244.
[44] *Id.*, 269-271.
[45] McCay (2002), at p. 374.
[46] *Id.*, at 361-63.

[47] Glendon, MA. 1991. *Rights Talk: The Impoverishment of Political Discourse*. New York: The Free Press. p. 14.
[48] *Id.*, at 154.
[49] *Id.*, at 155.
[50] *Id.*, at 20.
[51] Hunt, A. 1993. *Explorations in Law and Society: Toward a Constitutive Theory of Law*. New York: Routledge, Inc. pp. 141-42.
[52] Kronman, at 227.
[53] *Id.*, at 3.
[54] *Id.*, at 20.
[55] *Id.*, at 168.
[56] *Id.*, at 246-47.
[57] Kennedy, D. 1976. "Form and Substance in Private Law Adjudication." 89 Harv. L.R. 1685, 1687-88.
[58] *Id.*, at 1688.
[59] *Id.*, at 1712.
[60] *Id.*, at 1713-18.
[61] *Id.*, at 1712-1713.
[62] *Id.*, at 1777.
[63] *Id.*
[64] Kronman, at 248.
[65] Moore, SF. 2001. "Certainties Undone: Fifty Turbulent Years of Legal Anthropology, 1949-1999," Huxley Memorial Lecture, *Journal of the Royal Anthropological Institute* 7(1). Cited from excerpts in Moore, SF, ed. 2005. *Law and Anthropology*. Malden: Blackwell Publishing. p. 357
[66] *Id.*, at 356-57.
[67] Merry, SE. 1988. "Legal Pluralism." *Law and Society Review*, 22:5. p. 880.
[68] *Id.*, at 870.
[69] Sparrow, MK. 2000. *The Regulatory Craft: Controlling Risks, Solving Problems, and Managing Compliance*. Washington, D.C.: Brookings Institution Press. 2000.
[70] Scheberle, D. 2004. *Federalism and Environmental Policy: Trust and the Politics of Implementation*, 2nd ed. Washington, D.C.: Georgetown University Press. p. 25.
[71] Nedelsky, J. 1990. *Private Property and the Limits of American Constitutionalism: The Madisonian Framework and Its Legacy*. Chicago: University of Chicago Press. p. 14.
[72] Epstein, at 30.
[73] Glendon, at 23-24.
[74] Schorr, DB. 2005. "Appropriation as Agrarianism: Distributive Justice in the Creation of Property Rights." 32 Ecology L.Q. 3, 4-5.
[75] Kennedy, at 1719.

[76] Schorr, at 25-33; see also *Coffin v. Left Hand Ditch Co.*, 6 Colo. 443 (1882)
[77] Kennedy, at 1708.
[78] Epstein, at 10.
[79] *Id.*, at 30.
[80] Fischel, at 120.
[81] *Id.*, at 289.
[82] Harrington and Turem, at 204.
[83] Frank, J. (1930)1963. *Law and the Modern Mind.* Garden City: Doubleday Anchor Books. p. 37.
[84] Alexander, at x-xi. For a description of the social obligation norm in Germany and South Africa, two countries whose constitutions explicitly include this norm, see chapters three and four, respectively, of Alexander.
[85] *Id.*, at 223-24.
[86] *Lucas v. South Carolina Coastal Council*, 505 U.S. 1003, 1027 (1992).
[87] Carter, LH and Burke, TF. 2010. *Reason in Law*, 8th ed. New York: Longman Classics in Political Science.
[88] Kagan, RA. 2004. "American Courts and the Policy Dialogue: The Role of Adversarial Legalism," in *Making Policy, Making Law: An Interbranch Perspective.* MC Miller and J Barnes, eds. Washington, D.C.: Georgetown University Press. p. 33.
[89] Melnick, RS. 2004. "Courts and Agencies," in *Making Policy, Making Law: An Interbranch Perspective.* MC Miller and J Barnes, eds. Washington, D.C.: Georgetown University Press. p. 92.
[90] Sunkin, M. 2004. "Conceptual Issues in Researching the Impact of Judicial Review on Government Bureaucracies," in *Judicial Review and Bureaucratic Impact: International and Interdisciplinary Perspectives.* M Hertogh and S Halliday, eds. New York: Cambridge University Press. p. 54.
[91] *Id.*, at 68.
[92] Bogus, CT. 2001. *Why Lawsuits are Good for America: Disciplined Democracy, Big Business, and the Common Law.* New York: New York University Press. p. 52.
[93] Sunkin, at 45.
[94] Canon, BC. 2004. "Studying Bureaucratic Implementation of Judicial Policies in the United States: Conceptual and Methodological Approaches," in *Judicial Review and Bureaucratic Impact: International and Interdisciplinary Perspectives.* M Hertogh and S Halliday, eds. New York: Cambridge University Press. p. 84.
[95] Sparrow, at 239.
[96] *Id.*, at 240.
[97] Scheberle, at 20-21.
[98] Rossi, J. 2005. *Regulatory Bargaining and Public Law.* New York: Cambridge University Press. pp. 9-10.

[99] Smith, RM. 1988. "Political Jurisprudence, The 'New Institutionalism,' and the Future of Public Law." *The American Political Science Review*, Vol. 82, No. 1. pp. 92-98.
[100] Sparrow, at 2.
[101] *Id.*, at 2-3.
[102] Nakamura, RT and Church, TW. 2003. *Taming Regulation: Superfund and the Challenges of Regulatory Reform.* Washington, D.C.: Brookings Institution Press. p. 6.
[103] *Id.*, at 7.
[104] http://propertyrights.utah.gov
[105] Treanor, WM. 1995. "The Original Understanding of the Takings Clause and the Political Process." 95 Colum. L. Rev. 782, 887.
[106] Sterk, SE. 2004. "The Federalist Dimension of Regulatory Takings Jurisprudence." 114 Yale L.J. 203, 205.
[107] 30 U.S.C. § 1201.
[108] 16 U.S.C. § 1531.
[109] 30 U.S.C. § 1251-1279.
[110] 16 U.S.C. § 1539.
[111] Cook, TD and Campbell, DT. 1979. *Quasi-Experimentation: Design & Analysis for Field Setting*. Boston: Houghton Mifflin Company. p. 209.
[112] Gujarati, DN. 1995. *Basic Econometrics*, 3rd ed. New York: McGraw-Hill, Inc. p. 713.
[113] *Id.*, at 719.
[114] Seidman, I.E. *Interviewing as Qualitative Research: A Guide for Researchers in Education and the Social Sciences.* New York: Teachers College Press. 1991. p. 103.
[115] Odendahl, T. and Shaw, A.M. 2002. "Interviewing Elites," in *Handbook of Interview Research: Context and Method.* J.F. Gubrium and J.A. Holstein, eds. Thousand Oaks: Sage Publications. 2002.

CHAPTER 2

REGULATORY TAKINGS JURISPRUDENCE

The origins of regulatory takings lie in the Fifth Amendment protection of property rights, which prohibits "private property be[ing] taken for public use, without just compensation."[1] This constitutional protection clearly requires compensation when the government uses its eminent domain powers to physically seize private property for public use. However, the Amendment has been increasingly interpreted to include non-physical takings of property, where regulations leave property in the hands of the owner but remove either economic value or particular instances of property rights. When a property owner believes that such regulations have basically taken his or her property, the owner can argue that the government action is not rationally related to the government's stated ends, imposes an unfair private burden in the achievement of such public ends, and/or has not satisfied basic procedural requirements.[2] In such instances, the owner should be compensated for his or her loss. While "the legal tests of validity and invalidity are indeed not clear,"[3] an overview of the Supreme Court's self-admittedly inconsistent regulatory takings jurisprudence[4] is possible.

Although the ability of property owners to seek compensation for government intrusion upon their property dates as far back as the Bill of Rights, such litigation has been rare throughout the majority of American history, during which time "[f]ew cases were litigated under the clause, and there was no such thing as a 'regulatory taking' ... although state and local governments had been regulating private land uses, sometimes quite stringently, since the colonial era."[5] In the rare occurrence of a regulatory taking claim, early federal courts were unwilling to engage in judicial review under the Fifth Amendment. In 1887, a Kansas statute prohibiting the production of alcohol was challenged before the Supreme Court as a taking of private property.[6] Although the Court emphasized that such a remedy should be sought in the state courts,[7] the Court also declared that the "right to compensation...of private property taken for public uses is foreign to the subject of preventing or abating public nuisances."[8] The earliest regulatory takings cases also demonstrate an acknowledgement of the limits of private property and recognition of a nuisance exception to the takings clause.

The Supreme Court's first effort at qualifying the nuisance exception occurred in *Pennsylvania Coal v. Mahon* in 1922.[9] This decision declared that the Kohler Act, a Pennsylvania statute requiring coal companies to leave enough coal as to not threaten surface structures, constituted a compensable taking. Takings jurisprudence would henceforth be seen as a balancing act, focusing on the "extent of the diminution."[10] While still providing nothing more than vague generalities, *Pennsylvania Coal* established the regulatory takings framework under which future conflicts would be fought. "The general rule at least is that while property may be regulated to a certain extent, if regulation *goes too far* it will be recognized as a taking."[11]

Although the Supreme Court continues to recognize the simultaneous claims of property owners to their property rights and governments to their need to regulate property, the Court has articulated tests to measure this balance more specifically than simply asking whether the state has gone "too far." In the landmark *Penn Central* decision, a New York landmark and historical preservation law prohibited the owners of Grand Central Station from constructing a 53 story office building above the terminal.[12] The question before the Court was whether such building restrictions would require compensation. After seeing its regulatory takings jurisprudence as being based on "essentially *ad hoc*, factual inquiries,"[13] the Court declared that it had historically "been unable to develop any 'set formula' for determining when 'justice and fairness' require that economic injuries caused by public action be compensated by the government, rather than remain disproportionately concentrated on a few persons."[14] The Court, therefore, established the three-pronged *Penn Central* test: whether government action constitutes a compensable taking depends on the economic impact of the regulation, interference with investment-backed expectations, and the nature of the government's action, ranging from outright invasion to protection of the common good.[15] These tests are, of course, heavily dependent upon interpretation and have given the Court ample opportunity to produce rulings with a high degree of variance. "First, the Court has defined each factor in a variety of ways, without acknowledging the shifts in definition. Second, it is difficult to predict what weight the Court will give to each factor. At different times the Court has actually regarded each one of these so-called 'factors' as dispositive of whether a taking occurred."[16]

Two years after establishing its *Penn Central* test, the Court established a new, two-pronged takings test, referred to as the *Agins* test.[17] This test required the state to "substantially advance legitimate state interests" and to not "den[y] an owner economically viable use of his [sic] land."[18] The purpose of this new test and its relationship to *Penn Central* was not clarified, and subsequent use of the test failed to establish a proper interpretation of both parts of the *Agins* test and their relationship to one another.[19] Furthermore, the Court demonstrated confusion regarding the priority of each test over the other. In a series of cases heard in the 1980's, the Court considered whether a number of property-limiting regulations affected takings. In 1981, the Supreme Court evaluated a facial challenge to the constitutionality of the Surface Mining Control and Reclamation Act of 1977.[20] In determining whether environmental regulations limiting the extent of coal mining essentially took property from owners of coal mineral rights, the Court used the *Agins* test, asking whether the "economically viable use" of the land is denied the owner.[21] Additionally, in a partial dissent in *Pennell v. City of San Jose*, Justice Scalia argued that the *Agins* test should be used to find a taking in certain rent control ordinances.[22]

However, in cases dealing with zoning ordinances[23] and pesticide data-disclosure,[24] the Court relied on *Penn Central*.

The Court has recently moved toward a clarification of the proper role of the *Agins* test and toward a judicial preference for the *Penn Central* test by stating that the "substantially advances" component of *Agins* suggests a means/end testing inconsistent with the inquiry into whether property has been taken.[25] This ruling indicates that the Court will likely utilize *Penn Central* in future cases involving less-than-total diminishment of property value through regulation.[26] The possibility remains, however, that the Court could be asked to evaluate property-use regulations, wherein "the failure of a regulation to accomplish a stated or obvious objective would be relevant"[27] to general property rights challenges to the government's authority to enact specific property restrictions. Such challenges are more relevant in cases of alleged eminent domain abuse, where plaintiffs question the legal validity of a blatant governmental taking of private property, and less relevant to the question of compensation, where the legitimacy of the government's action is, theoretically, never challenged.

Despite such confusions, observable trends are present in this period of regulatory takings jurisprudence. The most obvious trend is a strong spirit of judicial deference to lawmaking bodies when determining whether a regulation or statute provides a public use, which is required by both the Fifth Amendment and the first prong of the *Agins* test. While determining whether the regulation of private property satisfied the public use requirement, the Court regarded the term "public use" as coterminous with state police powers, and deferred to the reasoning of state legislatures as better able to determine whether such a requirement has been met.[28] The Court further demonstrated a strong commitment to the ripeness standard, requiring that cases demonstrate a "concrete controversy."[29] In addition, property owners were required to receive a final decision from the agency and seek a possible variance to the regulation, which would allow the public good to be sought while leaving the property owner with economic productivity.[30] One consequence of the Court's focus on ripeness in regulatory takings cases is that the strategic use of the Takings Clause as the foundation for constitutional challenges to entire pieces of regulation has not been successful.

SHIFTS IN THE DOCTRINE

Victories have been won lately, however, in the Supreme Court by advocates of strong private property rights. Correlating with the appointments of conservative justices with leanings sympathetic toward private property[31] and a backlash to the rapid bureaucratization of environmental protection at the federal level, this shift, while far from total, has made the U.S. Supreme Court a substantially friendlier locale for regulatory takings challenges. Case decisions from the middle of the 1980's to the present have demonstrated a jurisprudential shift in regulatory takings cases visible in four areas: the level of judicial deference, the role of economics, the understanding of the nature of property, and the degree of scrutiny applied to questions of ripeness.

Judicial Deference

This string of recent cases, beginning in the late 1980's, has been argued in an atmosphere less deferential to state legislatures and agencies, which seek to create and enforce policies that limit the use of private property. In 1987, the Court considered whether a requirement by the California Coastal Commission that a specific property owner provide lateral beach access as a condition to a building permit for a parcel of beachfront property affected a taking.[32] Instead of interpreting the Commission's discretion as coterminous with its power to protect the common good in coastal land, the Court evaluated the wisdom of the Commission's policy, and determined that a lateral easement served neither the function of beach access nor the elimination of psychological barriers to such access, as claimed by the Commission.[33] Five years later, the Court would provide a clear justification for its willingness to second-guess the policy decisions of legislatures and agencies when those decisions limit a property owner's use of his or her property.[34] Such limits are generally justified as serving not only a public purpose, but also the essential purpose of preventing harm to the public and its property. The Court argued, however, that "[s]ince such a justification can be formulated in practically every case, this amounts to a test of whether the legislature has a stupid staff."[35] Therefore, the Supreme Court has taken on the self-imposed responsibility of doing "more than insist upon artful harm-preventing characterizations."[36]

Although the Court became decidedly less likely to facially accept a state's argument that it was preventing a public harm and, therefore, was not constitutionally required to compensate the property owner, this did not mean that states were prohibited entirely from such actions. The Court continues to recognize the limited nature of property rights, and further recognizes uncompensated limits can be placed upon property "if the logically antecedent inquiry into the nature of the owner's estate shows that the proscribed use interests were not part of his [sic] title to begin with."[37] In other words, the right to endanger the public is not part of my bundle of rights in a specific piece of property; therefore, when such action is regulated away, I deserve no compensation, because what was taken was not my property in the first place. The recent willingness of the Supreme Court to limit property by such means, however, should not be overstated. The Court has stated that "[a]ny limitation so severe cannot be newly legislated or decreed (without compensation), but must inhere in the title itself, in the restrictions that background principles of the State's law of property and nuisance already place upon land ownership."[38] In addition to limiting the nature of harms legislatures and agencies can declare, the Court also established standards by which policies aimed at protecting the public from such harms could limit property rights.[39] While prior decisions looked for a rational basis to justify policies that limit private property, the Supreme Court in *Dolan* introduced a stricter scrutiny for evaluating such policies.[40] Short of supplying a precise mathematical calculation, the Court now requires a policy to demonstrate a "rough proportionality" between the nature of the prevented harm and the extent of the requirements placed upon property owners.[41]

The Role of Economics

An increased scrutiny placed upon governments and their ability to limit the use of private property is indicative of a Court that has shifted its understanding of the nature of property and increased the significance of economic factors within that understanding. While the *Penn Central* and *Agins* tests stress both economic factors and the nature of regulatory action, including that which is regulated and the manner in which it is regulated, the Rehnquist Court increased the emphasis on the economic impacts of regulation in determining the existence of a regulatory taking. In *Lucas v. South Carolina Coastal Council*, the Court took a step toward clarifying the relationship between economic and non-economic factors in regulatory takings cases.[42] While property rights remain limited in the face of background principles of the common good, a *per se* taking occurs when regulation deprives the owner of all economically viable uses of the property.[43] The Court was particularly interested in protecting property in land, arguing that the "historical compact recorded in the Takings Clause that has become part of our constitutional culture" is inconsistent with the elimination by regulation of all economic value,[44] that is, without compensation. The Court does give examples of land uses that could be legally prohibited, even to the point of a total economic loss, which would not require compensation.[45] Such regulations limit the use of property to those uses that do not harm others or their property and simply "make the implication of those background principles of nuisance and property law explicit."[46] As stated above, however, such limitations on property cannot be "newly legislated,"[47] leaving it unclear how a legislature can make background principles explicit.

The Nature of Property

This increased focus on the role of economic factors in regulatory takings cases is correlated with a shift in the Court's doctrine on the nature of property. Throughout the history of its regulatory takings jurisprudence, the Court has sought the balancing of private property rights and public interests. One of the most significant facets of property rights considered by the Court is the right to exclude others, which the Court has regarded as "one of the most essential sticks in the bundle of rights that are commonly characterized as property."[48] In cases involving outright physical occupation, the Court has generally required the use of the states' eminent domain powers and the compensation of property owners.[49] In cases involving transition across private property, instead of physical occupation on such property, in order to guarantee public access to some public good, the private property right has been weighted more heavily by the Court in recent decisions.[50] Furthermore, the Court has regarded development as land's "essential use,"[51] requiring governments to provide stronger defenses for public and environmental protections.

During the aforementioned period of judicial deference in regulatory takings cases, the chronological order of the acquisition of property and the imposition of a regulatory limit on the use of property affected the legitimacy of a taking claim. Acquiring property under pre-existing regulations was generally understood as preventing the owner from having reasonable investment-backed expectations.[52] This so-called notice rule functions to define the background principals of property alluded to in *Lucas* by claiming that, "the underlying background principles of property must include all existing regulatory constraints at the time of acquisition."[53] Under such jurisprudence, property rights are positive rights, with origins in political processes, and the Takings Clause exists as a foundational law that governs the further maintenance of those rights. This position, however, has been recently challenged by the Court, which has stated that if the notice rule exception is seen as absolute, then "the postenactment transfer of title would absolve the State of its obligation to defend any action restricting land use, no matter how extreme or unreasonable. A State would be allowed, in effect, to put an expiration date on the Takings Clause."[54] By explicitly rejecting a Hobbesian understanding of the relationship between the state and property, and accepting a Lockean construction,[55] the Court has placed property rights into the realm of natural rights, which exist independent of and prior to the state.

It should be stated that the majority in *Palazzolo*, in keeping the seemingly required ambiguity found throughout regulatory takings jurisprudence, provided confusion over the role of the notice rule in a pair of concurring opinions. While the majority determined that the timing of Palazzolo's acquisition of the property (after regulations had been enacted) did not proscribe his taking claim, Justices Scalia and O'Connor disagreed as to the role of chronology more generally. Justice Scalia argued that timing has no bearing on the question, claiming that "[a] *Penn Central* taking … is not absolved by the transfer of title."[56] While Justice O'Connor agrees that post-enactment acquisition of title is "not talismanic under *Penn Central*,"[57] she does not appear ready to fully reject the notice rule. In her concurring opinion in *Palazzolo*, O'Connor stated:

> Today's holding does not mean that the timing of the regulation's enactment relative to the acquisition of title is immaterial to the *Penn Central* analysis. Indeed, it would be just as much error to expunge this consideration from the takings inquiry as it would be to accord it exclusive significance. Our polestar instead remains the principles set forth in *Penn Central* itself and our other cases that govern partial regulatory takings. Under these cases, interference with investment-backed expectations is one of a number of factors that a court must examine. Further, the regulatory regime in place at the time the claimant acquires the property at issue helps to shape the reasonableness of those expectations.[58]

A peculiar development resultant of the changes in the three factors described above is the development of an implicit test, or better, an implicit arrangement of tests, which has been used by the Court to determine whether the facts of a particular case constitute a compensable taking of property. Short of composing an expressed test, the following demonstrates the order of inquiry in which the Court has generally engaged and which lower federal courts have routinely followed in cases involving alleged regulatory takings. First, the Court has traditionally regarded a regulation which involves the physical invasion of private property by the government or a third party as constituting a taking, "no matter how minute the intrusion, and no matter how weighty the public purpose behind it."[59] In other words, physical invasion constitutes a categorical taking, just as total economic diminution constitutes a categorical taking in *Lucas*. The question of physical invasion, however, fits more comfortably within a discussion of eminent domain, and although it is generally the first inquiry made by the Court in regulatory takings, it is frequently handled quickly and inconspicuously.

FIGURE 2.1: Flowchart of Regulatory Takings Judicial Decision-Making

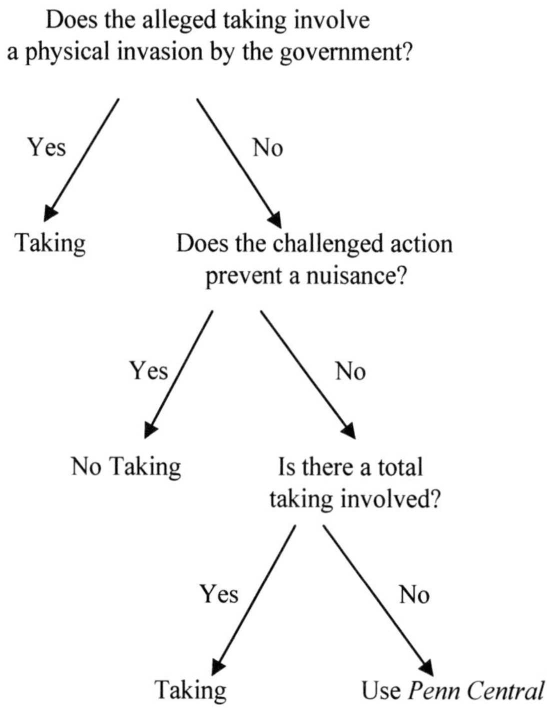

Once the generally facial inquiry into the existence of a physical invasion is complete, the Court has then generally turned to the far more delicate practice of determining whether the challenged regulatory action prevents a nuisance, which would absolve the government's duty to compensate for value lost. If the regulation is not aimed at nuisance prevention, then the Court inquires whether there has been a total taking. The ordering of these two steps might appear counterintuitive; one could reasonably assume that a per se, categorical taking, as described in *Lucas*, would be just that, categorical, and be a taking regardless of the involvement of a nuisance. Scalia is clear in *Lucas*, however, and although he limits the definition of nuisance to background principles in state property law, the consideration of the nuisance exception occurs logically prior to the consideration of a total taking, as the prevention of a nuisance will justify a total and uncompensated economic loss. Only after inquiries have been made into the existence of physical invasion, nuisance, and a total taking, and all three having been found lacking, should the courts utilize a *Penn Central* analysis.

Ripeness

Finally, more recent rulings in regulatory takings cases have potentially altered the environment in which the Court considers the question of ripeness, or whether a case is ready for review. Often described as one of the Court's "passive virtues,"[60] the ripeness doctrine acts as a judicial gatekeeper[61] and safeguard of the separation of powers by enabling members of the Court, "through avoidance of premature adjudication, from entangling themselves in abstract disagreements over administrative policies, and also to protect the agencies from judicial interference until an administrative decision has been formalized…."[62] Rooted in the constitutional limitation of the federal judicial power to true cases and controversies,[63] the ripeness doctrine serves the practical and prudential purpose of recognizing that "a court cannot properly adjudicate a case if the record before it is incomplete."[64] In cases involving regulatory takings, the ripeness doctrine is particularly significant, given the fact-based nature of regulatory takings decisions.[65]

Although neither *Penn Central* nor *Agins* is an actual ripeness case, the criteria used by the Court in these decisions laid the groundwork for the ripeness doctrine in regulatory takings cases. In *Penn Central*, the Court ruled that enactment of the New York historical preservation law did not constitute a taking, because the law did not interfere with the owners' then-present use of their property, nor did the denial of their application necessarily prohibit all use of the overhead airspace; an application for a smaller construction project might have been accepted.[66] Likewise, in *Agins*, the Court ruled that zoning ordinances, which include density restrictions, did not, on their face, constitute a taking[67] partially because the appellants never submitted a development plan, meaning there was no concrete controversy[68] and the appellants were still free to pursue the use of their property through the application process.[69] Although both cases were decided on the merits, *Penn Central* and *Agins* still figure prominently in the ripeness doctrine of regulatory takings jurisprudence, because the Court's requirement that an application be submitted, resubmitted, or modified became a central component in determining when a regulatory takings claim is ripe.[70]

After the Supreme Court alluded to ripeness guidelines in *Penn Central* and *Agins*, the Court began to rule specifically on the ripeness of regulatory takings cases. Early in its development of this ripeness doctrine, the Court was more likely to demonstrate a strict adherence to its ripeness requirements, which "reflected its respect for the autonomy and discretion of regulatory agencies by encouraging negotiation between landowners and regulatory agencies."[71] Subsequent rulings would "provide more protection for landowners' rights."[72] Initial decisions applied the doctrine of ripeness to prevent the Court from prematurely adjudicating cases, but did not help to standardize the ripeness doctrine, as applied to regulatory takings. In *Virginia Surface Mining* the Court ruled that a facial challenge to the Surface Mining Control and Reclamation Act was unripe because the "constitutionality of statutes ought not be decided except in an actual factual setting that makes such a decision necessary."[73] This decision mirrored the concrete controversy requirement in *Agins*[74] and would be used seven years later to rule in *Pennell* that a challenge to hardship provisions within a rental control ordinance was premature, because there was no evidence that the provision had ever been used.[75] In *San Diego Gas*, compensatory challenges to open space and industrial zoning restrictions were held unripe because the state appeals court had left the case open for a retrial due to confusion about the facts.[76] In its *Monsanto* decision, the Court ruled that a regulatory takings challenge to the data sharing provisions of federal pesticide laws were not ripe, because the owners of such intellectual property had not availed themselves to other options available for compensation.[77] While these three cases are important indicators of a Court attempting to work out a controllable role for itself in regulatory takings cases, the question of ripeness in each was answered by analyzing the specific facts of each case. For example, in *San Diego Gas*, the Court concerned itself with the standard of finality of state judicial decisions, as established for the

Court under U.S. statutory law,[78] and did not address the specific question of ripeness in regulatory takings cases. Little attention, however, was given to establishing a general ripeness doctrine for regulatory takings cases.

The Court's general ripeness doctrine would be established in two cases which still stand as the foundation of the ripeness doctrine of regulatory takings, known as the final decision requirement. In its *Williamson County*[79] and *MacDonald*[80] decisions, both of which dealt with challenges to zoning restrictions by developers, "the United States Supreme Court has articulated at least four distinct elements to consider in determining whether a landowner has obtained final decision concerning the development of his [sic] land sufficient to 'ripen' a takings claim."[81] The first element of the Court's final decision requirement is the need for a property owner to submit a proposal for use to the appropriate agency, as required in *Agins*.[82] The landowners in *Williamson County* and *MacDonald* both met this basic requirement,[83] but subsequent inaction on the part of the property owners resulted in the Court ruling that a final administrative decision had not been made and, therefore, the cases were not ripe for review.

In the event that a proposal for land use is submitted and rejected, the final decision requirement requires the property owner to "resubmit modified proposals that attempt to satisfy the...government's objection to the use or development as initially proposed."[84] The possibility of revised resubmittal of land use proposals "leave[s] open the possibility that some development will be permitted, and thus again leave...doubt regarding the antecedent question whether...property has been taken."[85] In addition to the possibility of resubmitting a proposal, property owners must be aware that some property regulations contain provisions to ameliorate total losses, provisions which must be pursued by property owners before a takings claim will be considered ripe. Some laws permit administrative agencies to permit variances to particular requirements of property regulations; without a pursuit of such variances on the part of the property owner, a governmental "denial of approval does not conclusively determine whether [the property owner] will be denied all reasonable beneficial use of its property,"[86] leaving a taking claim unripe. Furthermore, before compensation can be sought through judicial measures, the property owner must avail him/herself of administrative procedures for compensation allowed by the law or the regulation.[87] "If the government has provided an adequate process for obtaining compensation; and if resort to that process 'yield[s] just compensation,' then the property owner 'has no claim against the Government' for a taking."[88]

Shortly after the Court established its final decision doctrine to aid in the determination of the ripeness of regulatory takings cases, the Court began to issue decisions that abided by the requirements of *Williamson County*, but established exceptions to the final decision rule. In a series of significant decisions, the Court found regulatory takings challenges ripe for review, and occasionally proceeded to rule that a compensable taking had occurred. The Court softened its ripeness strictures through an increased focus of the issue of temporary takings and through the direct development of the futility exception to the final decision rule.

The issue of temporary takings is related, in theory and in judicial application, to the question of baseline determination in regulatory takings cases. The Court must occasionally consider what property baseline, as a whole, is to be used when determining the degree of economic impact caused by a regulation, in particular, to evaluate the *Penn Central* factor of economic impact.[89] In other words, the Court must determine, as the Court has put it, "the proper denominator in the takings fraction."[90] Within the context of a temporary taking, instead of asking how many acres should be considered as the plaintiff's total property, the Court must determine the "relevant denominator" of time against which to compare a property owner's rights in a "temporal slice."[91] If the Court finds that a regulation effects a total taking of <u>that</u> piece of property, for <u>that</u> period of time, then the final decision requirement can be side-stepped, because future resolution of a final decision does not affect past deprivations of property.[92]

The Court first considered ripeness in the context of temporary takings in its *First English* decision, which ruled a California state law limiting compensation for a regulatory taking to after a court has determined a regulation to be excessive, has issued declaratory relief or a writ of mandamus, yet the state continues to enforce the regulation, as inconsistent with the Fifth Amendment.[93] In the case, a flood control regulation prohibited the construction of buildings within a particular floodplain; the challenge to the regulation by a property owner within the floodplain was rejected by state courts because compensation was sought for denial of total use, without first seeking invalidation of the regulation.[94] The Court determined that, in this case, the state court ruling insulated the Supreme Court from the remedial questions involved, and made the question of whether a temporary taking (i.e. one which is halted by the invalidation of a regulation as excessive) is compensable, ripe.[95] "Although on remand the state courts could find that no taking had occurred,...the Court found that resolution of the takings claim would not address the issue of whether the just compensation clause required the government to pay for temporary regulatory takings."[96]

Additionally, the *Lucas* decision further strengthened the role of temporary regulatory takings in overcoming the ripeness hurdle. The state statute central to the case prohibited, without exception, construction of inhabitable structures seaward of an erosion baseline, and was passed in 1988 by the South Carolina legislature.[97] In 1990, after Lucas, who owned regulated property, challenged the law, the legislature amended the law to allow for the issuance of "special permits" for construction.[98] Although Lucas never applied for such a special permit, the Court stated that requiring him to do so to satisfy the ripeness standard would preclude him from challenging the deprivation of his property prior to the 1990 amendment.[99]

Lucas was also determined to be ripe for review through the utilization of the futility exception. In his dissent in *MacDonald*, Justice White argued that, while the final decision requirement of *Williamson County* is necessary to establish ripeness, resubmitting a denied proposal may not be necessary to establish a final decision. White stated, "Although a landowner must pursue reasonably available avenues that might allow relief, it need not, I believe, take patently fruitless measures."[100] His argument would prove prophetic as a more conservative Court would seek to reduce the "procedural merry-go-round" experienced by property owners[101] and reign in "over-zealous municipalities [that] can effectively filibuster development by perpetually delaying or denying plans and applications."[102] The futility exception excuses property owners from resubmitting proposals to arrive at a final administrative decision. To qualify for the futility exception, a property owner must demonstrate that the agency was powerless to adjust its position or that the filing of additional proposals would be so time consuming as to be cost prohibitive.[103] In *Lucas*, the Court stated that the property owner need not even file a development proposal with the council, since the strict and unalterable conditions of the 1988 Act would make such applications pointless.[104]

Although the futility exception has been brought in from lower court decisions, and attempts to codify its requirements have been unsuccessful,[105] it appears to be one of the less controversial components of the Courts ripeness and regulatory takings doctrines. In its *Suitum* decision, the Court unanimously agreed that a landowner did not need to file a second application for a building permit from the Tahoe Regional Planning Agency, because the strict requirements adhering to the agency's Stream Environment Zone (SEZ) classification left the property owner "definitively barred from taking any affirmative step to develop her land.... The only discretionary step left to [the] agency...[was] enforcement, not determining applicability.[106] The agency had argued that the property owner's access to Transfer of Development Rights (TDRs), which allowed her to sell the development rights that were abrogated by the regulation to developers in areas seeking denser development, should leave the case unripe, because the owner had made no effort to sell her TDRs, nor was their value known.[107] The Court disagreed, pointing to the facts that demonstrated that there was nothing disputed about her rights to TDRs or their value.[108] The only significant dispute between the Justices in the case concerned whether TDRs (and other regulatory or private compensatory provisions) should be considered in the "taking" or "compensation" part of evaluating regulations; if they should be considered in the compensation part of the equation, as was argued by the concurring justices, then the majority's evaluation of the value of the TDRs was unnecessary.[109]

Further evidence of the less-than-controversial nature of the futility exception can be found in the Court's 2001 *Palazzolo* decision. While not a unanimous decision, disagreement over *Palazzolo*'s ripeness was limited. In the decision, the Court ruled that a regulatory taking challenge to wetland regulations that prohibited a property owner from filling wetlands on his property for development purposes was ripe, because the "unequivocal nature"[110] of the regulations would make subsequent applications meaningless. The only dispute involving ripeness dealt with evaluating the facts of the case, not with whether the

MacDonald requirement of resubmitting a proposal should be strictly followed. Justice Ginsberg argued that "the Court's decision was inaccurate because the record was ambiguous with respect to the extent of permissible development,"[111] referring to developable upland portions of the property, which the plaintiff had included in earlier applications, but removed from the application before the Court.[112] The ripeness ruling in *Palazzolo* has been seen by some as a "specific ripeness ruling [which] is tied to the facts of the case and is thus unlikely to have much precedential effect adverse to government officials."[113] This sentiment was mirrored in the Court's *Tahoe-Sierra* decision one year later, in which a challenge to a severe development moratorium was considered unripe, despite the length of the moratorium and the Court's recent temporary takings doctrine, due to "the interest in facilitating informed decisionmaking by regulatory agencies."[114]

Finally, although it has not been utilized in any majority decisions by the Court in cases dealing with the ripeness of regulatory takings challenges, the argument put forth by Justice Scalia regarding the concrete controversy requirement of *Agins* should also be considered. In *Pennell*, the plaintiffs argued that hardship provisions of rent control ordinances unduly force private individuals to shoulder a public benefit.[115] The majority ruled that this facial challenge was unripe because there was no record of a concrete occurrence of the regulations application.[116] In his dissent, Justice Scalia argued that "knowing the nature and character of the particular property in question, or the degree of its economic impairment, will in no way assist this inquiry."[117] By arguing that a regulatory takings challenge can be considered ripe without reference to a specific application of the regulation, which the Court has historically used to determine "how far" a regulation has gone,[118] would add another exception to the Court's ripeness doctrine by eliminating the concrete controversy requirement by considering it "inconceivable…[to] say judicial challenge must await demonstration that this provision has actually been applied to the detriment of one of the plaintiffs."[119]

REGULATORY TAKINGS AND EMINENT DOMAIN

Although regulatory takings law and eminent domain law are closely related through their connection to the Takings Clause of the Fifth Amendment, it is important to recognize their distinctions. The difference between the bodies of law can be summarized by focusing on the essential argument made by claimants. In the case of regulatory takings, a plaintiff acknowledges the authority of the government to restrict property use, but argues that the restrictions amount to a taking and, thereby, require compensation. An eminent domain plaintiff, however, generally challenges the authority of the government to take property, even though such a taking is compensated. Apart from litigation aimed at determining just compensation, suits challenging a violation of eminent domain law gravitate around assessments of whether a particular governmental taking of private property satisfies the requirement of public use.

Definition of "public use," however, has been the subject of recent contestation within the Court. The Supreme Court's 2005 decision in *Kelo v. New London*[120] sparked a vitriolic reaction from property rights interests groups and the general public. Editorial titles, such as "Your Home Could be Up for Grabs"[121] and "Your Castle No More,"[122] summarize the sentiment of the backlash: the Supreme Court, with its decision in *Kelo*, has altered a pre-existing property protection and given the government an unprecedented degree of power over private property. Blame fell immediately on "activist justices" and residents of Weare, New Hampshire, attempted to evict Justice Souter from his home in the town "so that he can understand the importance of property rights and the error of the ruling."[123] The ruling, however, was clearly written in a spirit of deference and merely parroted past rulings.

Key to eminent domain jurisprudence is the definition of public use and whether the Court chooses to take a "broad view" or a "narrow view" of public use.[124] Narrowly interpreted, "public use" would require direct use of the property by the public, such as in instances of highway or park construction. The Court has, however, eschewed this reading and interpreted the phrase "public use" to mean "public purpose,"[125] thereby including transitions of property back to private hands for public purposes, such as the construction of privately run prisons. What remains clear is that a forced transition from one private owner to another, an A to B transfer, even with compensation, would not satisfy the Fifth Amendment since it would lack a public use or purpose.[126]

Past Supreme Court decisions provide clear examples of cases in which property is confiscated, compensation is paid, the property is transferred to another private individual, and the Court has interpreted the public use requirement as satisfied. The case with which most analyses begin is the 1954 *Berman* decision.[127] In this decision, the Court upheld the District of Columbia Act of 1945, an act of Congress aimed at relieving economic blight in Washington, D.C., through condemnation and possible transfer of title to private developers with the intention of sparking economic development. The question of the public nature of economic development, a question that would be central to *Kelo*, was answered by the Court through attention to police powers. The Court determined that it is legislative, not judicial, responsibility to determine the extent of police powers and the corresponding public interests,[128] as well the means of securing them.[129]

Thirty years later, the Court would rule on its *Midkiff* decision, which upheld efforts of the state of Hawai'i to combat oligopoly by compelling holders of feudal title to land to essentially sell their land to the state, which would sell it back to private citizens in order to redistribute land ownership.[130] In this instance, the property transfer scheme represents an A to B transfer, as the public would not have use rights to the transferred property, but the Court found that "the exercise of the eminent domain power is rationally related to a conceivable public purpose,"[131] namely, combating oligopoly. As in *Berman*, the Court in *Midkiff* prescribed a narrow role for itself in determining whether an eminent domain action has a nexus with public use, limiting that inquiry to whether "the legislature's purpose is legitimate and its means are not irrational,"[132] focusing on "the taking's purpose, and not its mechanics."[133] Generally, if there are instances of private benefit conferred by eminent domain powers, the action will still satisfy the public use requirement if private benefits are incidental to the actions, while public benefits are predominant and non-speculative.[134]

This is the legal background in which the Court made its *Kelo* decision in 2005. The case deals with the city of New London, Connecticut's, acquisition of 90 acres by purchase and compensated confiscation of the Fort Trumbull area, an area designated by the state as a "distressed municipality," for the execution of a development plan aimed at job creation, increase in tax revenues, and economic revitalization.[135] Intending to capitalize on the recent arrival of a neighboring Pfizer facility, the city developed a seven parcel plan including space for a conference hotel, restaurants, retail shops, a residential/commercial marina, public recreational walkways, new residential areas, a river walk, office and research space, parking, a museum, and supportive services for the neighboring, recently created, state park.[136] Petitioners in the case, who owned property being seized through eminent domain, argued that such planned uses failed to satisfy the public use requirement of the Fifth Amendment, and constituted an A to B transfer of property from one set of private hands to another.[137]

The *Kelo* plaintiffs asked the Supreme Court to perform two tasks that would prove difficult to do in the face of *Berman* and *Midkiff.* First, the plaintiffs stated that a bright-line rule should be established eliminating economic-development from the definition of public use.[138] The majority saw "no basis for exempting economic development from [the] traditionally broad understanding of public purpose."[139] Instead of referring to economic development as a public good, per se, the Court used language recognizing the distinction between private and public benefit, while acknowledging at least the possibility of their coexistence. "Quite simply, the government's pursuit of a public purpose will often benefit individual private parties.... 'The public end may be as well or better served through an agency of private enterprise than through a department of government – or so the Congress might conclude."[140] This language harkens back to previous rulings that allow for private benefit to accrue from public use, provided that benefit is incidental to a stated public purpose.[141] The presence of a formulated development plan, one which extended beyond the litigated properties and included an array of benefits beyond the challenged one, provided the predominance of public purpose.[142]

Second, the *Kelo* plaintiffs suggested that during tests of public use, the Court should at least ascertain the presence of a "reasonable certainty" that the expected public benefits will actually occur.[143] This point seems to be at the center of the public's confusion and ire. In ruling against the necessity of reasonable certainty, the Court observed the numerous stages of municipal decision-making and deferred to their judgment, stating, "When the legislature's purpose is legitimate and its means are not irrational, our cases make clear that empirical debates over the wisdom of takings...are not to be carried out in the federal courts."[144] By deferring to the municipality, the Court was perceived by some as approving the decision, as declaring it to be right. Critics of the Court's *Kelo* decision might claim that "New London can say that redevelopment program will 'create hundreds of jobs and substantial new tax revenue.' But saying it doesn't make it true—or even plausible.... The political power of faction is so great than [sic] those with influence will regrettably have their way. And yet the courts stand aside as if the legislature were composed of angels."[145]

The concern that municipal decision-making bodies can be captured by a wealthy and influential minority, which would guide the use of eminent domain power to create private benefit at public detriment, is legitimate. The Court's concern, however, as expressed in the *Kelo* majority opinion, is whether the judicial branch is an effective, or even an appropriate, control on such conditions. In acknowledging the diversity of conditions addressed by land use planning agencies, the Court declared that its "public use jurisprudence has wisely eschewed rigid formulas and intrusive scrutiny in favor of affording legislatures broad latitude in determining what public needs justify the use of the taking power."[146] Additionally, although local government may be dominated by elite interests, there is no reason to assume that courts are not equally susceptible. "Admittedly, in economic redevelopment projects, the poor are more likely to be displaced than the rich.... Cities are the most plausible governmental champions of the poor in our current political configuration, because their voices can be heard there."[147]

It is through this consideration of deference that a most significant connection can be drawn between eminent domain and regulatory taking laws. In deferring to legislative bodies for the determination of public use, the Court "emphasize[d] that nothing in [the] opinion precludes any State from placing further restrictions on its exercise of the takings power."[148] The ability or inability of voters to create consequences for bad or unpopular decisions forms much of the justification for judicial deference. The *Kelo* Court could have been even more comfortable in deferring to the "majoritarian" and municipal decisions in this case, given that a Connecticut statute defines economic development as a public use.[149] The backlash generated by the *Kelo* decision, however, manifested itself as citizens took up the Court's invitation to place further restrictions on state taking power. As discussed in the Introduction of this book, in the 2006 midterm elections, eleven state ballots contained initiatives to restrict eminent domain power through defining public use as not including economic development.[150] While the impetus to some of these initiatives could have been significant anecdotal accounts of particular egregious cases of eminent domain abuse, several initiatives expressly referenced the *Kelo* decision in their accompanying literature. Additionally, four of the eleven ballot initiatives contained regulatory takings language requiring that the state and municipal governments compensate property owners for land use restrictions (not takings) that decrease property value; two of the four passed.[151]

The public reaction to *Kelo* is an essential part in the understanding of the development of property law, generally, and regulatory takings law, specifically. The evolutions of both eminent domain and regulatory takings jurisprudences involve shifts in the ideas contained within them. Within courtrooms, deference has waned and scrutiny has heightened in regulatory takings cases as the Supreme Court has established greater property rights-based obstacles to property management. A corresponding increase in burden has not been placed by the courts upon governments seeking to use eminent domain powers. That shift has moved from the courtroom to legislative arenas. The end result is a multi-faceted property rights movement that has succeeded in establishing legal protections for private property against governmental efforts at the protection of common interests. The degree to which such shifts in legal protections actually manifest themselves in the policy outputs of governmental bodies charged with regulations that frequently confront private property is a separate question.

NOTES

[1] U.S. CONST. amend. V.
[2] Plater, ZJB, et al. 1998. *Environmental Law and Policy: Nature, Law, and Society.* 2nd ed. St. Paul: West Publishing Co. pp. 1037-38.
[3] *Id.*, at 1051.
[4] *Penn Cent. Transp. Co. v. New York City*, 438 U.S. 104, 124 (1978).

[5] Cole, DH. 2002. *Pollution and Property: Comparing Ownership Institutions for Environmental Protection.* New York: Cambridge University Press. p. 155
[6] *Mugler v. Kansas*, 123 U.S. 623 (1887).
[7] *Id.*, at 672.
[8] *St. Louis v. Stern*, 3 Mo. App 48, 53 (1876); *Mugler*, at 667.
[9] *Pennsylvania Coal v. Mahon*, 260 U.S. 393 (1922).
[10] *Id.*, at 413.
[11] *Id.*, at 415 (emphasis added).
[12] *Penn Central*, at 116-117.
[13] *Id.*, at 124.
[14] *Id.* See also *Kaiser Aetna v. U.S.*, 444 U.S. 164, 175 (1979).
[15] *Id.*
[16] Peterson, AL. 1989. *The Takings Clause: In Search of Underlying Principles, Part I—A Critique of Current Takings Clause Doctrine*, 77 CAL. L. REV. 1301, 1317.
[17] *Agins v. Tiburon*, 447 U.S. 255 (1980).
[18] *Id.*, at 260.
[19] Peterson, at 1328-30.
[20] See *Hodel v. Virginia Surface Mining & Reclamation Ass'n*, 452 U.S. 264, 295 (1981).
[21] *Id.*, at 296.
[22] 485 U.S. 1, 18 (1988).
[23] See, e.g., *Williamson County Planning Comm'n v. Hamilton Bank*, 473 U.S. 172, 191 (1985); *MacDonald, Sommer & Frates v. Yolo County*, 477 U.S. 340, 349 (1986).
[24] See, e.g., *Ruckelshaus v. Monsanto Co.*, 467 U.S. 986, 1005 (1984).
[25] *Lingle v. Chevron, U.S.A.*, 125 S.Ct. 2074, 2084 (2005)
[26] *Id.*, at 2087.
[27] *Id.*, Kennedy concurring
[28] See, e.g., *Hawai'i Housing Authority v. Midkiff*, 467 U.S. 229, 240 (1984); *Monsanto*, at 1014.
[29] *Virginia Surface Mining*, at 295; *see also Pennell*, at 10.
[30] See *Williamson County*, at 186; *MacDonald*, at 348.
[31] Brisbin, RA, Jr. 1990. "The Conservatism of Antonin Scalia." *Political Science Quarterly*, Vol. 105, No. 1; O'Connor, K. 1992. "The Effects of the Thomas Appointment to the Supreme Court." *PS: Political Science and Politics*. Vol. 25, No. 3.
[32] *Nollan v. California Coastal Comm'n*, 483 U.S. 825 (1987).
[33] *Id.*, at 839-40.
[34] See *Lucas v. South Carolina Coastal Council*, 505 U.S. 1003, 1029 (1992).
[35] *Id.*, at n.12
[36] *Id.*,

[37] *Id.*, at 1027.
[38] *Id.*, at 1029.
[39] *Id.*, at 1027.
[40] *Dolan v. City of Tigard*, 512 U.S. 374, 390 (1994).
[41] *Id.*, at 391.
[42] *Lucas*, at 1027-30.
[43] *Id.*, at 1020.
[44] *Id.*, at 1028.
[45] *Id.*, at 1029.
[46] *Id.*, at 1030.
[47] *Id.*, at 1029.
[48] *Kaiser Aetna*, at 176.
[49] See id. See also *Loretto v. Teleprompter Manhattan CATV Corp.*, 458 U.S. 419 (1982).
[50] *Nollan*, at 831; *Dolan*, at 383.
[51] *Lucas*, at 1031 (quoting *Curtin v. Benson*, 222 U.S. 78, 86 (1911)).
[52] See *Monsanto*, at 1006.
[53] Burling, JS. 2002. "Private Property Rights and the Environment After *Palazzolo*." 30 B.C. ENVTL. AFF. L. REV. 1, 31 .
[54] *Palazzolo v. Rhode Island*, 533 U.S. 606, 627 (2001).
[55] *Id.*
[56] *Id.*, at 637 (Scalia, J., concurring).
[57] *Id.*, at 634 (O'Connor, J., concurring).
[58] *Id.*, at 633. (O'Connor concurring)
[59] *Lucas*, at 1015; See, in general, *Loretto*.
[60] Bickel, AM. 1962. *The Least Dangerous Branch.* New Haven: Yale University Press. pp. 143-147.
[61] Hof, WM. 2002. "Trying to Halt the Procedural Merry-Go-Round: The Ripeness of Regulatory Takings Claims After *Palazzolo v. Rhode Island.*" 46 St. Louis L.J. 833.
[62] *Abbott Laboratories v. Gardner*, 387 U.S. 136, 148 (1967); see also Nichol, GR, Jr. 1987. "Ripeness and the Constitution." 54 U. Chi. L. Rev. 153, 161; Hitchcock, MB. 1998. "*Suitum v. Tahoe Regional Planning Agency*: Applying the Takings Ripeness Rule to Land Use Regulations and Transferable Development Rights." 28 Golden Gate U.L. Rev. 87, 93-94; Mixon, J and Waggoner, J. 1998. "The Role of Variances in Determining Ripeness in Takings Claims Under Zoning Ordinances and Subdivision Regulations of Texas Municipalities." 29 St. Mary's L. J. 765, 773; Hof, at 833-834; Strachan, GC and Strachan, A. 2002. "The Ripeness Doctrine in Regulatory Takings Litigation." 22 J. Land Resources & Envtl. L. 19, 21.
[63] U.S. Constitution. Art. III, § 2.
[64] Hof, at 837.
[65] *Penn Central*, at 124.

[66] *Id.*, at 136-137.
[67] *Agins*, at 257.
[68] *Id.*, at 260.
[69] *Id.*, at 262.
[70] Haffner, JC. 1997. "*Suitum v. Tahoe Regional Planning Agency*: The United States Supreme Court Revisits Ripeness in Regulatory Takings Context." 11 Tul. Envtl. L.J. 129, 133; Hitchcock, at 95.
[71] Hof, at 835.
[72] *Id.*
[73] *Virginia Surface Mining*, at 294-295.
[74] *Id.*, at 296.
[75] *Pennell*, at 9-10.
[76] *San Diego Gas & Electric Company v. San Diego*, 450 U.S. 621, 632 (1981).
[77] *Monsanto*, at 1019.
[78] 28 U.S.C. 1257; *San Diego Gas*, at Footnote 10.
[79] *Williamson County*.
[80] *MacDonald*.
[81] Strachan, at 24.
[82] *Agins*, at 260; Strachan, at 24.
[83] *Williamson County*, at 177; *MacDonald*, at 342.
[84] Strachan, at 24.
[85] *MacDonald*, at 353.
[86] *Williamson County*, at 194; see also Strachan, at 24.
[87] Strachan, at 25.
[88] *Williamson County*, at 194-195; *Monsanto*, at 1013.
[89] *Penn Central*, at 124.
[90] *Palazzolo*, at 631.
[91] *Tahoe-Sierra Preservation Council v. Tahoe Regional Planning Agency*, 535 U.S. 302, 355 (2002) (Thomas dissenting).
[92] *Lucas*, at 1012.
[93] *First English Lutheran Church v. Los Angeles County*, 482 U.S. 304, 308-311 (1987); see also *Agins v. Tiburon*, 24 Cal. 3d 266, 275-277 (1979)
[94] *Id.*, at 308-309; Pandolfi, T. 1989. "Putting the Cart Before the Horse: Just Compensation for Regulatory Takings in *First English Evangelical Lutheran Church v. County of Los Angeles*." 54 Brooklyn L. Rev. 1413, 1421.
[95] *Id.*, at 311-312.
[96] Pandolfi, at 1422.
[97] *Id.*, at 1008-1009.
[98] *Id.*, at 1010-1011.
[99] *Id.*, at 1011-1012.
[100] *MacDonald*, at 359 (White dissenting).
[101] Hof, at 848.
[102] Strachan, at 29.

[103] *Id.*, at 30; *Del Monte Dunes v. Monterey*, 920 F.2d 1496, 1501 (1990).
[104] *Lucas*, at 1012, Footnote 3.
[105] Hof, at 857-858.
[106] *Suitum v. Tahoe Regional Planning Agency*, 520 U.S. 725, 744 (1997).
[107] *Id.*, at 739-741.
[108] *Id.*
[109] *Id.*, at 747-748. (Scalia concurring)
[110] *Palazzolo*, at 619.
[111] Hof, at 865.
[112] *Palazzolo*, at 646-648 (Ginsberg dissenting). Note: Ginsberg referred to this tactic as a "bait-and-switch ploy" at 648.
[113] Dowling, TJ. 2002. "On History, Takings Jurisprudence, and *Palazzolo*: A Reply to James Burling." 30 B.C. Envtl. L. Rev. 65, 84.
[114] *Tahoe-Sierra*, at 338.
[115] *Pennell*, at 9.
[116] *Id.*, at 9-10.
[117] *Id.*, at 19 (Scalia dissenting).
[118] *MacDonald*, at 348.
[119] *Pennell*, at 16 (Scalia dissenting).
[120] 125 S. Ct. 2655 (2005)
[121] Trigaux, R. 2005. "Your Home Could be Up for Grabs," ST. PETERSBURG TIMES, June 24, at D1.
[122] Hudgins, E. 2005. "Your Castle No More," WASH. TIMES, June 27, at A20.
[123] "N.H. Town Votes on Justice Souter's House," Associated Press, March 14, 2006. (The above quotation came from a Los Angeles businessman named Logan Darrow Clements.)
[124] Berger, L. 1978. "The Public Use Requirement in Eminent Domain." 57 Or. L. Rev. 203.
[125] *Kelo v. City of New London*, 545 U.S. 469, 478; *Fallbrook Irrigation Dist. v. Bradley*, 164 U.S. 112 (1896).
[126] *Id.*
[127] *Berman v. Parker*, 348 U.S. 26 (1954)
[128] *Id.*, at 31.
[129] *Id.*, at 33.
[130] *Midkiff*, at 233-34. (In 1967, the year Hawai'i passed the Land Reform Act, 51% of land was privately owned, and 47% of land was owned by 72 individuals.)
[131] *Id.*, at 241.
[132] *Id.*, at 242-43.
[133] *Id.*, at 244.
[134] *Poletown Neighborhood Council v. City of Detroit*, 410 Mich. 616, 635 (1981).
[135] *Kelo*, at 473.

[136] *Id.*
[137] *Id.*, at 484.
[138] *Id.*
[139] *Id.*, at 485.
[140] *Id.*, at 486.
[141] *Poletown*, at 635.
[142] *Kelo*, at 488.
[143] *Id.*, at 487.
[144] *Id.*, at 488; *Midkiff*, at 242.
[145] Epstein, RA. 2005. "Can Your Town Take Your Home? Richard A. Epstein and J. Peter Byrne Debate." *Legal Affairs*, Feb. 21.
[146] *Kelo*, at 483.
[147] Byrne, JP. 2005. "Can Your Town Take Your Home? Richard A. Epstein and J. Peter Byrne Debate." *Legal Affairs*, Feb. 21.
[148] *Kelo*, at 489.
[149] *Id.*, at 476; Conn. Gen. Stat. § 8-186
[150] Passed: Arizona, Florida, Georgia, North Dakota, New Hampshire, Nevada, Oregon, and South Carolina; Failed: California, Idaho, Washington.
[151] Passed: Arizona and Nevada; Failed: Idaho and Washington.

CHAPTER 3

UNDERSTANDING AD HOC, FACTUAL INQUIRIES

Understanding the essence of law is an inherently complex endeavor. Early attempts at its articulation focused on universalizability despite the present awareness of diversity among systems of law. The legal positivism of Thrasymachus was rejected by Socrates and Aristotle who saw such diversity, caused by the rule of man, as opposed to the rule of law, as deviations from the natural. Analysis of the law would be made more complex as law became understood more and more as a specifically human institution. Montesquieu, for example, recognized a distinction between the laws of the "physical world" and the laws of the "intelligent world,"[1] and developed an understanding of laws as tied to the particular situations of particular peoples, as "consist(ing) in the various relations which the laws may bear to different objects."[2] This focus on legal diversity became the cornerstone of thinking about law in an anthropological sense.[3] While the shift toward a hermeneutical understanding of law grounds the study of law to particular experiences,[4] the position of law as something of substance for inquiry risks being lost.

This tension between the foci of justice and politics, between the "ought" and the "is," within the study of the essence of the law is paralleled in the study of regulatory takings. The law of regulatory takings has been studied and explained by individuals focusing primarily upon one side of an often conflictive dyad. Prescriptions offered by commentators have focused upon either right or efficiency, upon either law or economics. Through such a focus, even those most dedicated to normative argument are making statements about the nuts and bolts of regulatory takings law; by focusing upon either law or economics, one makes a claim as to what such conflicts are about in essence. What is being allocated when a regulatory takings case is decided: protection of individual or communal rights or a distribution of things?

The Supreme Court's own interpretation of regulatory takings cases presents a problem for attempts to formulate generalized knowledge of such conflicts and cases. Central to this confusion is the Court's 1978 *Penn Central* decision, which prescribed an "ad hoc" decision-making process based on "factual inquiries."[5] Such a test is a balancing test which frequently incorporates legal and economic criteria, although the significance of each may shift. Given the current state of property law in the U.S., with a freshly politicized emphasis on the strong protection of private property rights sparked by public reaction to the Court's 2005 *Kelo* decision,[6] attempts to develop an understanding of regulatory takings jurisprudence is merited, both politically and academically. Attempts to generate such knowledge through a dominant focus upon singular concepts of law or economics, however, may prove counterproductive. They certainly belie the balancing (albeit not always balanced) approach utilized by the Court. Although the Supreme Court's regulatory takings jurisprudence could capably ignore facets of the reality of regulatory takings, its legal reality as a complex jurisprudence cannot be ignored.

This chapter works through the admitted difficulties associated with regulatory takings jurisprudence by articulating already present methods of regulatory takings analysis and prescribing the use of other approaches that can shed meaningful light on the conceptualization of regulatory takings law. It begins with a summary of legal and economic analyses of regulatory takings conflicts. Such contributions, while prescriptive in nature, provide insight into the divergent manners in which compensatory property conflicts can be understood. This chapter then continues by considering the potential contributions to such understanding that can be made from other perspectives, viewpoints which have rarely been concerned with or considered by the issue of regulatory takings.

LAW, ECONOMICS, AND REGULATORY TAKINGS

A large amount has been written about regulatory takings in legal scholarship. The prevalence of regulatory takings literature within law reviews and legal journals may be partially due to a selection bias; the general absence of political analyses of regulatory takings, and the subsequent absence of the topic in political science journals (as well as the journals of most social sciences), could be causing non-law school academics interested in the topic to seek publication of their writings in law reviews. This creates a problem in determining what regulatory takings literature is, in fact, legal research, seeking to elaborate on the evolution of the law in practice, and what literature seeks to provide systematic explanation of that evolution. Obviously, both forms of research serve their own valid purposes, and just as obviously, it is difficult to establish a bright-line boundary between the disciplines. To be sure, the goals of this area of regulatory takings literature exist on a gradient. At one end of this spectrum exists a large amount of legal research that seeks to describe the basic trends of the decisions in the courts, and is written from a compliance perspective. Some of this literature focuses on the essentially chaotic and random nature of the jurisprudence[7] or on the role of the ideology of the individual justices.[8] Others act as case studies, focusing on the significance of particular decisions on a pre-existing and still evolving legal discipline.[9] Yet others construct the jurisprudence as embodying, to varying degrees, a consistent set of logically arranged ideas and legal concepts.[10]

Among those finding consistency within the regulatory takings jurisprudence, some explain this consistency through its connection to some underlying institutional or individual factor. This literature serves a different purpose than the aforementioned literature. The practice of regulatory takings law requires the lawyer to apply precedent to the particular facts of his or her litigated situation. Focusing on why the Court has ruled so in the past, especially if that explanation focuses on anything other than the facts or legal concepts, would be counterproductive. Social scientific literature, however, generally requires an explanation as to why the federal courts enforce the Fifth Amendment Takings Clause in a particular way. Examples of such explanations have centered attention on the institutional structure of the courts empowered by Congress to hear such cases,[11] the structure and requirements of the larger system of federalism,[12] and the various attitudes and values held by individual elites on the bench with the authority, as an individual, to directly affect the case outcomes.[13]

In addition to such descriptive scholarship, legal academics have also produced significant contributions to prescriptive or normative works on regulatory takings. Foundational to this literature are the writings of law professors Frank Michelman and Joseph Sax. Michelman seeks to merge utilitarianism with a Rawlsian fairness criterion,[14] which could be applied to regulatory takings jurisprudence. Michelman's approach avoids attempting to establish universalized decision rules, which have, in his view, "with suggestive consistency, yielded rules which are ethically unsatisfying," and at best would produce nothing "other than a partial, imperfect, unsatisfactory solution...."[15] To accomplish this goal, Michelman sets up "a quasi-mathematical structure" to lead "to the specific identification of 'compensable' occasions...."[16] Central to this quasi-mathematical structure are three key terms. "Efficiency gains" refer to the net benefit a project would bring, determined by the difference between the amount winners would be willing to pay for the benefit and the amount losers would demand to accept the costs.[17] "Demoralizing costs" include the amount "necessary to offset disutilities which accrue to losers and their sympathizers specifically from the realization that no compensation is offered"[18] and is extended to general social reactions, dealing with the perceived possibility that such actions could eventually be applied to them as well. In other words, "it is necessary to count the disutility of individuals who are adversely affected by government actions even if what was taken was not legally their property."[19] Finally, "settlement costs" are the total expenditures needed to offset demoralization through compensation.[20] This utilitarian calculus requires that governments avoid projects where the net benefits are exceeded by either demoralization or settlement costs.[21] (Economists concerned with efficiency generally stop at this point.)[22] However, governments can pursue activities when the net benefits exceed demoralization and settlement costs; if demoralization costs exceed settlement costs, the government should pay compensation; if settlement costs exceed demoralization costs, the government does not have to pay compensation.[23]

In addition to this utility determination, Michelman also argues for a fairness determination by focusing on two of Rawls' justice criteria: "(a) everyone has a chance to attain the positions to which differential treatments attach, and (b) the arrangement can reasonably be supposed to work out to the advantage of every participant, and especially the one to whom accrues the least advantageous treatment provided for by the arrangement in question."[24] Under such criteria, Michelman sets forth the following edict: "A decision not to compensate is not unfair as long as the disappointed claimant ought to be able to appreciate how such decisions might fit into a consistent practice which holds forth a lesser long-run risk to people like him than would any consistent practice which is naturally suggested by the opposite decision."[25] An ironic observation made by Michelman is that, due to the possibility of immediate utilitarian analysis and the necessity of patient, imaginative, and long-term consideration required of the fairness analysis, both approaches face the possibility of, occasionally, coming to different suggestions as to whether a particular policy should involve compensation or not.[26]

The presence of a legal consideration of justice in the takings analysis of Michelman cannot be ignored. In this regard, his analysis is not blindly reliant on economic calculations. His attempt to establish a fairness-criterion, however, does not change the fact that his analysis is fundamentally an economic one. The determination calculus developed by Michelman rests upon values determined by the degree of willingness to buy or sell. Justice, understood distributively, is ultimately assessed by measuring the degree to which value changes hands and not by the adherence to or breaking of the rights (and responsibilities) of ownership.

Like Michelman, Sax "illustrate(s) the difficulty of capturing in any bright-line fashion a standard that will sort out those situations in which compensation at least arguably ought to be paid, from those where compensation would certainly be inappropriate."[27] Furthermore, what remains implicit for Michelman, and is explicit for Justice Holmes in *Pennsylvania Coal*,[28] is also explicit for Sax, and that is the essential balancing nature of regulatory takings cases. In his writing, Sax has demonstrated an awareness of the economic perils faced by owners of regulated property, and is particularly concerned with the potential of downzoning to provide windfalls for early developers, while placing the burden of regulation (necessitated by earlier developers) upon those that develop later in time.[29] However, whereas Michelman analyzes regulatory takings cases through a concept of justice tied to the economic concerns of distribution of costs and benefits, Sax's analysis focuses squarely upon the law.

Sax's analysis of regulatory takings cases begins by observing the evolution of the jurisprudence from the first Justice Harlan to Justice Holmes. These justices represent the evolution of takings jurisprudence from a reliance on "traditional legal concepts…, such as appropriation of a proprietary interest, physical invasion giving rise to a prescriptive easement, and nuisance,"[30] exemplified by Harlan's opinion in *Mugler*,[31] to a focus on "the extensiveness of the economic harm inflicted by the regulation,"[32] exemplified by Holmes' opinion in *Pennsylvania Coal*.[33] The most onerous dimension of this evolution is the Court's subsequent reliance on the diminution of value theory, which still remains as one of the three prongs of the Court's main takings test, *Penn Central*. This theory holds "(1) that all legally acquired existing economic values are property, and (2) that while such values may be diminished somewhat without compensation, they may not be excessively diminished."[34] According to Sax, such a theory errs as a matter of law; Sax points to the legal minds that were influential in the forming of the Constitution and, more specifically, the Takings Clause, namely, Grotius, Pufendorf, and Vattel.

> We have become so indoctrinated with the idea that quantitative value maintenance is a constitutional principle and a dictate of "natural equity" that we have conveniently forgotten the extensive non-property background in our law. While it is true that the Roman tradition exalted the free market-private property concept, that tradition is just one of the roots of our legal system. Another and equally important part of the background, from which Grotius drew, must be recognized. That is the Christian tradition, which devised the legal concept of "just price."[35]

Sax argues that, since the dominant legal understanding of property at the time of the writing of the Takings Clause understood it as something which could legitimately be devalued by the state for public purpose, the intention of the clause was a protection against arbitrary takings, as opposed to general takings, "as a bulwark against unfairness, rather than against mere value diminution."[36]

Sax's criticism of the direction of regulatory takings jurisprudence is based on its deviation from historical legal principles; his prescription for such cases also adheres to the use of legal principles while seeking to define situations to which those principles should be applied. Sax's theory of takings cases can be understood as a middle ground between the deferential position of Harlan, which would only find a taking when the government had satisfied some abstract standard of appropriation or invasion, and the diminution of value position of Holmes, whose understanding of value as property constructed a compensation theory primarily concerned with the minimization of private loss.[37] Sax first draws a "distinction between the role of government as participant and the government as mediator in the process of competition among economic claims,"[38] and then proposes "that when economic loss is incurred as a result of government enhancement of its resource position in its enterprise capacity, then compensation is constitutionally required; it is that result which is to be characterized as a taking."[39]

By leaving the governmental role as mediator between competing interests outside of the bounds of constitutionally required compensation, Sax is relying on a notion of property as socially situated. He is critical of compensation paid for value loss in cases in which "claimants invariably sought to persuade the Court of the legality of the use they wished to make at the time their property was acquired."[40] This contractually obligatory understanding of property results in the aforementioned situations where early developers gain windfalls, while later regulations fall solely on the shoulders of later-in-time developers. For this reason, Sax suggests conceptualizing property in terms of time, not space. Instead of viewing property rights as fixed at the time of acquisition, a judge should see property as bestowing upon the owner particular rights contingent upon the social needs which give property its value in the first place.[41]

The differences between the analyses of regulatory takings of Michelman and Sax should be evident. Whereas Michelman's determination of whether compensation should be granted for a property use restriction depends solely upon the distributive impacts of such actions, Sax's determination hinges upon a legal assessment of rights in property, and compensation may be withheld from a property owner, even if that would prove costly, if the proscribed action was outside of such rights. This conclusion should not lead one to think, however, that a focus on the economic impact of alleged takings results in prescriptions of compensation, whereas a focus on the law of property rights/responsibilities would avoid such demands.

Richard Epstein is a strong advocate of property rights and posits such rights as fundamental in the American constitutional context.[42] Epstein's analyses of regulatory takings cases skew heavily toward the requirement of compensation, but the focus of such analyses is based not upon economic factors but upon legal factors. Like Michelman, Epstein is concerned with establishing a moral framework in which to discuss takings. There are, however, substantial differences between the two. First, whereas Michelman focuses attention on determining "whether the decision not to compensate is fair,"[43] Epstein states as the purpose of his work the discussion of "the proper relationship between the individual and the state."[44] The contrast between these two goals is elaborated by a second distinction. Although Michelman does not seek to espouse a utilitarian philosophy,[45] his formula remained faithful to the goals of efficiency and utility maximization. Epstein, on the other hand, bases his work on a concept of natural law, not based upon some divine mandate giving humanity ownership of property, but as based upon the assumption that property exists prior to the state.[46] Epstein does not base his normative consideration of the government's compensatory responsibility upon the efficient use of resources, but upon a notion of the proper relationship between property and the state. This relationship is rooted in the idea of first possession as the root of property, which he does recognize as having "very attractive utilitarian features that account for its persistence over time. It allows the transition from no ownership to ownership to take place without conscious government interference or authorization, which is critical to a Lockean theory that regards the state as the protector of property rights but not as their source."[47]

By positing property as logically prior to the existence of the state, Epstein structures normative debates on regulatory takings as based not on efficient use of resources or efficient exchange of goods, but on uncompromising a priori values. This places Epstein at strong odds with state confiscatory policies, even those aimed at protecting generally recognized common interests. At the center of his position is the state's reliance on declaring itself to be the title holder to property which might be called commons to impose policies and distributions aimed at protecting that resource's sustainability.[48] Epstein's criticism of this declaratory practice does not deal with the monetary and social costs to which such actions might lead; he raises "(t)he fatal objection to the declaration theory of private ownership...that it cannot explain how either a private party or the government can obtain *exclusive* rights to anything,"[49] which, according to Epstein, can only be accomplished through first possession.

While Epstein's natural law position advocates the protection of private property for reasons unrelated to economic consequence, the high valuation of property, which necessitates such natural law protection, relies heavily on utilitarian calculations. His preference for private ownership over pooled ownership relies on the claim that when "property rights are enforced, owners can make choices on efficient land use without having to overcome the conundrums of collective choice."[50] Placement of property into common ownership results in a situation where "(i)ll-defined rights replace well-defined ones, and transaction cost barriers are likely to exceed the gains that otherwise are obtainable from any shift in land use or ownership. Another negative-sum game."[51] When, however, such actions must be taken, when low levels of trust and a high degree of exchange complexity prevent efficient resource use through private exchange[52] and ownership must, therefore, shift to the public, Epstein prescribes that the "ideal solution is to leave the individual owner in a position of indifference between the taking by the government and retention of the property."[53] While Epstein may value property rights for practical, utilitarian reasons, his understanding of regulatory takings law rests on an inviolable legal concept of, what another scholar has termed, "Super Property."[54]

Economists have relied particularly on the use of contract theory as a model for interpreting regulatory takings cases. The trend with economic models to place primary significance on the actions of goal oriented and rational acting individuals generally results in a limited analysis of political institutions, except as providing boundaries within which individual economic actors act. "The standard form of contractual theory treats the content of the obligation as a matter of supreme indifference to the state agency charged with the validation or enforcement of the contract. The reason for this indifference to the content of a contract is the strong conviction that any voluntary transaction between two or more individuals will work to the advantage of both or all."[55]

William Fischel, although he dedicates a substantial amount of time and energy addressing political and legal questions, still roots his analysis at the level of individual pursuit of economic goals. For Fischel, political and legal questions are inherently economic questions: "The original Constitution was in large part an economic document. Under the Articles of Confederation, the American common market was retarded by an inability of the central government to perform important (economic) tasks.... Individual states often got in the way of mutually beneficial exchange by retarding interstate commerce for the usual prisoners' dilemma reasons."[56] Like Epstein's Lockean positioning of the government as intended to protect economic and contractual exchange, Fischel limits the property role for the Court through his reliance on John Hart Ely's process theory.[57] Whereas legislative bodies are more adapt at addressing the interests of the people, which in economic issues entails the creation of rules to govern contracts and exchange to enhance economic values of trust and predictability, judiciaries can avoid a "countermajoritarian dilemma" by using "judicial review not to reverse the decisions of legislators except when the legislators themselves are acting undemocratically."[58]

Fischel clearly works to fill in such gaps left by economists engaging in simplistic legal analysis and constructing courts as simultaneously third-party and primary enforcers of the Takings Clause.[59] Much of his effort to explain the specific details of the judicial role in regulatory takings may be explained by his avoidance of an uncompromising natural law approach to regulatory takings, and his concern with finding "a viable middle ground between judicial deference to the often unfair regulations that burden property owners and judicial imposition of compensation for every legislative infringement on private rights."[60] Beginning from his reliance on Ely's process theory, Fischel prescribes limiting the courts to what they do best: make sure that the pluralistic political process, which better addresses economic and social concerns of private property owners and the public,[61] is fair and allowing democratic participation in the balancing of such interests. In other words, in cases dealing with economic regulation, the role of the courts is to, for example, protect "the 'politically powerless' out-of-state interests from in-state parochialism."[62]

This approach, according to Fischel, significantly limits the role the courts should play in regulatory takings because property is not helpless in protecting its interests within pluralistic politics. Generally, and here Fischel constructs his argument most like an economist, general market forces will result in efficient regulations that are acceptable to all parties. Property owners, by definition, possess resources which give them a voice in pluralistic processes. Additionally, any jurisdiction seeking the regulation of a property use must confront the possibility that the regulated entity could always exit the jurisdiction, and take financial resources with it. The possession by property owners of the powers of exit and voice[63] can work to guarantee that economic regulations are acceptable, since they are the product of a property owner's seeking of areas where property can be most productively used and a jurisdiction's willingness to pay the balance between tax revenues and public goods. Courts have a role, however, and that is to protect property interests lacking voice, because the owner has no standing in a particular jurisdiction, or exit, because the particular property is inelastic.[64] This situation, according to Fischel, is more likely to occur at the local level; therefore, "(w)hen confronted with a regulatory taking claim, judges need to ask themselves whether the plaintiff has been forestalled from those options by the nature of his property and the nature of the political process."[65] Fischel's generalized prescription then becomes a request for greater judicial deference toward state and federal regulations, and a stricter scrutiny applied to local and municipal regulations.[66]

This question of the role of the courts in regulatory takings has been particularly perplexing in economic analyses. Epstein's general understanding of the proper relationship between property and the state is analogous to a highway system, where the government "determine(s) the rules of the road and not the composition of the traffic."[67] While this position could provide for a justification of an active, "night watchman"[68] judiciary, restricting the behavior of other branches, Epstein provides little advice to explain how and when the courts should enforce such rules; generally he is critical of Supreme Court justices that have placed substantive requirements on economic regulatory programs and sees such programs historically as ineffective.[69] Fischel limits judicial intervention into takings questions to those cases involving a Madisonian tyranny of the majority, identified predominantly as local conflicts. Others, however, criticize this assumption, arguing that democratic and economic influences have the strongest powers of "exit" and "voice" at the local level.[70] Sax positions the state, and thereby with it, the judiciary, as a mediator, not a participant, in economic exchange and, therefore, unless the state is actually enhancing its economic position, the courts are prescribed to not intervene in the majority of takings cases. This position does not clarify, however, the distinction between the state's roles as participant and mediator, and risks ignoring the same Madisonian concerns that form the heart of Fischel and Epstein's arguments.

Clearly the role of the judiciary as an enforcer of compensatory requirements diminishes as one moves from Epstein to Fischel to Sax. The more that one values strong, constitutionalized protections for private property as "the most effective way to successfully prevent factions from thwarting the proper running of majoritarian democracy,"[71] the more apt one is to request active protection of such rights from the judiciary. Courts, however, do not fit predominantly or even significantly into the theories of regulatory takings of Michelman, Sax, Epstein, or Fischel; nor, necessarily, should they. The arguments made by these individuals are essentially normative; each views the issue of regulatory takings as inherently involving a dispute between values, either economic or legal. All look to the courts to settle such disputes as enforcers of preexisting norms, as referees of a game fought outside of the courtroom. The Supreme Court's own jurisprudence, based upon ad hoc, factual inquiries, supports this position. To understand the depth and significance of the regulatory takings phenomenon, a more complete picture must be drawn, a picture that includes the courts in more than just an objective enforcer role, a picture drawn with tools other than separate basic notions of economics and law.

LEGAL PLURALISM

The concept of legal pluralism developed within the anthropological study of law and "is generally defined as a situation in which two or more legal systems coexist in the same social field."[72] Traditionally, the discipline focused on the analysis of legal systems in colonial societies and upon the interaction of European state law and indigenous non-state, normative codes of behavior.[73] This narrowly constructed, and frequently criticized, position evolved into an analytic approach to understanding the general coexistence of multiple legal forms across time and space,[74] a construction that challenges "the common-sense unity of the legal order."[75] Criticism of early legal pluralism focused on an overly state-centered perception of law and the frequent ignoring of the roles dominance and hegemony may play in legal systems.[76] Remaining aware of this tendency to simultaneously ignore and reify such hierarchy, legal pluralism "increasingly emphasized the dialectic, mutually constitutive relation between state law and other normative orders," focusing on "law as a symbolic and ideological system."[77]

At least two factors, therefore, are required for the analysis of a legal phenomenon through the lens of legal pluralism. Multiple legal traditions and sources of law must be present and those bodies of law must interact in some way. Both of these conditions are present in regulatory takings jurisprudence; the legally plural nature of regulatory takings cases is blatantly present in the Supreme Court's own established precedent on the matter. Stopping the analysis at this point would result in an understanding of regulatory takings that could have been derived using legalist logical assessment, meaning that legal pluralism had provided nothing novel. However, legal pluralism provides particularly insightful contributions to the understanding of regulatory takings through its focus on the social and symbolic nature of law.

Although contemporary studies of the United States and colonialism justifiably focus on the colonizing role of the U.S. in the rest of the world, the issue of regulatory takings highlights a legal dimension of the American experience as a colony. Much of American law, especially property law, finds its origins in British common law. As it was discussed above by Joseph Sax, the notion of property as restricted by the standards of the common well-being was prevalent in the common law tradition upon which American jurisprudence developed.[78] Specifically, American property law has always contained matters of private and public nuisance restricting the capacity of an owner to enjoy his or her property, and this nuisance law predates the American colonies.[79] Such tradition-based matters of property within the law conflict, however, with a codified protection of private property interests against public interests. From the common law and nuisance property traditions, such "constitutionalization of property perpetuates the false belief that it is possible (and desirable) categorically to isolate private interests from public involvement."[80] The question of regulatory takings inherently involves a confrontation between values rooted in the different traditions found within the U.S. legal system.

Although courtroom cases explicitly confront a constitutional protection of property with earlier legal property limitations, one must be careful to not polarize these legal traditions to an unacceptable degree. The U.S. Constitution and its Fifth Amendment property clause were not devices newly formed from the legal ether; they were historically precedent in the common law-based English colonial system. The Magna Carta and the 17th century colonial governments of Maryland and Pennsylvania had established due process requirements for governmental deprivations of property in land.[81] Just as the pre-constitutional legal history of the U.S. cannot be read without reference to limits on governmental authority, so too must a reading of the establishment of property's constitutional protection in the U.S. include an understanding of the limits of such protection. The constitutional establishment of property rights, along with the establishment of all other rights, "does not imply unrestrained liberty to enjoy the maximum economic advantages of property under all circumstances."[82] As stated above, the traditional legal understanding of property at the time of the founding of the Constitution contained an understanding of the limits of the right of enjoyment, limits aimed at the protection of larger common interests.[83]

This understanding of property within the legal realms of British common law and American constitutionalism is at the heart of most analyses of regulatory takings jurisprudence. This is most evident when one considers law-centered approaches. The above-described regulatory takings jurisprudence analyses of Joseph Sax and Richard

Epstein, while vastly different from one another on the issue of compensation qualification, are quite similar in their reliance on predominantly legal factors as analytical bases. Their understandings of property are vastly different; Sax views property rights as predicated upon social and political contingency, while Epstein's natural law construction of property rights leaves property unconditioned by such contingencies. Their similarity comes in each of their defenses for their own understandings of property.

Sax has been critical of judges and legal scholars that have interpreted the Fifth Amendment to require compensation in situations distinguishable only by the extent of economic value lost to the regulation, what is known as the diminution of value theory.[84] This theory was made most fully manifest in the Supreme Court's *Lucas* decision, which established a categorical rule for compensation in situations in which regulation deprived the owner of all economic value.[85] Sax claims that such a rule operates on the erroneous assumption that "economic values as such are entitled to constitutional protection,"[86] and inquiry into the compatibility of property use and the common good may not be warranted. Beyond being an indefensible philosophical position or inconsistent with a proper definition of property,[87] Sax regards the diminution of value theory as providing "a highly unreal view of the actual working of the compensation rule in American law,"[88] a body of law constructed by American and British minds concerned more with the arbitrary seizure of land, instead of with the mere loss of value.[89]

Richard Epstein's position on takings is practically antithetical to that of Sax, at least when one considers their case-by-case desired outcomes. What remains consistent between the two, however, is a fundamental appeal to law to decide such cases. Like Sax, Epstein sees the solution to takings cases lying in the property interpretation of the history of American property law, a history that incorporates both the framing of the Constitution and the common law which predated it. Unlike Sax, however, Epstein's interest in common law is the legal tradition of appropriation, under which "the general rule of acquisition is a rule of first possession."[90] When this tradition forms the foundation of property law, "possession is said to give the first possessor rights against the rest of the world."[91] This is the idea that is seen as central to the property theories of Locke and Blackstone, the individuals seen by Epstein as the dominant influences of the framers of the Constitution.[92] Furthermore, the Constitution is a document of limited powers, highlighted by an "effort to limit the power of the sovereign by ruling certain areas out of the bounds to collective governance."[93] Under this system, the Bill of Rights forms the ends or purposes of the government,[94] and the Constitution is preeminently concerned with the protection of individual rights, including property, against the collective.

Both Sax and Epstein defend their divergent prescriptions for regulatory takings jurisprudence with appeals to logical, legal constructs. Both acknowledge the existence of common law limitations to property and the constitutionalization of property rights by the Fifth Amendment; the argument of neither relies on the claim that one of these aspects of law is non-existent or irrelevant. The solution, for both, involves a search for the proper relationship between the two bodies of law in a manner which upholds both traditions and develops a consistency between them. The appropriateness of this approach as a matter of normative discourse is not the purpose here; as a matter of description, the assumption of cohesiveness between divergent bodies of law is problematic, which is a topic to be discussed later. For the moment, it is important to note that the idea of a consistent merging between common law limitations on and constitutional protections of property rights is an idea that is prevalent in the regulatory takings decisions issued by the U.S. Supreme Court.

The dominant methodology utilized by the Supreme Court in establishing its regulatory takings jurisprudence can be best described as a methodology of balancing.[95] From its inception with the 1922 decision in *Pennsylvania Coal v. Mahon*, the Court recognized the inherent limits to property rights and that the state may regulate those rights to protect the public, but further added that the Fifth Amendment should restrict regulations that go "too far."[96] Alone, this dictum provides little elaboration of the balance between public good and private right deemed appropriate by the Court. Holmes, the author of the *Pennsylvania Coal* decision, did identify factors that were key considerations: what was the diminution in value, was there a threat to the general public, did owners enjoy an "average reciprocity of advantage," and were distinct contractual relations destroyed?[97] The

Court did little, if anything, however, to prioritize these factors or relate them to one another in any meaningful way.

A similar approach was taken by the Court in *Penn Central*.[98] The Court, likewise, made efforts to balance property rights with the demands and needs of the public, but this time identified only three factors in making such a determination: the economic impact of the regulation, if the regulation interfered with "investment-backed expectations," and the nature of the government's action.[99] Again, there was no indication by the Court about whether one factor weighed more than another or how many factors had to be satisfied to constitute a taking. Through the Court's description of its doctrine as ad hoc and factual, however, a case-by-case approach was institutionalized. By declaring its approach to be case-by-case and centered on a few specific factors, the Court presents its approach as persistently balancing between two bodies of law, which are differently applicable to different situations.

The root consistency in the Court's regulatory takings jurisprudence can be best seen, ironically, when the doctrine has shifted. When the Supreme Court established its categorical rule for takings in its 1992 *Lucas* decision,[100] shockwaves were felt in the environmentalist, planning, and property rights communities. A brief overview of law review articles published shortly after the *Lucas* decision indicates that a substantial amount of commentators viewed the decision as shifting regulatory takings jurisprudence strongly in the direction of the protection of private property rights at the expense of governments' willingness or ability to regulate property.[101] Other commentators noted, however, that although the decision on its own was deferential to the concerns of the property owner, the case was unlikely to cause a major shift in the doctrine.[102] Despite Scalia's efforts to create a category of constitutional property rights fully isolated from common law limitations, he nevertheless acknowledged that even total economic losses may not warrant compensation when an "inquiry into the nature of the owner's estate shows that the proscribed use interests were not part of his [sic] title to begin with."[103] Although Scalia stated that these "background principles" of state common law must pre-exist the regulation and not be "newly legislated,"[104] the logical conclusion of the case is that inquiries into the limits of property rights are inherently prior to questions of constitutional protection.

This admission of the Scalia decision was criticized by proponents of strong constitutional property protections as "a rejection of the self-regarding base of takings law and…an assumption of a communitarian view."[105]

As the chief judicial institution in the U.S., the Supreme Court plays a significant role in the construction of regulatory takings jurisprudence. Looking to the cases used by the Court in that activity, one sees a foundational thread that runs through the cases, although particular Courts have been deferential to property interests to varying degrees over time. By its own implicit admission, the Court is engaging in a legally pluralistic enterprise, balancing its regulatory takings doctrine between common law property limitations and constitutional property protection. This process, however, defies its own labeling under the title of legal pluralism by creating the image of a singular and consistent body of law, altered only through the varied interpretations and applications of fallible justices.

Legal pluralism carries the analysis of regulatory takings jurisprudence beyond this convergence by moving the focus of analysis away from the thing in itself, the end law, and toward the process, the dialectic relationship between the two interacting bodies of law. Instead of understanding the regulatory takings doctrine through a "postulational examination of how logical principles inform structure of thought and practice," the use of legal pluralism directs the investigator into a "hermeneutic search for the ideas that underlie the social institutions and cultural formulations of law."[106] In other words, the use of legal pluralism can turn an understanding of regulatory takings from a comprehension of the legal principles developed through past cases, and from a concern over the economic/regulatory impacts of those cases (although such inquiries are still important), toward a focus on the manners in which the law shapes and is shaped by efforts to define the key terms of jurisprudence. Regulatory takings law, then, is not a logically derived central path between common law and constitutional law, but a fluid and evolving interaction between those sides.

An area of regulatory takings law that deserves attention due to its susceptibility to the ebbs and flows of hermeneutic forces is the question of rational expectations. The second prong of the *Penn Central* test directs justices to consider the impact on investment-backed expectations caused by a regulation. This component of the takings test was a new addition by the *Penn Central* Court, and directs focus toward the existent or speculative nature of the owner's expectations.[107] Although the Court did not expressly necessitate such expectations to be reasonable, the standard of reasonableness is applied throughout the decision, especially in reference to property uses.[108] Lower federal courts have expressly applied a reasonableness standard to expectation analysis, since not doing so "would reward parties who make bad investments."[109]

The reasonableness standard has been interpreted to include the regulatory environment in place at the time of title acquisition. In other words, the challenge to regulations that restrict the use of property must consider the reasonableness of the owner's expectations, which itself is judged in reference to already existent regulations. This has not been without controversy. In 2001, Justice Kennedy's majority opinion in *Palazzolo* ruled that the presence of pre-existing regulations does not automatically prevent a regulatory takings challenge.[110] Despite the efforts of Justice Scalia's attempt to systematically remove any consideration of pre-existing regulations from a takings consideration,[111] the dominant interpretation of *Palazzolo* follows Justice O'Connor's concurrence, as discussed in Chapter Two, encouraging a consideration, albeit a non-dispositive consideration, of the state of regulations at the time of property acquisition in assessing the reasonableness of a property owner's expectations.[112] Subsequently, lower federal courts have been unwilling to find takings in regulations that even unexpectedly impose restrictions on property when the use of that property is for a practice that has historically been heavily regulated, and the expectations of owners must be conditioned by such a possibility.[113]

Through the establishment of rules over the reasonableness of expectations held by property owners, the Court has done more than determine whether takings have occurred in individual cases. The Court has been a participant among participants in the historical process of defining expectations and, thereby, property generally. Such is not a novel practice; engagement in the definition of property is as old as property itself. The practice only appears invasive from the assumption that the definition of property is settled. This assumption is prevalent in the ownership model of property, an understanding of property in which academia, law, and economics are frequently mired.[114] The origins of this position is often attributed to Blackstone, whose explanation of property centered on despotic dominion over a thing owned and total exclusion of the rights of others to that thing.[115]

Singer describes this understanding of property as "misleading and morally deficient," but "pervasive."[116] Economists, for example, adhere faithfully to the model, and the only role posited for law is the placement of limits on the use of property when market forces fail to produce efficient results.[117] This understanding of property is essentially self-interested, and ignores the idea that the right to property also entails an obligation on the part of the owner.[118] For this reason, purely economic models provide insufficient analyses of regulatory takings, for they focus on the efficiency of result, without attention to other norms of ownership, which regulation frequently implies.

The ownership model of property is also frequently associated with constitutional protections of property. Scholars have posited property as primary among the concerns of the framers, especially those of Madison. Madison's concern with faction focused on the threat of majority faction, under which property is "peculiarly vulnerable to the collective power."[119] With his fundamental concern being the tyranny of the majority over property, Madison "suggests that once we recognize that there are rights distinct from, and potentially threatened by, democracy, the solution must be to contain democracy…."[120] The purpose of the Fifth Amendment, then, is to define property as something that "the society, or its representative, the state, cannot touch…."[121]

The Supreme Court has occasionally (albeit not fully) utilized this interpretation. An alternative interpretation of the ownership model of property was developed by legal realist scholars, and is frequently referred to as the bundle of rights theory.[122] This model was designed to demonstrate the multidimensional nature of property by analogizing property rights to sticks in a bundle; these sticks could be individually separated or alienated, yet the owner is still left with a bundle. The Court has, however, on occasion, countered the bundle of rights design with conceptual severance, "the idea that each incident or set of incidents of ownership in the bundle of rights itself constitutes a fully protectable property interest."[123] Advocated most vocally by Justices Scalia and Thomas,[124] conceptual severance has been utilized temporally to find a complete deprivation of property over a temporary period of time,[125] and has been used by the Claims Court to find a total taking of property in a partial reduction in water rights.[126]

This interpretation of the role of the property in the Constitution is referred to as Super Property, and sees "the constitutional right of property [as] a 'precommitment device,' that is, a voluntarily self-imposed constraint by which one prevents oneself from engaging in activities that are harmful to oneself but that are otherwise difficult to resist."[127] The conceptualization of property as ownership, that is, as antithetical to obligation and restriction, and protected by a Constitution that places the burden of proof for the legitimacy of restriction squarely upon the state that seeks the protection of the common good,[128] seems to be a vision of property appealing to the American populace. Utilizing the tools of legal pluralism, along with contributions from critical legal studies, this construction can be seen less as a conclusion of a legal, logical formulation, and more as a "complex process...in which a dominant hegemony will articulate values and norms in such a way that they take on significant trans-class appeal."[129]

A legally pluralistic analysis of regulatory takings begins with attention directed toward the process by which the boundaries between common law and constitutional law are negotiated. That process is less a logical project and more the product of shifts in cultural and psychological symbolism. Such a project is inherently interpretive, and attempts "to reconstruct intentional states of mind and cultural or political contexts in the hope that [they] can induce with some confidence the reasons that led a particular person to adopt a particular course of conduct."[130] This focus on intentional states of mind "suggests that what matters is less whether or not a constitutional property clause exists than how it is interpreted...[and acknowledges] the path-dependent role played by background history and political-legal culture in the interpretation process."[131] The tendency of perceptions of property expectations and the permissibility of regulation to be influenced by such perceptive factors is documented; the willingness of property owners to accept regulation is frequently affected by the perception of the risk the regulation seeks to ameliorate in terms of degree, likelihood, or even existence.[132] In this regard, the law goes beyond the formation of "institutions that situate the rational choice activities of resource users,"[133] and actually shapes the perceptions of property owners about reasonable expectation and regulation.

This inquiry can be applied to the regulator as well as the regulated. A potential criticism of economic analyses of regulation, which focus on whether or not market failures are corrected, as well as the more social scientific analyses of regulation, which generally focus on the inability of pluralistic politics to protect public interest (often explained through the phenomenon of agency capture), is that an ends-focused approach, while asking legitimate and interesting questions, misses the opportunity to consider how process-oriented questions can bring to light a whole new series of issues.[134] In particular, economists who focus on economic regulation exclusively through contract theory tend to regard "(t)he contract and the regulatory ends it reflects...to exist independent of the mechanisms of regulatory evolution and enforcement."[135] This ends-oriented research agenda has placed undue (or better yet, misplaced) emphasis on courts as external enforcers of contractual commitments and ignores the solutions-seeking and decision-making processes within agencies, which may have a greater impact on property dispute outcomes than courts. Such an "incomplete contract perspective" emphasizes the role that bargaining plays in the ultimate outcomes of regulations through a focus on the impermanent and imperfect nature of regulatory "contracts," which are generally changing as political, economic, and informational contexts change.[136] So although emphasis is directed away from the courts as enforcers of the balance between forms of property in the common law and constitutional law, judicial decision-making may have a greater impact on the outcomes by changing the perceptions of private property and public good that are in play in a bargaining process.

Finally, consideration has to be given to groups acting outside of the immediate circle of a regulatory takings case (the property owner, the regulator, and the court). Interest groups have an interest in the conceptualization of property and rational expectations for its use that extends beyond the facts of a particular case. Their role is reflected by the more recently developed concern over hegemony within legal pluralism. Interest groups can pursue or assist litigation with the goal of shifting recognized standards of reasonable expectations that may have more lasting effects in courts or in the general public. The immediate public reaction to the Supreme Court's recent *Kelo* decision, an eminent domain case that left eminent domain jurisprudence fundamentally unaltered,[137] and the subsequent mobilization of property rights in the form of state voter initiatives in the 2006 elections, demonstrate the potential such litigation has for social mobilization efforts. Such efforts can be seen as attempts to establish a hegemonic power of one legal tradition over another. Legal pluralism acknowledges the likelihood that, "while there is competition and contradiction among the systems, in reality these legal arenas are almost exclusively the domain of the powerful."[138] Additionally, while recognizing the tendency of hegemony, legal pluralism, through its intentional focus on the interactions between bodies of law, allows us to not forget about subsumed traditions and "reflects alternative sites of counter-hegemonic discourse...."[139]

NOTES

[1] Montesquieu, C. 2002. *The Spirit of Laws*. Amherst: Prometheus Books. p. 2
[2] *Id.*, p. 7.
[3] Moore, SF, ed. 2005. *Law and Anthropology*. Malden: Blackwell Publishing Ltd. p. 12.
[4] Geertz, C. 1983. *Local Knowledge: Further Essays in Interpretive Anthropology*. New York: Basic Books, Inc. p. 232.
[5] *Penn Cent. Transp. Co. v. New York City*, 438 U.S. 104, 124 (1978).
[6] *Kelo v. City of New London*, 545 U.S. 469 (2005)
[7] See, e.g., Peterson, AL. 1989. "The Takings Clause: In Search of Underlying Principles." 77 Calif. L. Rev. 1301; Coursen, DF. 1999. "The Takings Jurisprudence of the Court of Federal Claims and the Federal Circuit." 29 Envtl. L. 821; Johnson, L. 2004. "After Tahoe-Sierra, One Thing is Clearer: There is Still a Fundamental Lack of Clarity." 46 Ariz. L. Rev. 353.
[8] Power, G. 2009. "Regulatory Takings: A Chronicle of the Construction of a Constitutional Concept." 23 BYU J. Pub. L. 221.
[9] See, e.g., Lazarus, RJ. 1993. "Putting the Correct 'Spin' on *Lucas*." 45 Stan. L. Rev. 1411; Johnson, at 36; Kmiec, DW and Kmiec Turner, K. 2005. "Property Lost: The Takings Clause in the 2004 Term." 8 PREVIEW 471.
[10] See, e.g., Peterson, at 7; Treanor, WM. 1995. "The Original Understanding of the Takings Clause and the Political Process." 95 Colum. L. Rev. 782.
[11] See, e.g., Marzulla, RJ and Marzulla, NG. 1991. "Regulatory Takings in the United States Claims Court: Adjusting the Burdens That in Fairness and Equity Ought to be Borne by Society as a Whole." 40 Cath. U.L. Rev. 549.

[12] See, e.g., Sterk, SE. 2004. "The Federalist Dimension of Regulatory Takings Jurisprudence." 114 Yale L.J. 203.
[13] See, e.g., Davis, S. 1986. "Federalism and Property Rights: An Examination of Justice Rehnquist's Legal Positivism." *The Western Political Science Quarterly*. Vol. 39, No. 2; Davis, S. 1992. "Rehnquist and State Courts: Federalism Revisited." *The Western Political Quarterly*. Vol. 45, No. 3; Kendall, DT and Lord, CP. 1998. "The Takings Project: A Critical Analysis and Assessment of the Progress So Far." 25 B.C. Envtl. Aff. L. Rev. 509.
[14] Fischel, WA. 1995. *Regulatory Takings: Law, Economics, and Politics*. Cambridge: Harvard University Press. p. 142.
[15] Michelman, F. 1967. "Property, Utility, and Fairness: Comments on the Ethical Foundations of 'Just Compensation' Law." 80 Harv. L.R. 1165, 1171.
[16] *Id*, at 1214.
[17] *Id.*
[18] *Id.*
[19] Fischel, at 145; See also, Kupiec, JA. 2008. "Returning to Principles of 'Fairness and Justice': The Role of Investment-Backed Expectations in Total Regulatory Taking Claims." 49 B.C. L. Rev. 865.
[20] Michelman, at 1171.
[21] *Id.*, at 1215
[22] Fischel, at 144.
[23] Michelman, at 1215; Fischel, at 146.
[24] Michelman, at 1220.
[25] *Id.*, 1223.
[26] *Id.*, 1223-1224.
[27] Sax, JL. 1996. "Takings Legislation: Where it Stands and What is Next." 23 Ecology L.Q. 509, 514.
[28] *Pennsylvania Coal v. Mahon*, 260 U.S. 393 (1922).
[29] Sax, JL. 2005. "Why America has a Property Rights Movement." 2005 U. Ill. L. Rev. 513, 516-517.
[30] Sax, JL. 1964. "Takings and the Police Power." 74 Yale L. J. 36, 37.
[31] *Mugler v. Kansas*, 123 U.S. 623 (1887).
[32] Sax (1964), at 41.
[33] *Pennsylvania Coal.*
[34] Sax (1964), at 50.
[35] *Id.*, at 55.
[36] *Id.*, at 57.
[37] *Id.*, at 42.
[38] *Id.*, at 62.
[39] *Id.*, at 63.
[40] Sax (2005), at 519.
[41] *Id.*, at 518-519.

[42] Alexander, GS. 2006. *The Global Debate over Constitutional Property: Lessons for American Takings Jurisprudence.* Chicago: University of Chicago Press. p. 101.
[43] Michelman, at 1221.
[44] Epstein, RA. 1985. *Takings: Private Property and the Power of Eminent Domain.* Cambridge: Harvard University Press. p. 3.
[45] Michelman, at 1228.
[46] Epstein, at p. 5.
[47] *Id.*, 216-217.
[48] *Id.*, 218.
[49] *Id.*
[50] *Id.*, 265.
[51] *Id.*
[52] Epstein, RA. 2005. "Takings, Commons, and Associations: Why the Telecommunications Act of 1996 Misfired." 22 Yale J. on Reg. 315, 323-325.
[53] Epstein (1985), at p. 182.
[54] Alexander, at 37.
[55] Epstein (1985), at pp. 321-322.
[56] Fischel, at p. 102.
[57] Ely, JH. 1980. "Democracy and Distrust: A Theory of Judicial Review." Cambridge: Harvard University Press.
[58] Fischel, at p. 120.
[59] Rossi, J. 2005. *Regulatory Bargaining and Public Law.* New York: Cambridge University Press. p. 11.
[60] Fischel, at p. 1.
[61] *Id.*, 316.
[62] *Id.*, 133.
[63] *Id.*, 289.
[64] *Id.*, 290.
[65] *Id.*, 324.
[66] *Id.*, 289.
[67] Epstein (1985), at p. 332.
[68] Alexander, at 63
[69] Epstein (1985), at 332-333.
[70] Alexander, at 38.
[71] *Id.*, at 37.
[72] Merry, SE. 1988. "Legal Pluralism." *Law and Society Review*, 22:5. p. 870.
[73] Fuller, C. 1994. "Legal Anthropology, Legal Pluralism and Legal Thought." *Anthropology Today.* Vol. 10, No. 3, June. p. 10.
[74] Hunt, A. 1993. *Explorations in Law and Society: Toward a Constitutive Theory of Law.* New York: Routledge. p. 9.
[75] *Id.*

[76] Fuller, at 10.
[77] Merry, at 880.
[78] Sax (1964).
[79] Dukeminier, J and Krier, JE. 1998. *Property*, 4th ed. Aspen: Aspen Law and Publishers. pp. 747-48.
[80] Alexander, at 4.
[81] Ely, JW, Jr. 1992. *The Guardian of Every Other Right: A Constitutional History of Property Rights*. New York: Oxford University Press. p. 13.
[82] *Id.*, at 9.
[83] Sax (1964), at 57.
[84] *Id.*, at 51
[85] Lucas v. South Carolina Coastal Council, 505 U.S. 1003 (1992).
[86] Sax (1964), at 51.
[87] *Id.*
[88] *Id.*, at 53.
[89] *Id.*, at 57.
[90] Epstein (1985), at vii.
[91] *Id.*
[92] *Id.*, at 16.
[93] *Id.*, at 17.
[94] *Id.*, at 18.
[95] Alexander, at 73.
[96] *Pennsylvania Coal*, at 415.
[97] Alexander, at 74.
[98] *Penn Central.*
[99] *Id.*, at 124.
[100] *Lucas.*
[101] See, e.g., Belsky, MH. 1994. "The Public Trust Doctrine and Takings: A Post-Lucas View." 4 Alb. L.J. Sci. & Tech. 17; Bayne, KA. 1993. "*Lucas v. South Carolina Coastal Council*: Drawing a Line in the Sand." 42 Cath. U.L. Rev. 1063; Haffner, PF. 1993. "Regulatory Takings—A New Categorical Rule." 61 U. Cin. L. Rev. 1035.
[102] See, e.g., Protos, JD. 1993. "*Lucas v. South Carolina Coastal Council*: A Tremor on the Regulatory Takings Richter Scale." 43 Case W. Res. 651; Lazarus.
[103] *Lucas*, at 1027.
[104] *Id.*, at 1029.
[105] Smith, MB. 1994. "Defining Property in the Post-Lucas World." 1994 U. Ill. L. Rev. 443, 460; see also Epstein, RA. 1993. "*Lucas v. South Carolina Coastal Council*: A Tangled Web of Expectations." 45 Stan. L. Rev. 1369.
[106] Guillet, D. 1998. "Rethinking Legal Pluralism: Local Law and State Law in the Evolution of Water Property Rights in Northwestern Spain." *Comparative Studies in Society and History*, Vol. 40, No. 1. p. 42.

[107] Alexander, at 71.
[108] *Penn Central*, at 119.
[109] *Cane Tennessee, Inc. & Colten Inc. v. United States*, 57 Fed. Cl. 115, 123 (2003)
[110] *Palazzolo*, at 627.
[111] *Id.*, at 637.
[112] *Id.*, at 633.
[113] *Apollo Fuels, Inc. v. United States*, 381 F.3d 1338, 1350 (2004)
[114] Singer, JW. 2000. *Entitlement: The Paradoxes of Property*. New Haven: Yale University Press. p. 6.
[115] Blackstone, W. 1979(1765). *Commentaries on the Laws of England*, Vol. 1. Chicago: University of Chicago Press. p. 135
[116] Singer, at 6.
[117] *Id.*, 4.
[118] *Id.*, 16.
[119] Nedelsky, J. 1990. *Private Property and the Limits of American Constitutionalism: The Madisonian Framework and Its Legacy*. Chicago: University of Chicago Press. p. 208.
[120] *Id.*, 209
[121] *Id.*, 208.
[122] Singer, at 9.
[123] Alexander, at 78.
[124] *Id.*, at 80.
[125] *First English Lutheran Church v. Los Angeles County*, 482 U.S. 304, 308-311 (1987).
[126] *Tulare Lake Basin Water District v. United States*, 49 Fed. Cl. 313 (2001).
[127] Alexander, at 37.
[128] Singer, at 30.
[129] Hunt, at 230.
[130] Gillman, H. 1999., "The Court as an Idea, Not a Building (or a Game): Interpretive Institutionalism and the Analysis of Supreme Court Decision-Making." *Supreme Court Decision-Making*. Chicago: University of Chicago Press. p. 78.
[131] Alexander, at 29-30.
[132] Thompson, BH. 2000. "Tragically Difficult: The Obstacles to Governing the Commons." 30 Envtl. L. 241.
[133] McCay, BJ. 2002. "Emergence of Institutions for the Commons: Contexts, Situations, and Events." *The Drama of the Commons*. Ostrom, E, et al., eds. Washington, D.C.: National Academy Press. pp. 361-362.
[134] Rossi, at 9-10.
[135] *Id.*, at 11.
[136] *Id.*, at 12-13.
[137] *Berman v. Parker*, 348 U.S. 26 (1954).

[138] Moore, EP. 1993. "Gender, Power, and Legal Pluralism: Rajasthan, India." *American Ethnologist*, Vol. 20, No. 3. (Aug). p. 523.
[139] Guillet, at 43.

CHAPTER 4

REGULATORY TAKINGS AND THE QUESTION OF IMPACT

The attempt to answer questions of judicial impact is one fraught with difficulties. The institutional structure of the U.S. judiciary is set up in a manner which counters the ability to cause an impact; limits on rights, constraints from other branches, and a lack of implementation powers all may act to constrain courts.[1] Even when a court can overcome such constraints, one is still left considering the question of causality. "In a case where an agency reconsiders and changes an individual decision following a successful judicial review application by the person directly affected by the decision, the causal link may be easily enough established. But, where the impact is a change in more general modes of working, the contribution of judicial review may be much harder to trace."[2] The previous chapters dealing with the doctrine and theory of regulatory takings focused upon the complex and evolving nature of this body of law. Given the complex natures of regulatory takings law, environmental law, and the interests held by environmentalists, communities, property-owners, developers, property rights organizations, etc., measuring the impact of regulatory takings litigation on the implementation regime of any body of environmental policy will necessarily be more difficult than simply determining the outcome of particular conflicts.

Such measurements are especially difficult to determine given the particularly complex relationship between the U.S. judiciary and environmental regulatory agencies. Robert Kagan has conceptualized the policymaking role of the U.S. judiciary as one of adversarial legalism, wherein the lines of separation of powers are not boldly drawn and "policymaking, implementation, and dispute resolution [are] characterized by frequent resort to highly adversarial legal contestation."[3] The origins of adversarial legalism lie in institutions as old as the nation itself: "a politically selected judiciary, with powers to make policy through common law and constitutional adjudication, and a highly entrepreneurial, politically engaged legal profession."[4] Additionally, the U.S.'s environmental regulatory regime developed during a "vast expansion of government programs and bureaucracy" aimed at nationalizing regulatory power due to "differences among the states...hav[ing] become suspect."[5] Given the interwoven relationship between environmental agencies and the courts, and since "one cannot understand the nature of the impact of judicial review on administrative procedures without first understanding the nature of administrative procedures,"[6] inquiry into such judicial impact will involve a focus on an array of potential events and targets, some with more obvious causal links than others.

Given the complex relationship between the judiciary and environmental regulatory agencies, traditional pre-litigation/post-litigation quantitative measurements of impact should be considered a necessary but insufficient component of impact analysis of regulatory takings litigation, itself a complex array of various legal, social, and economic factors. When institutional relationships are straight-forward and one-dimensional, result-oriented measurements of impact do not present much of an interpretive problem. When the relationship is multi-dimensional, however, theoretical and descriptive analyses become more necessary to find results that may not be obvious and to understand and assess those that are. As was discussed earlier, the development of regulatory takings jurisprudence cannot properly be understood without reference to shifts in the social meaning/value context that surrounds property and its regulation. Therefore, inquiry into the impact of regulatory takings litigation on the implementation of environmental protection policy must focus on these factors through attention to the decision-making processes of those involved in implementation and enforcement.

Within the public law subfield of political science, the studies of judicial impact and judicial decision-making have remained separate. This chapter takes the levels of analyses applied to the decision-making processes of justices and applies them to those who are in the position of regulator, the individuals who are simultaneously charged with the implementation of environmental policy and challenged by litigation to accompany such implementation with compensation. The central argument of this chapter is that the tool of interpretive decision-making analysis is essential to answer the question of regulatory takings impact. Interpretivism, which has been increasingly utilized in studies of judicial decision-making, can also be applied to those that, in turn, must make regulatory decisions in the light of judicial decisions. Through interpretivism, such decisions are understood in the context of a larger social and legal network of meaning. This chapter discusses the development of judicial interpretivism within the study of judicial decision-making, and then proceeds to consider the ways this decision-making model sheds light on the question of judicial impact, especially in the field of regulatory takings.

DECISION-MAKING MODELS

The explanation of judicial decision-making is a hotly contested subject at political science conferences and within public law journals. Despite the contentious nature of the exercise, there appears to be, at the root of all the approaches to decision-making analysis, a common agreement: all of the components of judicial decision-making to which scholars have pointed have an actual presence in political and legal reality. Segal and Spaeth, arguably the strongest proponents of their own decision-making model, state, "A model represents reality; it does not constitute reality itself. A model purposefully ignores certain aspects of reality and focuses instead on a selected set of crucial factors."[7] This statement illustrates that the debate surrounding judicial decision-making models has less to do with whether or not a judge is solely influenced by the factor highlighted by a particular scholar, and has more to do with whether or not that one of several factors is of the highest theoretical significance.

Furthermore, judicial decision-making models are frequently applied solely to judicial decision-makers. However, the activity of interpreting legal issues is one that is hardly limited to the interior of a courtroom. When considering the impact that a particular case may have, on society as a whole, it becomes evident that the act of judicial interpretation is engaged in, not only by the interpreting population of the courts, but also by the implementing and consuming populations of the regulators and the regulated.[8] For that reason, judicial decision-making models should also have something to say about the interpretive behaviors of non-judicial actors.

While judicial decision-making models are frequently taught and explained in an easily distinguishable chapter format, the fact is that the division lines between various schools of thought on the question are vague and frequently crossed. An early source of division can be seen beginning with the influence of realism on American legal and political academies in the early twentieth century. The diminishment of idealized notions of political phenomena and a redirected emphasis on the forces of human-created institutions fundamentally altered the study of politics, and "within the legal academy Legal Realists such as Oliver Wendell Holmes, Karl Llewellyn, and Jerome Frank dispatched traditional mechanistic and formalistic conceptions of the law, and instead emphasized the creativity found in judging."[9]

The "mechanistic and formalistic conceptions of the law" which legal realists sought to replace have frequently been associated with the legal model of judicial decision-making, which some critics, desiring to describe the legal model as irrevocably rooted in pre-realist academia, have defined as "postulat[ing] that the decisions of the Court are based on the facts of the case in light of the plain meaning of statutes and the Constitution, the intent of the framers, precedent, and a balancing of societal interest."[10] However, such portrayals of the legal model are, at best, incomplete, and are likely rooted in the methodological schism between political scientific analyses and the "somewhat idealized and distorted notion of the role of law"[11] utilized by those directly involved in the legal profession where "precedent, *stare decisis*, and formalism continue to be the way most law students experience law and the way judges describe what they do in written opinions."[12] Looking back at the transition from legalism to legal realism, a mutually exclusive relationship between the two camps need not necessarily be constructed. Instead of interpreting the legal model as focusing exclusively on the doctrine of law while ignoring the influences of justices as political actors, "it is better understood as a commitment to apply a set of *a priori* 'interpretive canons or principles' (some of which are substantively political) in deciding cases. Thus, the distinction is between a 'principled' rather than a 'result-based' process of decision-making, not between political and apolitical models."[13] Hart's legal positivist jurisprudence remains consistent with both the legal model and legal realism through an adherence to the role of law, whereby judges make decisions based on the non-arbitrary rules of recognition, change, and adjudication, and a recognition of the purely legal manner in which such rules come to be.[14] Despite the efforts of advocates of legalism to maintain a presence for law within political science, legalism was pushed further into the margins of the systematic study of judicial behavior.

With the valuation of positivist methodology that accompanied the behavioralist revolution of the mid-twentieth century, came an intensified focus of legal realism on the theorization and operationalization of the political nature of justices' behavior. As the focus moved from the law to the justices themselves, the overarching goal of legal realists became the "analysis of judicial behavior which will contribute to theorizing about judicial decision-making and, in a larger context, about the role of the judiciary in the American system of government."[15] In pursuit of this analysis, behavioralists stressed traditional scientific values, such as prediction, explanation, observable and quantifiable data, and theoretical orientation.[16] Influences from behavioral psychology would direct studies of judicial decision-making toward a focus on the attitudes, or "set of interrelated beliefs about at least one object and the situation in which it is encountered,"[17] of justices, free from the influence of legal or institutional factors that would prevent them from following their attitudes.[18] This model of judicial decision-making is called the attitudinal model, and it "holds that the Supreme Court decides disputes in light of the facts of the case vis-à-vis the ideological attitudes and values of the justices. Simply put, Rehnquist votes the way he does because he is extremely conservative; Marshall voted the way he did because he is extremely liberal."[19]

An obvious advantage of the attitudinal model is that it purports to explain judicial decision-making by reference to the key component of the foundational assumptions of legal realism, namely, the political ideologies of flesh-and-blood justices and, in so doing, aligns its explanation with common anecdotal experiences and public perceptions of judicial behavior. The fundamental assumption of the attitudinal model, that justices seek to manifest their own policy preferences in their judicial decisions, is generally not even challenged by critics of the model, who generally concede that, "at some level, all political behavior must be explained with some reference to individual values, attitudes, or personalities."[20] However, just as any attempt to explain judicial decision-making without reference to attitudes or values will remain incomplete, so too, argue critics, will any attempt which ignores "contexts such as institutional settings…inevitably be incomplete for at least two reasons."[21]

The first reason why institutions must be included in any accurate explanation of judicial decision-making is that "institutional settings are an omnipresent feature of our attempts to pursue a preferred course of action."[22] When a justice must make a decision about a particular case, the justice is already positioned within a "complex political system within which he [sic] must function [which] compels a Justice who wishes to act rationally in terms of achieving his [sic] policy goals to weigh a number of factors in addition to the specific legal issues in individual cases."[23] Institutionalist critics of attitudinal models may maintain the assumption that justices are driven by a desire to politically establish their preferred policy positions through case decisions, but they temper the impact of such a desire by considering it within a framework of institutional constraints which limit the degree to which a justice can, in fact, pursue his or her policy preferences in a judicial setting. In so doing, such an approach establishes "hypotheses about how Justices will behave or have behaved, based on how they *can* act."[24]

These rational choice models of judicial decision-making criticize attitudinal models by positioning the attitudinal judge within the institutional constraints of the political world. Rational choice models are often included as part of the camp known as "new institutionalism," which is "a challenge to the reductionist and instrumentalist conception of politics that characterized behavioralism, and a renewed appreciation for constitutive and normative conceptions of politics and the role that institutions played in the latter."[25] The end result of such analysis differs significantly from that of the attitudinal models. Since the focus of analysis has shifted from political ideologies to institutional constraints, rational choice scholars often see judicial decisions not as sincere, maximally preferred position statements, but as the product of strategy, as an acceptable, but less than maximum, position arrived at through bargaining and satisficing.[26] Although policy preferences remain as the most significant theoretical factor, the presence and constraint of institutional factors make the model more reflective of a complex political environment.

Rational choice analyses of judicial decision-making are generally focused on one of two types of institutional constraints which guide and direct the judges' decisions. One set of institutions which force justices to behave strategically in the pursuit of their policy preferences includes external constraints. The separation of constitutional power among different branches means that "the Supreme Court is embedded in a political system in which the legislative and executive branches of government have the capacity to overturn, circumvent, or even ignore its decisions."[27] Such limiting external constraints would clearly direct a policy-oriented justice toward satisficing; his or her decision would have to be "a position that is as close to its ideal point as possible, without being so far from Congress that it is overturned."[28] In addition to political constraints, members of the Court could also be constrained by the institution of law. While some rational choice scholars do not see legal institutions as providing a significant constraint on justices' policy pursuits,[29] except in situations where the policy question is not of major interest to a particular justice,[30] others argue that the law sets up an institution of legitimacy in the public eye, and such legal traditions as *stare decisis* and *sua sponte* limit the ability of justices to pursue their policy preferences.[31]

In addition to external constraints, internal constraints are described by rational choice scholars as being significant factors in the judicial decision-making process. One of the most key internal institutional components of the Supreme Court is the presence of nine justices and the necessity of a majority opinion; "the strategic approach recognizes that the behavior of individual justices is shaped in part by the actions and preferences of their brethren. As a result, a justice's choices during the selection and consideration of cases will depend in large part on the choices made by the other justices."[32] The requirement that any individual justice must achieve agreement with at least four other justices if he or she is going to manifest a personal policy preference results in various decision-making behaviors observed by rational choice scholars. Such behavior includes bargaining with other justices to overcome disagreements, forward thinking to anticipate the actions of other justices, manipulating the agenda to make it more favorable to one's preferred position in light of other justices' likely positions and actions, and strategic opinion writing with the goal of constraining the likely actions of other justices.[33]

While the rational choice model of judicial decision-making adds a depth and complexity to such models that legalist and attitudinal models lack, one of its clear weaknesses is that "the strategic model can only claim to shed light on those features of institutional politics that are properly considered strategic."[34] The second reason why the inclusion of institutional factors is necessary for an analysis of judicial decision-making is that "institutions not only structure one's ability to act on a set of beliefs; they are also a source of distinctive political purposes, goals, and preferences."[35] As opposed to attitudinal and rational choice approaches, which hold the rational self-maximizing actor as a constant, a second new institutional approach works to understand the formation of the values and ideologies which guide judicial decision-making. Known as the historical-interpretive model of judicial decision-making, theoretical primacy is moved toward institutions, while still acknowledging the presence of attitudes. "Rather than focus on ostensibly universal motivations such as rationality or selfishness..., interpretivists try to reconstruct intentional states of mind and cultural or political contexts in the hope that [they] can induce with some confidence the reasons that led a particular person to adopt a particular course of conduct."[36]

"The interpretive turn"[37] in the analysis of judicial decision-making can be conceptualized as providing a middle ground between attitudinal and rational choice reliance on individual motivation and the overly deterministic nature of Marxist and Weberian historical determinism.[38] While room for agency and strategy exists within historical interpretivism, as it does within the rational choice model, foundational theoretical value is given to institutions, which are themselves constitutive of attitudes, values, and ideologies. Within this model, institutions are considered as establishing "an identifiable purpose or a shared normative goal that, at a particular historical moment in a particular context, becomes routinized within an identifiable corporate form as the result of the efforts of certain groups of people."[39] Such historically and culturally rooted institutions are crucial to an understanding of how justices' attitudes, values, and perceptions and definitions of problems are formed. Such social definitions are central to the justices' own perception of themselves and their role as justices. Such constitutive institutions, including the institutions of laws and norms, remain external to the Court, but are as necessary for an understanding of judicial behavior as the "idiosyncratic attitudes of particular justices."[40]

Although the historical interpretive model rejects the notion of a decision-making actor free from institutional contexts, it is not a deterministic model and allows for human agency. The model does revive an interest in law and precedent from the legal model, but "making legal ideology or judicial opinions the object of serious inquiry need not imply a belief in the science of law or mechanical jurisprudence."[41] Theoretical room still exists for human agency in the form of strategy within institutionalized contexts, as well as within the possibility of establishing new or changing old institutional contexts. Institutions "are themselves created by past human political decisions that were in some measure discretionary, and to some degree they are alterable by future ones. They also have a kind of life of their own."[42] An analysis involving a mutually constitutive relationship between actors and institutions is going to be methodologically complex, and may have difficulty achieving the perceived standards of a behavioralist academy. Although the model lacks the unidirectional parsimony of the other decision-making models, its descriptive nature does not make it any less empirical. "[E]fforts to reinvigorate qualitative inquiries into norms, values, and ideologies within public-law scholarship do not really represent efforts by legal scholars to be political or moral philosophers. Rather, they are attempts to integrate the study of ideas in law with *descriptive* studies of the historical evolution of political institutions and behavior."[43]

The key contribution of interpretivism in the study of judicial behavior mirrors its main critique of the attitudinal model: one cannot conceptualize attitudes without first conceptualizing institutions. Gillman's contribution to this discipline, as discussed above, is the recognition that an understanding of judicial decision-making requires a focus upon the institutions that shape concepts involved in the decision-making process. This step adds analytic complexity to decision-making analyses by adding to the behavioral variables of policy preferences and strategies a recognition that the law does matter in such analyses. Such an observation is not purely novel; salvaging a place for law distinct from politics, while recognizing the contributions of legal realism, is a central part of Hart's post-legal realism.[44]

Additionally, proponents of Critical Legal Studies (CLS) have understood the phenomenon of law in a manner simultaneously malleable and confining. The dilemma of being forced to choose law as either a "true form of doctrine" and "some established version of social order" or "the inconclusive contest of political visions" is rejected.[45] While hardly representing a single, unified mode of legal thinking, CLS begins with a reliance on Marxist historical materialism and a focus on the ideological nature of law. The point is not to "throw aside the generalisations and abstractions elaborated by bourgeois jurists, whose starting point was the needs of their class and of their times. Rather, by analysing these abstract categories, it should demonstrate their true significance and lay bare the historically limited nature of the legal form."[46] The structure seen beneath such legal abstraction, for CLS, is class rule; more to the point of the question of judicial impact is the manner in which law performs such functions. In CLS, "an adequate understanding of the legal system must account for the way the rule of law ideal is rooted in a particular form of social life."[47] The interconnectedness of law and society is best articulated, from the CLS perspective, as social forces as constitutive of law as a means of reproducing those same social forces. Such social relations cannot be "explained without regard to the meanings the men [sic] who participate in those relations attribute to them."[48] As perception becomes an essential, albeit insufficient, component of legal understanding, law becomes "analogous to the duck-rabbit figure which, without any alteration in the lines that compose it, can change its overall appearance, depending on how one perceives it."[49]

It is at this point that the historical-interpretive model of judicial decision-making merges with Critical Legal Studies to demonstrate its connectedness with the question of impact. For both schools of thought, law as an institution cannot be understood absent attention to cultural, social, psychological, and symbolic contexts. Additionally, these dimensions of the law affect the application of the law. Unger, for example, regards legal behavior as constituting a double life, simultaneously enforcing and defining legal custom.[50] When judicial decision-making inquiries are expanded beyond the role of judges and consider the behavior of other legal actors, including inspectors, enforcers, lawyers, and regulated individuals, the interpretation of laws is seen not only as affecting immediate situations, but also as shaping the historical context in which future legal decisions will be made. As judges interpret laws in particular cases, they are shaping and creating legal contexts; such contexts further shape the manner in which regulators and the regulated understand the meaning of the law and the meaning of social relations under the law.

The question of impact is, therefore, an inherently complex question. One must consider traditional indices of impact, such as compliance or non-compliance of litigants or related parties to a case or collective doctrine, realizing that such impact has the potential to be shaped, i.e. made more or less likely, by extraneous circumstances. Additionally, one must also recognize that such circumstances, i.e. the social and legal environment, can be shaped by judicial decisions. This shaping can occur at the frequently hard to measure symbolic level; a decision or a family of decisions may shape the way a population as a whole understands a legal question, perhaps in a manner inconsistent with the text of that decision. What follows is a consideration of the ways in which the social, legal, and cultural environment involved in the questions of regulatory takings are susceptible to shifts brought about by the actual regulatory takings case decisions made in courtrooms.

IMPACT AND REGULATORY TAKINGS

One type of impact that could be caused by a body of litigation is a behavioral adjustment on the part of the agency based upon the agency's overall level of acceptance of the judicial decision.[51] Such evidence is often easiest to identify. For example, official statements by Fish and Wildlife Service (FWS) personnel that the agency will not follow through on plans to change the listing status of certain gray wolf populations from endangered to threatened, although they "continue to believe the reclassification was both biologically and legally sound,"[52] due to a district court ruling that the particular change was unreasonable and contrary to Congressional intent[53] would be a fairly clear example of an agency adjusting its behavior due to a judicial decision. A procedural change in regulations to circumvent such a decision would also be such an example of impact.

The search for such direct, behavioral judicial impacts corresponds easily with a basic understanding of the nature of judicial impact. Such an understanding looks for litigious events in which the Court rules on a case and the litigants, and all similarly situated parties, alter their behavior accordingly or in some manner directly attributable to the decision. While such occurrences certainly occur, this type of impact cannot describe in detail the complex relations between courts and the outside world. In addition to failing to consider why such compliance or non-compliance occurs, this construction of impact also ignores the presence of multiple other factors and relations that likely shape the probability of compliance. The situation is the same for regulatory takings and judicial impact. While one might safely speculate that a particular agency of the government would comply with a judicial order to compensate an individual property owner being regulated, a far more interesting question is whether this will result in the same agency, and other similarly situated agencies, being shy about property regulation in the future. Short of evidence in the form of an agency memo directing regulatory personnel to reduce regulatory behavior and citing a takings case loss as the reason (or directing a regulatory increase citing a win), broad direct behavioral adjustments in regulatory takings cases should not be expected.

Agency behavior might also change in "unofficial" ways, i.e. in ways which do not directly attribute changed behavior to a case, but nonetheless, "*actions changed* in such a way as to conform with the Court, regardless of what was said"[54] as a reason for the behavior. This sort of impact is more consistent with the impacts allegedly associated with regulatory takings litigation. If a regulatory takings case is ruled upon in such a manner as to require compensation for a regulatory action commonly engaged in by a particular agency, "the mere threat of challenge may exert an inhibiting effect on policy and influence decision-making, and the degree to which it does so is likely to vary depending on the precision of the threatened challenge, the nature of the litigant and the sensitivity of the issues involved."[55] The conclusion of such behavior as observable impact cannot be made simply upon correlation, but must be theoretically explained, i.e. "the mechanisms or links of influence must be clearly specified."[56] Therefore, decision-making models should remain a part of efforts to study judicial impact.

The decision-making model most useful in assessing such impacts is the rational choice model. As described above, in the context of judicial decision-making, a judge seeking the satisfaction of his or her own policy preferences will manifest those preferences into the decision, taking into account the external and internal institutions shaping the degree to which such preferences can be achieved. This model can also be used to explain the behavior of those reacting to that judicial decision, namely, key regulatory agency personnel. In other words, the product of strategic decision-making, i.e. the judicial decision, becomes a key institution in the strategic decision-making of another person or group. Another shift that occurs in the move of the rational choice model from judicial to regulatory behavior involves the goals pursued. Advocates of the rational choice model of judicial behavior commonly point to factors such as background, personal attributes, values, role perception, and group interactions as important to explaining behavior.[57] While such factors may make sense from a rational choice perspective when considering regulatory decision-making, additional factors, such as the availability of resources and political pressure from state legislatures and interest groups[58] are likely to influence agencies to a greater degree than judges.

In terms of the impact of regulatory takings cases, a rational choice model could be useful in highlighting instances in which the presence and awareness of agency losses by similarly situated agencies in such cases reduces the willingness of regulatory personnel to regulate private property if doing so brings the possibility of having to pay for it. This model prevents the researcher from being reduced to searching for the "silver bullet" memo that directly accounts for judicial impact. Instead, a more general approach is taken, in which an aversion to overly costly regulation is assumed and fluctuations in regulatory output are measured. One could theorize that regulatory agencies, already confined by finite budgets, will reduce their regulatory outputs in the face of regulatory takings challenges to maximize their use of available resources by either avoiding costly regulation of making up for the costs of litigation and compensation accrued through regulation deemed necessary.

Any rational choice analysis of regulatory takings impact, however, must account for the complex institutional structure surrounding regulatory decision-making. Bureaucratic reaction to a judicial decision may occur across multiple levels of political division, across longer periods of time, and sometimes leave less obvious causal calling cards. The availability of monetary and personnel resources may be affected by compensatory losses and the perceived availability of such resources may be affected by the perceived threat of regulatory takings lawsuits; however, such budgetary restrictions have other potential sources, which may produce the same outcome. Furthermore, communication between courts and agencies is multi-faceted. An agency may directly interact with a court or the counsel may act as a liaison between the two. Additionally, agencies frequently interact with political institutions other than courts. Agencies are enabled through state and federal legislatures and they are governed by executives. State agencies, which implement most regulatory policy, encounter varying degrees of oversight from federal agencies. Given this complex array of institutional interactions, the impact of regulatory takings litigation from courts to agencies may occur along multiple pathways. One possible route, meant to only provide a possible example, could be a state legislature reacting to the potential costs in regulatory takings litigation that it has observed and, in reaction, legislatively restricting regulatory behavior through mandatory cost/benefit analyses to minimize state expenditures.

Finally, extra-judicial forms of impact should be considered. A highly visible court decision may alter public consciousness about a particular legal question in a manner fully unrelated to the facts of the case. The Supreme Court's 1978 decision in *TVA v. Hill*[59] ordered the construction of the nearly completed Tellico Dam halted to protect the snail darter, a small fish. Despite the eventual, but relatively quick, completion of the dam through Congressional override of the Court's decision,[60] the image of the fish that stopped the dam, a dam which was not stopped, serves as a powerful cultural icon portraying the Endangered Species Act in a particularly politicized way.[61] Within the realm of property law, a more recent example can be found in the Supreme Court's recent decision in *Kelo*,[62] which was discussed in earlier chapters. Obviously, the more a regulatory statute exists in a collective public consciousness, the more likely its corresponding litigation is to rise to the level of widespread public awareness and subsequent political action.

Two versions of extra-judicial impact, which affect regulatory change through cultural and social avenues, are particularly relevant to regulatory takings litigation. One avenue begins in the courts, moves through cultural/social areas, and comes back to regulatory behavior through non-judicial political institutions. When considering the larger political, social, and cultural impacts of a judicial decision, one observes "that the impact of decisions is not necessarily directly linked to the legal success or otherwise of the challenge.... Moreover, it cannot be assumed that a failure in the courts will necessarily be altogether unwelcome."[63] Even unsuccessful litigation can serve a larger political purpose of rights mobilization and redirect political energies, so that "legal mobilization may contribute in different ways and with varying impacts at different points in ongoing struggles."[64] Such political or legal mobilization works by crystallizing political resources through litigation so that such resources, even if they come about through a legal defeat, may be used to seek victories through other political or legal avenues. The existence of several litigation-focused interest groups with policy goals centered on private property rights and limited government involvement in economic areas means that the necessary institutional structure exists for social mobilization of "private property rights consciousness" to maneuver through multiple political arenas.

Extra-judicial impact of regulatory takings litigation can also occur in a manner that does not involve the formation of overt political efforts to mobilize regulatory change. As with political mobilization, social or cultural mobilization begins with litigation, win or lose, forging a shift, crystallization, polarization, etc. of social and cultural modes of understanding. However, instead of such social capital being used in political efforts to bring about change, the shift in understanding changes the overall social context in which the key components of such litigation are understood.

Such questions involve institutionalism and interpretivism as they "try to reconstruct intentional states of mind and cultural or political contexts in the hope that [they] can induce with some confidence the reasons that led a particular person to adopt a particular course of conduct."[65] Lawsuits can do more than alter the official rules of implementation for a particular statute or regulatory program; lawsuits can also shift the way people, from the public at large to key decision-makers to members of a specific regulated community, perceive the spirit, purpose, or value of the law as well as the rights possessed in relation to that law. "Rights can only be operative as constituents of a strategy of social transformation as they become part of an emergent 'common sense' and are articulated within social practices."[66] Through the forging of "common sense," as it is "questioned, disputed, affirmed, developed, formalized, contemplated, even taught,"[67] understandings of how the law operates and to what property owners are entitled in the face of the law, media accounts and even anecdotal experiences may exert a greater impact on the eventual political course taken to shape the law.[68]

Regulatory takings jurisprudence involves not only a balancing of public and private interests, but a confrontation between different bodies of law: common law notions of nuisance (themselves coming from multiple and conflicting sources),[69] a public trust doctrine originating in Roman Law,[70] and a constitutional protection of private property. Thinking about regulatory takings law should "involve a shift away from functionalist thinking about law...and a shift toward hermeneutic thinking about it—as a mode of giving particular sense to particular things in particular places."[71] Of particular interest is the reliance of the federal judiciary on the *Penn Central* assessment of the presence and reasonableness of investment-backed expectations[72] in determining when regulation amounts to a taking. The purpose of such a requirement is clear: without such a requirement, property owners could get compensation for regulated property for uses that were neither reasonable nor intended. A cyclical relationship exists between the courts and this matter of law: while the Court must interpret what property expectations are reasonable, such rulings shape the very definition of "reasonable." Fluctuations in the understanding of reasonable property expectations within various populations, such as regulatory agencies and regulated industries, could affect the level of regulation, agency/public relationships, economic activity, and rates of litigation.

The following chapters discuss two separate regulatory regimes, those involving the environmental regulation of surface coal mining and the protection of endangered species. In each example, a history is detailed, considering the complex relations between regulatory agencies, regulated populations, and the courts. Special attention is given to the history of regulatory takings cases under each statute, for obvious reasons. Finally, the question of the impact of such litigation is considered, with a focus on the previously discussed types of impact one might expect to find.

NOTES

[1] Rosenberg, GN. 1991. *The Hollow Hope: Can Courts Bring About Social Change?* Chicago: University of Chicago Press. pp. 10-21.
[2] Cane, P. 2004. "Understanding Judicial Review and Its Impact," in *Judicial Review and Bureaucratic Impact: International and Interdisciplinary Perspectives*, M Hertogh and S Halliday, eds. New York: Cambridge University Press. pp. 33-34.
[3] Kagan, RA. 2004. "American Courts and the Policy Dialogue: The Role of Adversarial Legalism," in *Making Policy, Making Law: An Interbranch Perspective*." MC Miller and J Barnes, eds. Washington, D.C.: Georgetown University Press. p. 14.
[4] *Id.*, at 25.
[5] Melnick, RS. 2004. "Courts and Agencies," in *Making Policy, Making Law: An Interbranch Perspective*." MC Miller and J Barnes, eds. Washington, D.C.: Georgetown University Press. p. 90.
[6] Sunkin, M. 2004. "Conceptual Issues in Researching the Impact of Judicial Review on Government Bureaucracies," in *Judicial Review and Bureaucratic Impact: International and Interdisciplinary Perspectives*, M Hertogh and S Halliday, eds. New York: Cambridge University Press. p. 45.
[7] Segal, JA and Spaeth, HJ. 1993. *The Supreme Court and the Attitudinal Model*. New York: Cambridge University Press. p. 32.

[8] Canon, BC and Johnson, CA. 1999. *Judicial Policies: Implementation and Impact*, 2nd ed. Washington, D.C.: Congressional Quarterly Inc. pp. 18-22.
[9] Clayton, CW. 1999. "The Supreme Court and Political Jurisprudence: New and Old Institutionalisms," in *Supreme Court Decision-Making*. Cornell W. Clayton and Howard Gillman, eds. Chicago: University of Chicago Press. p. 16.
[10] Segal and Spaeth, at 32.
[11] Perry, HW, Jr. 1991. *Deciding to Decide*. Cambridge: Harvard University Press. p. 140.
[12] Clayton, at 17.
[13] *Id.*, at 26.
[14] Hart, HLA. 1994. *The Concept of Law*. 2nd ed. New York: Oxford University Press.
[15] Murphy, WF. 1970. *Elements of Judicial Strategy*. Chicago: University of Chicago Press. p. 3.
[16] Segal and Spaeth, at 67; See also Somit, A and Tanenhaus, J. 1967. *The Development of Political Science*. Boston: Allyn and Bacon. pp. 177-78.
[17] Rohde, DW and Spaeth, HJ. 1976. *Supreme Court Decision Making*. San Francisco: W. H. Freeman Press. p. 72; See also Segal and Spaeth, at 69.
[18] Segal and Spaeth, at 69.
[19] *Id.*, at 65.
[20] Gillman, H and Clayton, CW. 1999. "Beyond Judicial Attitudes: Institutional Approaches to Supreme Court Decision-Making," in *Supreme Court Decision-Making*. Clayton, CW and Gillman, H, eds. Chicago: University of Chicago Press. p. 3.
[21] *Id.*
[22] *Id.*
[23] Murphy, at 199.
[24] *Id.*, at 201.
[25] Clayton, at 30.
[26] Mohr, LB. 1976. "Organizations, Decisions, and Courts." *Law and Society Review*. 10: 621-642. pp. 629-634; Perry, at 192-195; Baum, L. 1998. *The Puzzle of Judicial Behavior*. Ann Arbor: University of Michigan Press. pp. 89-91.
[27] Maltzman, F, et al. 1999. "Strategy and Judicial Choice: New Institutional Approaches to Supreme Court Decision-Making," in *Supreme Court Decision-Making*. Clayton, CW and Gillman, H, eds. Chicago: University of Chicago Press. p. 48.
[28] *Id.*
[29] Murphy, at 14.
[30] Perry, at 10.
[31] Epstein, L and Knight, J. 1998. *The Choices Justices Make*. Washington, D.C.: CQ Press.

[32] Maltzman, at 51.
[33] Epstein and Knight (1998), at 56-107.
[34] Gillman, H. 1999. "The Court as an Idea, Not a Building (or a Game): Interpretive Institutionalism and the Analysis of Supreme Court Decision-Making," in *Supreme Court Decision-Making*. Clayton, CW and Gillman, H, eds. Chicago: University of Chicago Press. p. 67.
[35] Gillman and Clayton, at 4-5.
[36] Gillman (1999), at 78.
[37] Hiley, DR; Bohman, JF and Shusterman, R, eds. 1991. *The Interpretive Turn*. Ithaca: Cornell University Press.
[38] Smith, RM. 1988. "Political Jurisprudence, The 'New Institutionalism,' and the Future of Public Law." *The American Political Science Review*, Vol. 82, No. 1. pp. 92-98.
[39] Gillman (1999), at 79.
[40] Gillman, H. 1993. *The Constitution Besieged*. Durham: Duke University Press. p. 17.
[41] *Id.*, at 16.
[42] Smith, at 95.
[43] *Id.*, at 90.
[44] Hart, at 13.
[45] Unger, RM. 1983. *The Critical Legal Studies Movement*. Cambridge: Harvard University Press. p. 15.
[46] Pashukanis, Evgeny B. *The General Theory of Law and Marxism*. New Brunswick: Transaction Publishers. 2002. p. 64.
[47] Unger, RM. 1976. *Law in Modern Society: Toward a Criticism of Social Theory*. New York: The Free Press. p. 57.
[48] *Id.*
[49] Altman, A. 1990. *Critical Legal Studies: A Liberal Critique*. Princeton: Princeton University Press. p. 130.
[50] Unger (1976), at 49.
[51] Canon, BC. 2004. "Studying Bureaucratic Implementation of Judicial Policies in the United States: Conceptual and Methodological Approaches," in *Judicial Review and Bureaucratic Impact: International and Interdisciplinary Perspectives*, M Hertogh and S Halliday, eds. New York: Cambridge University Press. p. 80.
[52] Statement of Craig Manson, Assistant Secretary of the Interior for Fish, Wildlife and Parks. http://www.fws.gov/midwest/wolf/esa-status/manson_stm_dec05.htm. Dec. 16, 2005.
[53] *Defenders of Wildlife v. Secretary, United States Department of the Interior*, Civil No. 03-1348-JO, United States District Court for the District of Oregon (2005).
[54] Rosenberg, at 109.
[55] Sunkin, at 48.

[56] Rosenberg, at 108-109.
[57] Epstein, L and Knight, J. 2000. "Toward a Strategic Revolution in Judicial Politics: A Look Back, A Look Ahead." *Political Research Quarterly*. Vol. 53, No. 3. (Sept.). p. 630
[58] Teske, P. 1991. "Interests and Institutions in State Regulation." *American Journal of Political Science*. Vol. 35, No. 1. (Feb.).
[59] 437 U.S. 153 (1978)
[60] For a retelling of this complex story of pork-barrel politics, see Peterson, S. 2002. *Acting for Endangered Species: The Statutory Ark*. Lawrence: University of Kansas Press.
[61] For a few examples of the use of the snail darter as a symbol of ESA run amuck, see these varied examples: Johnson, J. 2006. "Environmentalists fight to save 'species over people' law that infuriates land developers." *Financial Times*, April 21. p. 6; Balko, R. 2004. "Property Rights Form Foundation of Freedom." *Fox News*, March 25; "Land Use and Endangered Species Insurance." 2005. *California Insurance Law & Litigation Alert*, November 30. p. 15.
[62] *Kelo v. New London*, 545 U.S. 469 (2005).
[63] Sunkin, at 52-53.
[64] McCann, MW. 1994. *Rights at Work: Pay Equity Reform and the Politics of Legal Mobilization*. Chicago: University of Chicago Press. p. 11; see also Scheingold, SA. 1974. *The Politics of Rights: Lawyers, Public Policy and Political Change*. New Haven: Yale University Press.
[65] Gillman (1999), at p. 78.
[66] Hunt, A. 1993. *Explorations in Law and Society: Toward a Constitutive Theory of Law*. New York: Routledge. p. 247.
[67] Geertz, C. 1983. *Local Knowledge: Further Essays in Interpretive Anthropology*. New York: Basic Books, Inc. p. 76.
[68] Haltom, W and McCann, M. 2004. *Distorting the Law: Politics, Media, and the Litigation Crisis*. Chicago: University of Chicago Press. p. 9.
[69] Bone, RG. 1986. "Normative Theory and Legal Doctrine in American Nuisance Law: 1850-1920," 59 S. Cal. L. Rev. 1101.
[70] Parenteau, PA. 2002. "Unreasonable Expectations: Why Palazzolo Has No Right to Turn a Silk Purse Into a Sow's Ear," 30 B.C. Envtl. L. Rev. 101.
[71] Geertz, at 232.
[72] *Penn Central Transportation Co. v. New York City*, 438 U.S. 104, 124 (1978).

CHAPTER 5

The Surface Mining Control and Reclamation Act

Enacted in 1977, the Surface Mining Control and Reclamation Act (SMCRA) is unique among mining laws. "Whereas other forms of mining are subject to a mix of federal and state requirements on both private and public lands, coal mining is regulated under...a comprehensive federal law that applies on all lands throughout the United States."[1] The law was created, among other reasons, to fix the lack of uniformity among state efforts to regulate surface coal mining.[2] The end result was a law that required that all surface mining of coal in the United States be done so under a permit to guarantee that the end effects of the mining would not cause irreparable damage to the environment, agriculture, or the public. When thinking of such permits, it is best to not think of a driver's learning permit or any other permit that fits on one piece of paper. SMCRA permits can be large, filling a few large three-ring binders. This is because the requirements placed upon surface coal mining are numerous, scientific in nature, and exact. Some mining operations "were especially vociferous in their opposition because compliance costs posed significant economic hardships for their marginally profitable mines."[3]

Miners who have been confronted by the restrictions and requirements of SMCRA have occasionally resorted to regulatory takings litigation. Such claims generally focus on the value of coal rendered not mineable by regulations aimed at protecting the environment and public health. Given the size of some coal mining operations, and the massive scope of environmental harm potential in such operations, the financial strain placed upon the government when it regulates coal mining has the potential to be great. The question that emerges is to what extent could such litigation impose such a cost on the regulatory government that it, in turn, reduces it implementation of SMCRA?

This chapter investigates that question by measuring the impact of regulatory takings litigation on the policy outputs of state and federal agencies charged with the implementation of SMCRA. This chapter begins by explaining the statutory framework of SMCRA and discussing the case history of regulatory takings challenges to the Act. Next, the impact of such decisions are measured in the context of SMCRA through the use of time-series cross-sectional regression analysis (TSCS). Finally, the results of those regressions are evaluated in the context of what is known about SMCRA implementation, knowledge which has been gained through research interviews with regulatory personnel in state and federal coal mining agencies. Ultimately, although the regression analyses demonstrate a chilling effect on regulation through an increase of surface mining permits issued brought on by successful regulatory takings challenges, those conclusions remain suspect due to issues of stationarity, heteroskedasticity, and serial correlation and evidence from the interviews. This does not, however, mean that such litigation cannot have a chilling effect on regulation, although particular features of SMCRA seem to, at least partially, insulate the Act from such challenges.

STATUTORY FRAMEWORK OF SMCRA

Enactment of the Surface Mining Control and Reclamation Act (SMCRA) in 1977 only occurred after a tragic collapse of a coal waste dam in West Virginia in 1972, killing 125 people, the introduction of more than 100 bills in Congress on surface mining, and two vetoes by

President Ford of similar, previous legislation.[4] Although it is a product of a moment in American political history which produced the foundational statutes of the environmental regulatory regime, SMCRA does not enjoy the same recognition of other environmental laws, such as the Clean Air Act; the Clean Water Act; the Comprehensive Environmental Response, Compensation, and Liability Act (a.k.a. Superfund); and the Endangered Species Act. Such ambivalence to SMCRA, however, is undeserved; the law broadly covers the environmental, aesthetic, health, safety, cultural, and historical impacts of the production of the nation's largest source of domestic energy, regulates it across all lands of the United States, and "contains inspection and enforcement provisions, which, in many ways, are more progressive that those found in any other major environmental statute."[5]

SMCRA is comprised of two main parts. Title IV contains the provisions of the Abandoned Mine Lands (AML) program, which uses a tax on coal production to reclaim lands on which coal mining had occurred prior to enactment of SMCRA and had since been abandoned.[6] Title V provisions of the Act deal with the regulation of active surface coal mining and the surface effects of underground coal mining.[7] The dangers associated with abandoned coal mines are tremendous; not only do abandoned mines constitute an ongoing environmental risk due to such harms as erosion or acid mine drainage (AMD), but they also pose a risk to the safety of individuals who could drown in dangerous pools or fall off of crumbling high-walls. However, the focus of this research is on the active regulatory component of SMCRA, which has significantly more intersections with regulatory takings litigation than the AML program.

"Like many environmental laws, congressional architects chose a partial-preemption regulatory approach for implementing SMCRA.... (T)his approach returns regulatory control to the states, but only after the states adopt enforcement programs that meet national standards."[8] Having assumed the power to regulate surface coal mining from the states, SMCRA only allows the states to reassume regulatory authority upon approval of the Secretary of the Interior, which requires that the state establish a surface mining regulatory program which "provides for the regulation of surface coal mining and reclamation operations in accordance with the requirements of" the federal law.[9] Even after primacy has been achieved by a state, SMCRA provides significant federal oversight powers to ensure compliance with federal standards. The Secretary is empowered to "make those investigations and inspections necessary to insure compliance with"[10] SMCRA, and is further empowered to provide for federal enforcement if the state program is determined to not be effectively enforcing the law in a manner consistent with the requirements of SMCRA.[11]

Central to the Title V regulatory provisions, and central to potential regulatory takings challenges, are the permitting practices used to implement the law. To insure that surface coal mining is conducted in a manner that balances environmental, agricultural, and energy interests,[12] SMCRA requires that any surface coal mining operation, or underground coal mining operation with surface effects, be conducted with an approved permit, granted by either the federal Office of Surface Mining (OSM) or the state regulatory authority. Issuance of such a permit is conditioned upon the ability of the surface mining operator to conduct such operations in a manner which insures the ability of the operator to reclaim the land, i.e. "to restore the approximate original contour of the land;"[13] "minimize the disturbances to the prevailing hydrologic balance;"[14] "control or prevent erosion and siltation, pollution of water, damage to fish or wildlife or their habitat, or public or private property;"[15] "assume the responsibility for successful revegetation;"[16] "restore the land affected to a condition capable of supporting the uses which it was capable of supporting prior to any mining or higher or better uses;"[17] and "conduct surface coal mining operations so as to maximize the utilization and conservation of the solid fuel resource being recovered so that reaffecting the land in the future through surface coal mining can be minimized."[18] To guarantee post-operations reclamation will occur, operators must post a reclamation bond which will be forfeited if reclamation efforts are abandoned.[19]

In addition to establishing a number of requirements which must be met by any surface coal mine operator, SMCRA also places upon regulatory personnel a strict set of inspection and enforcement requirements. Regulatory authorities are required to conduct, on average, monthly partial inspections and annual full inspections of all surface coal mining operations, and are further required to conduct such inspections irregularly and without prior notice.[20] In the event that the regulatory authority observes a violation of the permit which "can reasonably be expected to cause significant, imminent environmental harm to land, air, or water resources," or "creates an imminent danger to the health or safety of the public," the agent is required to immediately issue a cessation order (CO), which halts all relevant mining or reclamation practices until the violation is rectified.[21] If the violation does not present an imminent risk, the issuance of a notice of violation (NOV) is required, which, if the violation is not corrected within the time-frame established by the NOV, will result in the issuance of a CO.[22]

Surface coal mining operators, facing the broad requirements of SMCRA placed upon their planned mining activity, have occasionally brought regulatory takings challenges against the regulatory actions of either OSM or state regulatory authorities. Such challenged actions generally restrict the areas from which operators may legally attempt to extract coal, areas which can be considered the property of the operators, who have acquired either mineral rights or property rights in fee simple. These access restrictions are either the product of a determination by regulatory decision-makers that particular practices, which result in leaving some coal behind, must be a condition of a permit to protect environmental or other interests, or the area has been declared as land unsuitable for mining (UFM). Under the UFM designation provisions of SMCRA, individuals may petition the regulatory agency to designate a particular area as unsuitable for surface mining if mining activities in the area would result in significant damage to natural, historic, aesthetic, cultural, scientific, or resource values, or result in an unacceptable risk to public safety due to increased flooding or geological instability.[23] Furthermore, Congress declared certain areas to be unsuitable for surface mining, including lands in the National Parks System and other federal lands programs and lands within specified buffer zones of public roads, occupied dwellings, public buildings, schools, churches, community or institutional buildings, public parks, and cemeteries.[24] These unsuitability designations, however, are subject to valid existing rights (VERs). These rights are defined by OSM regulations as "a set of circumstances under which a person may, *subject to regulatory authority approval*, conduct surface mining operations on lands" on which Congressional designations "prohibit such operations."[25] The existence of a VER is determined through OSM's "Good Faith/All Permits" standard, which allows for the possibility of surface mining operations when "all permits and other authorizations required to conduct surface coal mining operations had been obtained, or a good faith effort to obtain all necessary permits and authorizations had been made, before the land came under the protection of" SMCRA.[26]

SMCRA AND REGULATORY TAKINGS

The determination of the extent of property rights in the form of coal lease or ownership rights is not only a component of the surface coal mining permitting regime, but it is also the first step used by federal courts to determine whether restrictions placed upon surface coal mining to protect the environment and insure the possibility of reclamation result in a compensable taking of the operator's property due to the resultant inaccessibility of some coal. Over the last few decades, several challenges to regulatory decisions under SMCRA and its corresponding state statutes have been heard by the U.S. Court of Federal Claims and the U.S. Court of Appeals for the Federal Circuit. These decisions comprise an important piece of the larger legal context in which the regulation of coal mining and regulatory takings litigation meet.

In fact, the telling of the legal history of regulatory takings litigation almost always begins with a case involving the regulation of coal mining. In its 1922 *Pennsylvania Coal*[27] decision, the Supreme Court for the first time ruled that a regulation of property effected a compensable taking under the Fifth Amendment. Well before SMCRA, Pennsylvania sought to control subsidence under private property caused by anthracite coal mining by enacting the Kohler Act, which required coal mining operators to leave behind enough coal to support the surface structure supporting private property.[28] Although the Court in *Pennsylvania Coal* recognized that "government hardly could go on if to some extent values incident to property could not be diminished without paying for every such change in the general law,"[29] the Court ruled that the Kohler act went "too far"[30] in that regard.

Sixty-five years later, the Supreme Court issued its decision in *Keystone*,[31] a case involving another Pennsylvania statute controlling for subsidence and with facts very similar to those of *Pennsylvania*

Coal.[32] While the facts of *Pennsylvania Coal* and *Keystone* were indeed quite similar, the Court in *Keystone* argued "that the similarities are far less significant than the differences, and that Pennsylvania Coal does not control this case."[33] In its consideration of the Subsidence Act, which "prohibits mining that causes subsidence damage to three categories of structures,"[34] the Court demonstrated "hesitance to find a taking when the State merely restrains uses of property that are tantamount to public nuisances...."[35] Central to the Court's argument was the characterization of the Subsidence Act as a statute protecting the common good and the Kohler Act as protecting the property of a privileged few.[36] Given the high demand for cleaner burning anthracite coal, the State of Pennsylvania sought to increase revenues through the Fowler Act. "The Fowler Act, adopted on the same day as the Kohler Act, enacted tax on anthracite coal. It was not an ordinary tax, though. Coal mining companies did not have to pay it *unless they wanted relief from the obligations of the Kohler Act.*"[37] The presence of the Kohler Act had less to do with the protection of public safety and more to do with persuading anthracite coal miners to pay the tax. "Because many cities banned the burning of the smoky bituminous coal, demand for anthracite was inelastic. Much of the burden of the regulation and tax would thus be shifted forward to consumers in other states."[38]

The nuisance exception, which holds that the "right to compensation...of private property taken for public uses is foreign to the subject of preventing or abating public nuisances,"[39] as stated in *Keystone* would be a common component of regulatory takings decisions involving SMCRA. Such challenges would begin with the first major takings challenge to SMCRA, the Supreme Court's 1981 *Virginia Surface Mining* decision.[40] This case involved a facial challenge to SMCRA's Title V performance requirements, with plaintiffs arguing that the Act itself was "an uncompensated taking of private property by requiring operators to perform the 'economically and physically impossible' task of restoring steep-slope surface mines to their approximate original contour."[41] The Court's decision upheld the constitutionality of SMCRA, stating that "constitutionality of statutes ought not be decided except in an actual factual setting that makes such a decision necessary,"[42] but still allowed for the possibility that a particular case of SMCRA implementation could require compensation for a taking of private property.

Given such a legal possibility, several regulatory takings challenges have been brought before the U.S. Court of Federal Claims and, on appeal, to the Court of Appeals for the Federal Circuit. In 1989, Whitney Benefits challenged the application of SMCRA restrictions on its long-held mining interests in 1327 acres of coal under an alluvial valley floor (AVF) in the Powder River Basin in Wyoming.[43] Surface mining of coal under AVFs west of 100th meridian is prohibited by SMCRA if such activity would "interrupt, discontinue, or preclude farming."[44] After seeking to take advantage of a SMCRA exchange program, which permitted the Secretary to exchange available federal coal deposits for restricted AVF deposits if "substantial financial and legal commitments were made by an operator prior to January 1, 1977,"[45] but, ultimately being unsatisfied with the government's offer,[46] Whitney Benefits sued under a takings claim. The United States claimed that the property in coal was valueless,[47] given the difficulty in mining beneath AVFs, but the Claims Court countered that "(p)laintiffs adequately showed dealing with alluvial water as a mining cost and that it would be taken care of in normal mine operations."[48] The Appeals Court upheld the finding of a taking, stating that "(b)efore SMCRA was enacted, Benefits had a property right it could expect to exercise, i.e., to surface mine the Whitney coal. The moment SMCRA was enacted, Benefits no longer had that property right, for it had no permit and could not possibly under the statute obtain one for a mine that would obviously violate the conditions expressly set forth in SMCRA."[49] The Appeals Court, therefore, ruled that Whitney Benefits was "entitled to $60,296,000, plus pre-judgment interest…."[50]

In subsequent regulatory takings challenges to SMCRA, the federal courts were more likely to rule against plaintiffs, generally recognizing "that the goals of regulations embedded with SMCRA are of such a protective public nature that non-compensated restrictions on the property rights of coal mining operations are justified."[51] The U.S. Court of Federal Claims has regularly ruled that regulatory restrictions on coal mining "represented an exercise of regulatory authority indistinguishable in purpose and result from that to which plaintiff was always subject under…nuisance law."[52] Even in situations where the Claims Court does find a compensable taking in the implementation of SMCRA, the U.S. Court of Appeals for the Federal Circuit has traditionally overturned such decisions.[53] A number of observable consistencies have emerged from this body of federal rulings, which might be considered surprising, given the "essentially ad hoc, factual"[54] nature of regulatory takings jurisprudence.

When confronted with a regulatory taking challenge to SMCRA, the federal courts have consistently utilized a two-tiered approach, as articulated in *Chancellor Manor v. U.S.*[55] "First, a court should inquire into the nature of the land owner's estate to determine whether the use interest proscribed by the governmental action was part of the owner's title to begin with."[56] This inquiry asks whether such uses were already limited by "the restrictions that background principles of the State's law of property and nuisance already place upon land ownership."[57] If the owner never possessed a property right in the restricted use, then the court need not undertake the second tier of the analysis. If, however, "the claimant can establish the existence of such an interest, the court must then determine whether the governmental action at issue constituted a compensable taking...."[58] This generally involves determining whether there was a categorical, per se taking, involving a loss of "all economically beneficial uses in the name of the common good,"[59] or engaging in a *Penn Central* analysis, weighing the economic impact, interference with reasonable investment-backed expectations, and the nature of the government action.[60]

When the federal courts have considered takings challenges to SMCRA, their first tier inquiries into the nature and extent of the property rights of the owner of the particular interest in coal have focused on the nuisance exception to regulatory takings. If the purpose of restrictions placed on coal mining is to prevent a nuisance to the public, then such a restriction—"even a restraint barring all such use—cannot become the basis of a compensable taking,"[61] because such a regulation would be considered nothing more than "a traditional exercise of police power to protect public safety, health and welfare from the 'unacceptable risks' that coal mining operations...would pose."[62]

A clear example of a court's use of the nuisance exception can be found in the Claims Court's decision in *M&J Coal*. Little dispute was present as to what was owned by whom: the coal rights in central West Virginia obtained by M&J were originally purchased through mineral severance deeds which severed the underground mineral estate from the surface estate, and freed the owner of the mineral estate from liability "for any injury or damage done to the overlying surface, or to anything therein or thereon.... (M&J) assumed they could subside structures where the surface owners had conveyed the right to subjacent support, and as to those structures required by law to be protected, the angle of draw would be 15 degrees."[63] Eventually, but suddenly, M&J's mining practices began to subside the Dingus and Tarley residences:

> "When it happened, my daughter was taking a bath and I was working in the kitchen starting dinner," said Margaret Tarley. "It sounded like a gunshot. I went down into the basement. When I came back up into the kitchen, I could see the walls pulling apart. It was scary. We moved in three hours. We were lucky. We had mine subsidence insurance." The Dingus family next door wasn't as lucky.... "We spent the next 12 days in a motel. Charles Sorbello, who owns the company, handed me six $50 bills and paid our motel bill of $739. That's all we got." Dingus had no subsidence insurance.[64]

After the state refused to engage in any enforcement actions against M&J, OSM issued a CO against the company and required the creation of a new subsidence control plan, which increased the angle of draw from 15 to 30 degrees and prohibited M&J from damaging single family dwellings.[65] Even after OSM took enforcement action against M&J, subsidence continued as damage was caused to a section of a public road and a town's new water tower began to tilt, which were damages prohibited by West Virginia state law.[66]

Given the new mining restrictions placed upon the company, M&J "alleged that OSM's enforcement actions which required plaintiffs to increase the draw angle under protected structures and to protect single family dwellings deprived plaintiffs of 99,700 tons of coal they otherwise would have mined, and resulted in $580,000 in lost profits."[67] In other words, M&J argued that OSM actions took their property in the support estate, which was part of their severance deed, and transferred it to the surface estate owners, a property taking which should be compensated. The Claims Court disagreed and focused on the first-hand accounts of the subsidence provided by Mr. Tarley, which described a severed gas line, which could have exploded, deep cracks in the yard, which had already claimed the life of a dog and could easily do the same to child, and electric lines from the house, which were "stretching tight as a fiddle string."[68] It was OSM's response to the need for public safety which distinguished the case from the facts of *Whitney Benefits*,[69] and insulated the enforcement actions from regulatory takings claims. On appeal, the Appeals Court upheld the finding of no taking, stating that, although the deed possessed by M&J included the support estate, "M&J's acquisition of rights by deed did not give it the right to mine in such a way as to endanger the public health and safety."[70]

In other cases involving nuisance determinations, the Claims Court has sought to ground a particular nuisance in something more referential than a declaration of a threat to public safety. In particular, the Claims Court has looked for definitions of nuisance in state common law, heading Justice Scalia's requirement that nuisance restrictions "inhere in the title itself, in the restrictions that background principles of the State's law of property and nuisance already place upon land ownership."[71] "Thus, if the Government shows that the activity it was regulating constituted a nuisance in the state's common law, it can avoid paying compensation because the right to engage in the activity was excluded from the owner's title."[72] In its 1999 *Rith Energy* and 2002 *Apollo Fuels* decisions, the U.S. Court of Federal Claims ruled that certain coal mining operations "constitute(d) an enjoinable nuisance under state law."[73] In *Rith*, although initial testing by the company demonstrated a low risk of AMD, subsequent testing demonstrated a 500% variance in the tests[74] and OSM determined that the mining activities presented too great a risk of contaminating the Sewanee Conglomerate aquifer.[75] In *Apollo Fuels*, OSM designated an area unsuitable for surface mining (although it allowed for underground mining from outside the area) due to the risk that AMD posed to the endangered blackside dace, the Cumberland Gap Historical Park, and, most importantly (according to OSM), the water supply aquifer for the town of Middleboro.[76] In both cases, the Claims Court looked to Tennessee common law and the Tennessee Water Quality Control Act (TWQCA) to determine that water pollution was an actionable nuisance under state law.[77] In both cases, the Appeals Court upheld the findings of no takings, but ignored the nuisance question, engaging instead in *Penn Central* analyses, which will be described below.[78]

A final note on the nuisance exception in regulatory takings challenges to SMCRA: despite the substantial impacts that can be caused by coal mining, the nuisance exception has not always been sufficient to insulate SMCRA enforcement from a takings claim, much less from the necessity to engage in *Penn Central* or categorical taking analyses. The nuisance exception seems to be weakest when the courts apply nuisance criteria to the act of mining instead of the externalities of mining. In the cases described above, the Claims Court looked to issues such as subsidence of property and AMD as the potential nuisances. In *Whitney Benefits*, the Appeals Court looked at the provisions of SMCRA and observed that "Congress expressly permitted, in the grandfather clause, the continued mining beneath AVFs of all grandfathered mines and all mines found by State Authorities to have minimal AVF involvement, hardly the action of one out to abate a 'nuisance.'"[79] Likewise, in *Eastern Minerals*, the Claims Court has stated that mining itself does not constitute a nuisance.[80] In this case, OSM denied a permit to the company due to concerns about noise and hydrological impacts on a nearby public park, which is protect by SMCRA from adverse effects of mining.[81] The Claims Court read these concerns as speculative, which coupled with the historical presence of mining on the property, led the court to conclude that the government had not demonstrated that the plaintiffs' proposed mining activities would constitute a nuisance.[82]

When a court determines that a proposed mining activity would not result in the creation of a nuisance, or elects not to consider making that determination, and the proposed activity is, therefore, part of the owner's bundle of property, the courts then determine whether a compensable taking of that property has occurred. As stated above, the court first considers whether a categorical taking has occurred; just as when the restriction involves prevention of a nuisance not inherent in the owner's title, a more detailed consideration of the extent of the property value's diminution is not necessary if the diminution is total or the property is physically invaded by the government.[83] If the owner is left with some viable use of his or her property, i.e. in the absence of a categorical taking, the court then utilizes the three-pronged *Penn Central* analysis, which considers the economic impact of the restriction, interference with investment-backed expectations, and the nature of the governmental action.[84]

The test for a categorical taking and the economic impact prong of the *Penn Central* test are related; if the impact is not a total loss, hence, not a categorical taking, then the impact is considered and balanced with the remaining two *Penn Central* prongs. The Claims Court has found a particular implementation of SMCRA to result in a categorical taking,[85] and given the large scale on which surface coal mining can occur, the potential compensatory liability of the government is significant. Therefore, the role of courts in determining the relevant parcel to be considered in a takings analysis should be considered a key plot point in any storytelling of takings cases. Furthermore, determination of the relevant parcel is essential; to determine the economic impact of a particular regulatory restriction, one must first determine the total property interest or, as the Supreme Court has put it, "the proper denominator in the takings fraction."[86] This property fraction exists both spatially and temporally, and plaintiffs in takings cases involving SMCRA have argued that, for purposes of a takings analysis, the relevant parcel should only be considered to be the area restricted by regulation[87] and property value should only be evaluated by the court from the date of regulation forward.[88]

Federal courts, however, have been reluctant to follow plaintiffs' lead, heading the Supreme Court, which "has counseled against labeling the property subject to the regulation as the appropriate parcel, noting that '[t]o the extent that any portion of property is taken, that portion is always taken in its entirety,'"[89] further noting that "defining the property interest taken in terms of the very regulation being challenged is circular."[90] In *Benchmark Resources*, for example, the U.S. Court of Federal Claims declined to focus solely on the area of the plaintiffs' property designated as UFM, and considered the presence of coal property outside of the designated area, as well as the permissibility of alternative mining techniques within the designated area.[91]

Since the Claims and Appeals Courts hearing SMCRA takings cases have been hesitant to view the regulated parcel, spatially and temporally, as the relevant denominator parcel, findings of categorical takings have been rare. This still leaves the possibility, however, of a less-than-total diminution in value that, when balanced with the other *Penn Central* factors, can result in a taking. In evaluating the economic impact of regulations on the parcel as a whole, courts have been forced to consider the remaining value of other interests in coal, as well as the remaining value of non-coal interests. In *Rith*, the company was able to extract substantial amounts of coal under its permit, prior to the discovery of excessive AMD and subsequent regulation by OSM.[92] In *Cane and Colten*, both companies possessed separate tracts of coal-bearing lands, which the Claims Court determined were treated by both companies as single investment opportunities.[93] Additionally, the presence of non-coal values to the regulated land, in such areas as timber and development, have generally been considered by court, in evaluating both the economic impact of regulation and the possibility of a categorical taking.[94]

On this last issue, courts have been more hesitant about adding non-coal value to the relevant parcel than additional, accessible coal value. In *Whitney Benefits*, the government argued that the presence of surface rights, on which one could engage in agricultural activities, should prevent the company from making a claim of a total taking. The Claims Court disagreed, stating that the surface rights were purchased merely as a means to facilitate access to the company's property in coal and, since the company was only claiming that their property in coal was taken, the surface property should not be considered in the relevant parcel.[95] "Courts have been willing to designate the area subject to government regulation as the appropriate denominator if the area contains the whole of a claimant's viable economic interests."[96] Only if the separate property parcel has been rendered valueless by the regulation of the main parcel or the owner can demonstrated that the separate parcel was purchased as a separate investment[97] will such separate parcels be omitted from the property denominator.

The Courts have not provided a set figure or percentage for determining whether an economic impact exceeds an acceptable level and, therefore, constitutes a taking. In *Cane and Colten*, the Claims Court has stated that the ability of the owner to recoup his or her investment "can sometimes be relevant. For example, if a party were able to recoup its investment after the government action, it is less likely that a taking has occurred."[98] However, the Claims Court immediately cautioned against the overuse of such a determinant, stating that the opposite, ruling for a taking if investments cannot be recouped, "would reward parties who make bad investments."[99]

The preceding dictum regarding bad investments is a component of the federal courts' regulatory takings jurisprudence that recognizes the inherent risk involved in coal mining and increases the burden placed upon plaintiffs alleging takings by SMCRA implementation. Although the second prong of the *Penn Central* test requires the court to judge something subjective, i.e. the expectations of the plaintiff, a reasonableness standard has been applied to those expectations, since behavior that may indicate an expectation of a lesser regulatory presence "could serve equally well as evidence of an improvident investment."[100] In assessing the investment-backed expectations of coal mining operators, the Courts have recognized that coal mining is quite complex and operators must be aware of the potential risks that may limit their activities as to avoid causing public nuisances. In *M&J*, the Court of Appeals ruled that any permit issued by the state was always conditioned by the need to protect public safety.[101] The Courts in the *Rith* decisions observed that the company had been made aware of the presence of the aquifer.[102] Therefore, "when Rith purchased its coal leases it did not have any reason to expect that it would be permitted to mine in a way that was likely to produce acid mine drainage;"[103] such activity would have violated state nuisance law.[104]

In addition to the complexities of coal mining, the Courts have also pointed to the historical presence of a regulatory regime surrounding coal mining. The presence of a regulatory agency, with the vested power to use its discretion to determine whether particular coal mining activities will be permitted, is part of the economic environment in which operators initially pursue mining investments. Part of that environment must include "an uncertainty that was part of the business risk that plaintiffs took when they made their investment."[105] Therefore, the reasonable investment-backed expectations of individuals and companies entering into or continuing business in the heavily regulated coal mining industry must account for potentially restrictive regulations as "easily foreseen, not necessarily as a certainty, but as a reasonable possibility."[106]

The Courts have paid particular attention in these cases to the chronology of property acquisition and regulatory enactment. Referred to by some as the notice rule,[107] the Courts have stated that "if at the time of sale an existing law or regulation precluded a certain use, that use was never a 'stick' in the purchaser's 'bundle of rights.'"[108] In the major Claims Court case that awarded compensation due to SMCRA restrictions, *Whitney Benefits*, plaintiffs acquired mining rights prior to the enactment of SMCRA.[109] Furthermore, evidence of congressional history that indicated that Congress directly considered the impact on Whitney Benefits coal resulted in a decision by the Claims Court that the plaintiff's property in coal was taken on the date of the enactment of SMCRA.[110] In cases where plaintiffs acquired their coal rights after the enactment of SMCRA, mining operators and investors have not fared as well. In *Cane and Colten*, the Claims Court drew special attention to the investor's lack of experience in coal mining[111] and stated that a

> reasonably prudent individual investing $5 million would, in the court's view, become acquainted with all of these regulations, as well as the possible impact of the adjacency of a major state park. Cane did not do so in this case. Because a reasonably prudent investor could not have believed that its investment was without regulatory risk, Cane cannot now claim that it had reasonable investment-backed expectations that were unexpectedly impacted by government action.[112]

There are, however, limits to the notice rule acknowledged by the Courts. In *Eastern Minerals*, the predecessor case to the eventual *Cane and Colten* cases, the Claims Court found a taking in the restrictions placed upon the plaintiffs. The Claims Court stated that "(m)ere awareness that Eastern's permits could be affected by future regulations does not destroy plaintiffs' property interests. Plaintiffs who choose to do business in a heavily regulated industry do not forfeit all property interests."[113] Although the case was eventually overturned by the Court of Appeals for the Federal Circuit, it did mirror the Supreme Court's eventual ruling in its 2001 *Palazzolo* decision, especially O'Connor's concurrence in which she called for a consideration of acquisition timing and existing regulatory environment in the determination of reasonable expectations of property use.[114]

Justice O'Connor's interpretation of *Palazzolo*'s holding, that the chronology of property acquisition and regulatory enactment is neither irrelevant nor deterministic in a takings decision, remains present in the takings jurisprudence as it relates to SMCRA. The appeal of the

Claims Court's decision in *Rith*, which relied heavily on the fact that "SMCRA was enacted eight years before Rith purchased the coal leases...(and, therefore,) Rith could not reasonably have expected that it would be free from regulatory oversight,"[115] was decided almost two months before the Supreme Court handed down its decision in *Palazzolo*. The case was appealed back to the Court of Appeals so that the case could be decided again, this time in the light of *Palazzolo*. The Court of Appeals upheld its previous finding of no taking, interpreting the *Palazzolo* decision as having "rejected the argument that when governmental action regulates the use of property, a person who purchases property after the date of the regulation may never challenge the regulation under the Takings Clause.... In rejecting such a 'blanket rule,' however, the Court did not suggest that the reasonable expectations of persons in a highly regulated industry are not relevant to determining whether particular regulatory action constitutes a taking."[116] Although the acquisition of mining rights in the regulatory presence of SMCRA may not eliminate takings claims in reaction to regulatory restrictions, the well established presence of SMCRA within an industry that is heavily regulated indicates that "investment-backed expectations are an especially important consideration in the takings calculus. A party in Rith's position necessarily understands that it can expect the regulatory regime to impose some restraints on its right to mine coal under a coal lease."[117]

The final prong of the *Penn Central* test focuses on the nature of the government action. While the explanation of this test in the *Penn Central* decision focused on such criteria as whether the regulation involved a public use or a physical invasion,[118] a broader set of questions asked by the Courts targets the timeliness and completeness of the government's regulatory actions. When the Courts consider such questions, they are working to protect the property rights of coal operators from potential stall and delay tactics of regulatory personnel. In regulatory takings jurisprudence the issues of temporary takings and ripeness are closely related. The ripeness doctrine protects the separation of powers by preventing courts, "through avoidance of premature adjudication, from entangling themselves in abstract disagreements over administrative policies, and also to protect the agencies from judicial interference until an administrative decision has been formalized...."[119] The general rule for ripeness in a regulatory takings case is the requirement of a final decision by the regulatory agency, thus preserving the possibility that property can still be used profitably through variances and approved re-submittals.[120] The requirement for repeated submittals of permit applications is tempered by the futility exception, which removes the requirement of re-submittal to reach a final administrative decision by recognizing that there may be situations "in which there was no indication that upon application the property owner would not be allowed to develop his [sic] property in some economically beneficial manner, and…further application would allegedly be futile."[121] In addition to the futility exception, the property owner is protected by being allowed to issue a challenge of a temporary taking. If the administrative delay is excessive, courts can rule that such delays took plaintiff's property for the period of time during which the permitting process prevented the owner from using his or her property. Such delays, however, must be "extraordinary" in nature to amount to a compensable taking.[122]

The ripeness requirement has been used by the Courts to insulate implementation of SMCRA from takings claims. In the *Stearns* decisions, a coal company sold surface rights to the U.S. Government for the creation of a national forest, well before enactment of SMCRA, but retained its mineral rights.[123] After the eventual enactment of the "good faith, all permits" requirement for VER, it was determined by OSM that the company did not satisfy the test and, therefore, did not have VER.[124] However, OSM stated that the plaintiff could still apply for a permit to mine and, referencing the historical presence of mining in the area and the general good track record of the plaintiff, stated that this permitting process "was essentially a rubber stamp."[125] In the trial, the Claims Court stated that the VER determination had "reversed the basic structure of rights between surface and subsurface owners" and a focus on the possibility of still receiving a permit "misses the point. Ownership and use are not synonymous. The fact that my neighbor always lets me use his lawnmower does not mean I own it."[126]

This decision, however, was overruled by the Court of Appeals for the Federal Circuit, which declared the case to be unripe. The decision hinged on defining the conflict as a regulatory takings case, not a physical invasion of property.

> Here, the government has not occupied Appellee's mineral property or the accompanying implied appurtenant easement.... Appellee's argument to the contrary is little more than an incredible attempt to transform a regulatory taking claim into a per se physical taking. Under Appellee's theory, the implied appurtenant easement that attends the mineral estate creates a power in Appellee to be free from regulation that addresses the circumstance of access to that mineral estate.[127]

Once the Appeals Court determined that the issue at hand belonged to a regulatory takings inquiry, the simple absence of a final administrative decision, leaving the possibility of profitable use of the property open, rendered the case unripe.[128]

Whereas the ripeness doctrine protects OSM and the various state regulatory authorities from premature takings claims, the futility doctrine has been used to limit that protection. In the *Whitney Benefits* case, the government argued that the case was not ripe since it had not been able to effectively evaluate the AVF overlying the company's property in coal. "The Government (did) not suggest, and did not suggest at trial, any basis whatever on which a permit could be legally granted to surface mine Whitney coal.... Indeed, the record is clear that any such application was obviously and absolutely foredoomed on the day SMCRA was enacted."[129]

Not all UFM designations make application for mining futile and, therefore, takings claims ripe. In *Benchmark Resources*, a UFM designation specified areas that were "unsuitable for coal mining operations using conventional overburden mixing techniques for reclamation,"[130] meaning that submitting a permit application would not necessarily be futile. However, by deciding that any attempt on the part of Whitney Benefits to secure a surface mining permit for the coal underlying the AVF would be futile and that the regulatory takings challenge was, therefore, ripe for consideration, the Court of Appeals judged the regulatory behavior of the government by stating that it had "carried its attempt to deny the impact of SMCRA on Whitney coal to unreasonable lengths in an apparent hope of postponing the day of reckoning into eternity."[131]

In the various cases arising out of the regulatory restrictions placed upon the coal properties at issue in *Eastern Minerals*, the ripeness of the takings claims and the behavior of the regulating agency were constantly in question. This issue begins with the fact that Eastern Minerals allowed its lease to expire, wishing to avoid rent liabilities during the regulatory process.[132] The Claims Court stated that this action was caused by the government's delay in the permitting process[133] and any further permit-seeking actions on the part of the company would have been futile.[134] On appeal, however, the Court ruled that such reasoning was "speculatory,"[135] and "the futility exception can never excuse the prerequisite that there exist a valid property interest for all takings cases."[136]

In addition to its ruling that the case brought by Eastern Minerals lacked a property interest, the Appeals Court also considered whether delays in the actions of the government took plaintiffs' property temporarily prior to them abandoning their lease. The Court ruled that the delays were not extraordinary, and further stated that "it is the rare circumstance that we will find a taking based on extraordinary delay without a showing of bad faith."[137] The bad faith requirement also excused a lengthy decision-making process over a subsequent UFM petition on the property.[138] Proving that regulatory delays were extraordinary due to bad faith may prove quite difficult for coal mining operators. The courts tend to defer to the decision-making expertise of regulatory agencies, especially "when the permitting process requires detailed technical information necessary to determine environmental impacts."[139] Furthermore, there always remains the possibility "that delay in the permitting process may be attributable to the applicant as well as the government."[140] The Appeals Court ruled that the delays encountered in Eastern Minerals' application process were at least partially caused by failures to properly respond to technical deficiency letters (TDLs) and administrative violations on the part of the investor.[141]

In addition to federal cases involving regulatory takings challenges to the implementation of SMCRA, a few cases from state courts are also worth mentioning. In 1998, a Pennsylvania Commonwealth Court ruled that a UFM designation by the state's Department of Environmental Regulation had taken a mining company's property in the mineable coal within the designated area.[142] The decision turned on the Commonwealth Court's declaration of the separated coal estate as the relevant parcel for the takings denominator, despite the fact, as pointed out by a dissenting judge, that alternative uses of the property existed, and only a portion of the land was affected.[143] The Pennsylvania Supreme Court reversed and remanded the decision, taking issue with the Commonwealth Court's determination of the property denominator. The Court observed that property can be conceptualized vertically, horizontally, and temporally,[144] and then noted that the U.S. Supreme "Court has refused to allow: vertical severance of the mineral estate in Keystone; vertical segmentation of air and surface rights in Penn Central; or temporal division of property in Tahoe-Sierra. Thus, in this case, the relevant parcel cannot be vertically segmented and must be defined to include both the surface and mineral rights."[145] The Court then considered whether the restrictions placed on plaintiffs' property was necessary to prevent a nuisance, namely, the potential AMD that the state sought to prevent through its UFM designation. Just as with the federal courts, the Pennsylvania Supreme Court ruled against the finding of a taking by considering whether the externalities of mining ("pollution of public waterways"), as opposed to the mining itself constituted a taking.[146] Additionally, the Court considered the level of burden placed upon the state in proving its finding of a nuisance; the Court stated, "We see no reason to require the Commonwealth to prove that the alleged pollution is practically certain to occur. It is enough if the Commonwealth can prove what its technical study found, that further mining in the UFM area had a 'high potential to cause…(AMD) that would adversely affect the use of the stream as an auxiliary water supply.'"[147]

More recently, the Ohio Supreme Court heard a takings challenge to a UFM designation by the state Department of Natural Resources to protect a sole-source aquifer for the Village of Pleasant City.[148] Unlike the Pennsylvania Supreme Court, the Ohio Supreme Court ruled that the designation constituted a categorical taking of the company's coal estate property. In determining the relevant parcel in the vertical context, the Court stated that "mineral rights are recognized by Ohio law as separate property rights" and the company "acquired all the property at issue herein, whether in fee or through coal leases or purchases, for the sole purpose of surface-mining the coal from these premises."[149] Horizontally, the Court ignored the 1/5 of the property outside the UFM area, stating "when the UFM designation prevented (the company) from mining a majority of its coal reserves within the regulated area, it made mining those minimal reserves outside the UFM-designated area economically impracticable."[150] Although this determination of the relevant parcel relies on precedent from U.S. Claims and Appeals Courts, it runs counter to the U.S. Supreme Court's reluctance to regard only the regulated property as the relevant parcel.[151] Therefore, instead of utilizing a *Penn Central* analysis, under which the Court still could have found the economic impact to be so great as to warrant the finding of a taking, a categorical analysis was used, and resulted in the finding of a total taking.[152] Additionally, the Court still had to determine whether an uncompensated, total taking would be permitted under the nuisance exception, but in making that determination, analyzed whether mining itself was the nuisance, as opposed to the AMD the state sought to prevent. The Court "concluded that coal mining is not an absolute nuisance, because it can be conducted safely when care is taken" and the company "had acted in a reasonable manner in mining the property and until the UFM designation was issued was allowed to mine the property pursuant to permits."[153] Absent from the opinion and, in particular, the very short section dealing with the nuisance question, was any discussion about whether the Court considered factual evidence about the feasibility of safe mining practices in the UFM area.

BEHAVIORAL ADJUSTMENTS

To test the hypothesis that the aforementioned regulatory takings challenges to SMCRA implementation affected the policy outputs of the agencies charged with such enforcement, cross-sectional time-series regression analyses were conducted to assess regulatory output trends before and after such cases. The dependent variable is the number of surface mining permits issued by OSM and the various state regulatory authorities. Data was collected from 1978 to 2004 from the Annual Reports of the Office of Surface Mining and the Energy Information Administration. Panels were comprised of a sample of SMCRA implementing agencies in 21 states, focusing on the historically productive states of the three coal producing regions of the United States: the Appalachian, the Interior, and the Western regions.[154]

FIGURE 5.1: Coal Producing Regions of the United States

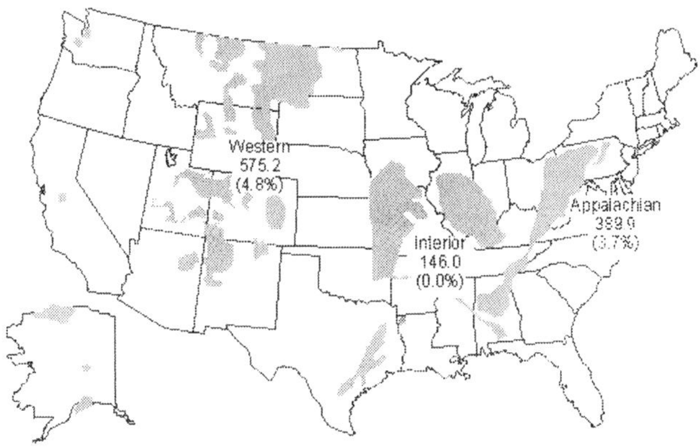

Source: Energy Information Administration
Numbers indicate 2004 coal production in million short tons and percentage change from 2003

The geographic regions are characterized by differing factors, each making the question of permitting unique. Geologically, Appalachian coal seams are smaller, positioned more deeply, are under complex topographies and hydrologies, and contain higher amounts of sulfur. Western coal seams, conversely, are larger, nearer the surface, are predominantly under flat and arid lands, and are valued for their low sulfur content. Historically, coal mining has been more predominant in Appalachia, where underground mining was common; however, starting in the 1970's, coal production has moved west, utilizing surface mining techniques almost exclusively, seeking large deposits of low sulfur coal to satisfy demand brought on by an oil embargo and stricter environmental regulations.[155] Figure 5.2 demonstrates the current disparity between Western and Appalachian surface coal mining by comparing the production of coal of Wyoming, currently America's largest producer of coal, by far, and Kentucky.

FIGURE 5.2: Comparison of Wyoming and Kentucky Coal Production (1978-2004)

Wyoming

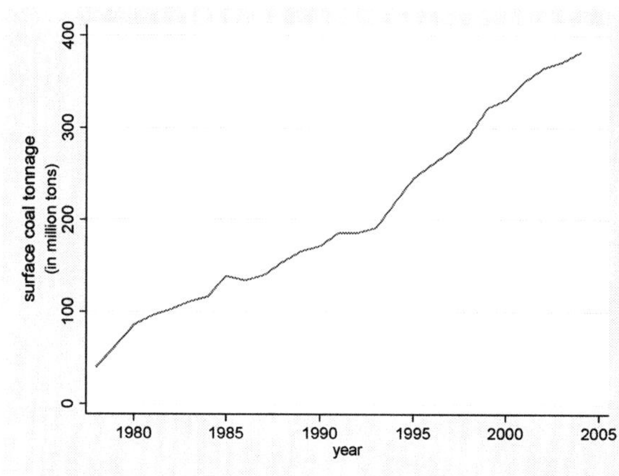

Kentucky

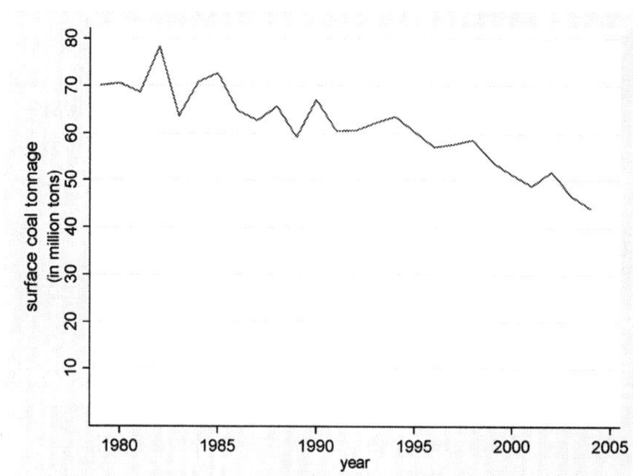

Source: Annual Reports of the Office of Surface Mining

FIGURE 5.3: Efficiency of U.S. Surface Coal Mining (1978-2004)

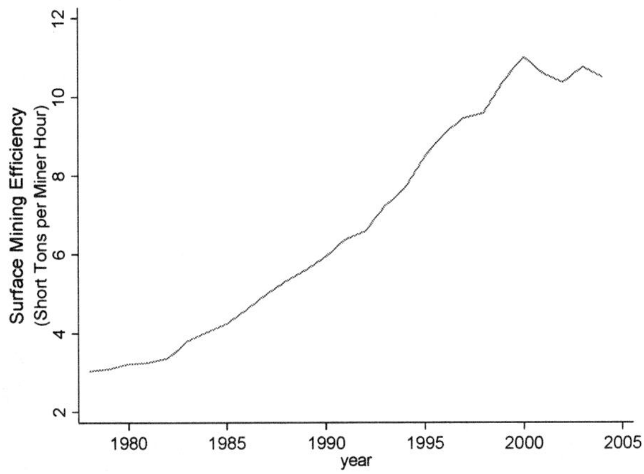

Source: Energy Information Administration

FIGURE 5.4: Price of U.S. Coal (1978-2004)

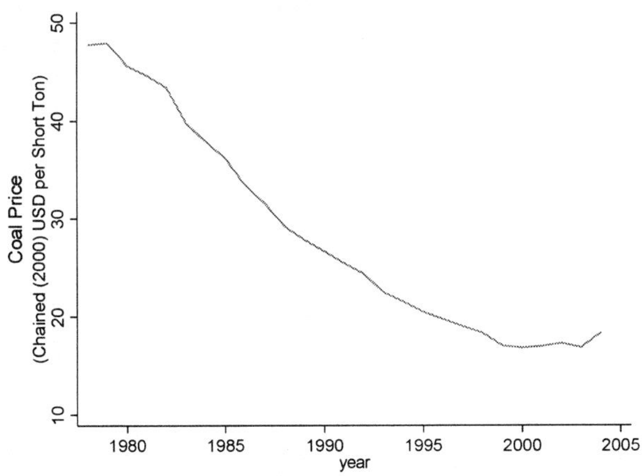

Source: Energy Information Administration

Additionally, developments in surface mining technology have increased efficiency, as demonstrated in Figure 5.3, making Western coal more attractive economically. The accessibility of Western coal seams, located in sparsely populated, flat, arid areas, compared with the difficulties associated with extracting Appalachian coal from under varying, populated terrains,[156] has also affected the types of companies involved in coal mining. To simplify this difference, Western coal companies tend to be very large operations, possessing sufficient expertise and capital to extract large amounts of coal from very large seams, while Appalachian coal companies, although they are becoming more corporatized, are significantly smaller, and are frequently limited to extracting coal left behind by previous mining enterprises. This means that, although the vast majority of America's coal comes from Western states, regulatory bodies are much larger in the East, regulating several smaller operations; regulatory authorities in Western states frequently regulate fewer than 10 single surface mining operations. Finally, since coal is a commodity, it can be assumed that changes in demand brought about by changes in the price of coal will likely also affect the amount of pressure on coal mining companies to seek permits in the first place. Figure 5.4 indicates that the price of coal has dropped over the lifetime of SMCRA, although a recent spike in the price has fallen outside of the timeframe of other collected data.

Before assessing the impact of regulatory takings litigation on the SMCRA permitting process, it was important to establish a baseline for understanding changes in the dependent variable, i.e. the number of permits issued by each state agency, was a function of other, independent variables. Arguably, one could reasonably expect that the number of permits issued by a state is related to the amount of coal produced through surface mining and the availability of federal funds.[157] Permitting activity could also be a product of the demand for such permits, which could be affected by the U.S. price of coal and changes in the efficiency of surface mining techniques. Furthermore, various political factors could affect permitting trends. One might expect a Democrat as President or Governor to produce more stringent environmental enforcement and, therefore, fewer permits. The same could be said for state regulatory agencies experiencing increased oversight activities from the federal OSM. The number of notices of violation issued by a state agency might serve as a general indicator of the amount of general activity of a state office. Finally, regional differences, indicated by the coal-producing region to which the state belongs must be considered.

Coefficients for these variables were determined by subjecting the data to a Prais-Winsten, panel corrected standard error (PCSE) regression, which controls for first order autocorrelation amongst the panels.[158] The results of those regressions are summarized in Table 5.1. These results indicate that, without considering the impact of regulatory takings litigation, the SMCRA permitting process is a function of several factors. Most noticeably, regional variance was significant, with the Appalachian region demonstrating high permitting activity, and the West low. There was also an observable decrease in permitting activity under Democratic control of state governors' offices.

TABLE 5.1: Prais-Winsten PCSE Regression (AR1) Results (Issuance of SMCRA Permits)

	Coefficient	Stand. Error	P>|Z|
Surface Coal Tons	-0.064	0.028	0.020
Oversight Visits	-0.171	0.072	0.017
Federal Funds	3.987	0.474	0.000
Notices of Violation	0.063	0.027	0.020
U.S. Price of Coal	-2.683	1.130	0.018
Dem. Governor	-28.993	9.314	0.002
Appalachian Region	78.797	8.161	0.000
Western Region	-33.585	6.871	0.000
Cons	58.043	25.818	0.025
Y=Permits Issued			R^2=0.8132

Dummy variables were then constructed to measure the impact of the presence of a judicial precedent finding a taking in the implementation of SMCRA. The cases that established a federal precedent were *Whitney Benefits* (1990-present), *Cane* (1997-2001), and *Stearns* (2003-2004). Additionally, state and cumulative impacts were considered through the creation of a variable for total cases, which indicates the total number of takings precedents, federal and state, at a point in time, for each state agency. The regression results when these variables were included can be seen in Tables 5.2 and 5.3.

As the regression results from Tables 5.2 and 5.3 demonstrate, there does appear to be a significant impact on permitting activity caused by regulatory takings cases which are decided in favor of the claimants. In particular, the *Whitney* and "total cases" variables produced statistically significant positive coefficients, which is consistent with the general hypothesis. One should also note that, with the addition of the *Whitney* variable, the U.S. price of coal dropped out of the equation. However, with the addition of the total cases variable, for total cases, surface mining efficiency became significant. The negative coefficient for mining efficiency is likely an indicator of a move toward larger coal extraction technologies, and not a per se indicator of a negative effect of efficiency on SMCRA permitting activity.

TABLE 5.2: Prais-Winsten PCSE Regression (AR1) Results (Impact of *Whitney* Decision)

	Coefficient	**Stand. Error**	**P>|Z|**
Surface Coal Tons	-0.059	0.029	0.041
Oversight Visits	-0.180	0.070	0.010
Federal Funds	4.039	0.460	0.000
Notices of Violation	0.063	0.027	0.021
Dem. Governor	-30.967	9.262	0.001
Appalachian Region	79.884	8.285	0.000
Western Region	-34.830	6.652	0.000
Whitney Decision	43.888	13.258	0.001
Cons	-35.624	11.712	0.002
Y=Permits Issued			R^2=0.8158

TABLE 5.3: Prais-Winsten PCSE Regression (AR1) Results (Impact of Multiple Regulatory Takings Decisions)

	Coefficient	Stand. Error	P>|Z|
Surface Coal Tons	-0.056	0.026	0.029
Oversight Visits	-0.185	0.070	0.008
Federal Funds	4.023	0.461	0.000
Notices of Violation	0.064	0.027	0.016
Mining Efficiency	-12.350	5.959	0.038
Dem. Governor	-28.106	8.984	0.002
Appalachian Region	79.037	8.265	0.000
Western Region	-33.887	6.896	0.000
Total Cases	55.31	18.448	0.003
Cons	34.399	32.342	0.288
Y=Permits Issued			R^2=0.8209

As the TSCS regressions indicate, there appears to be a statistically significant positive relationship between successful regulatory takings challenges and the issuance of surface mining permits under SMCRA. Such conclusions should be made cautiously, though, as time series analyses are particularly susceptible to spurious regressions and cointegration of variables,[159] and knowledge about stationarity in TSCS data is in its infancy.[160] Table 5.4 summarizes the results of Dickey-Fuller and correlogram for stationarity of the data. The results indicate a high presence of non-stationary data, indicated by a Dickey-Fuller tau-statistic (Z(t)) that fails to achieve the critical value at, at least, the 5% confidence level, or a Q statistic that is statistically significant. If the PCSE (AR1) regressions were insufficient to control for all non-stationarity, then there is likelihood that the relationship observed between variables is a function of their joint function of time.

Furthermore, post-regression error variance analyses indicate that results derived from this data may be questionable. ANOVA testing for panel heteroskedasticity for all three models demonstrate a high probability of unequal error variance among the panels beyond the corrections of the Prais-Winsten PCSE regression. Furthermore, the errors in the model for each state appear to be serially correlated across time. For the regressions performed in Tables 5.1 and 5.2, the error terms for the data of a majority of the states was correlated to previous error terms. Serial correlation was observed in the data of only three of the nineteen states within the data set after testing for the cumulative effect of total taking cases (Table 5.3).

TABLE 5.4: Results of Dickey-Fuller and Correlogram Testing for Stationarity

State	Z(t)*	Q(L1)	Prob>Q
AL	-2.492	15.515	0.0001
AR	-3.759	9.7109	0.0018
CO	-2.541	20.679	0.0000
IA	-2.832	20.620	0.0000
IL	-3.056	5.9303	0.0149
IN	-4.994	0.00857	0.9262
KS	-3.315	17.721	0.0000
KY	-3.693	6.0405	0.0140
MD	-3.9	2.7927	0.0947
MO	-4.193	21.971	0.0000
MT	-4.638	0.16092	0.6883
NM	-4.101	1.1351	0.2867
OH	-3.12	4.0283	0.0447
OK	-2.442	16.391	0.0001
PA	-3.196	6.0427	0.0140
TN	-1.881	20.085	0.0000
UT	-0.963	16.874	0.0000
VA	-4.08	8.4968	0.0036
WA	-3.122	10.353	0.0013
WV	-2.869	5.6707	0.0173
WY	-3.769	5.2322	0.0222

***Interpolated Dickey-Fuller**

1% C.V.	5% C.V.	10% C.V.
-4.371	-3.596	-3.238

ASSESSING THE IMPACT

To develop a better understanding of the internal workings of SMCRA and how the various past, and possible future regulatory takings challenges, could affect permitting activities, elite interviews were conducted with key personnel in federal OSM and state regulatory authority offices. Subject selection was made based on permitting responsibilities. Interview requests were sent to directors of SMCRA implementing offices, both federal regional OSM offices and state regulatory offices, under varied state regulatory bodies, such as a Department of Natural Resources or a Department of Environmental Protection. Efforts were made to solicit interviews from states with either significant coal production or a history of coal production and from states that represent the different coal producing regions of the United States. Interviews were conducted in person and by telephone in 2006. While not every office responded to interview requests, interviews were conducted with personnel in state SMCRA implementing agencies in ten states, representing the Appalachian, Interior, and Western coal production regions. Interviews were also conducted in five federal OSM offices, including two regional offices and three field offices. Since state agencies have their own unique arrangements, it is difficult to generalize about the titles and ranks of interview respondents. The most common titles of interview respondents in state offices were director, chief, and program manager. Interviews were conducted with directors of federal OSM offices. Requests were also made to speak with legal counsels from these offices, but such requests were only granted in to state offices and two federal offices.

One feature of SMCRA regulation that emerged from the interviews was bureaucratization. This feature was found to exist both externally and internally to the regulatory regime. Externally, SMCRA regulation occurs within a larger bureaucratic context, involving other regulatory agencies, enforcing various statutes of federal, state, and municipal origins. Surface mining procedures present a number of risks to the area's hydrology, agriculture, biodiversity, and history, risks which SMCRA requires mining operations to control. Even absent of SMCRA, these risk producing activities would require various permits and activities. Discharge permits would be required by the Clean Water Act. Considerations may have to be made under the Archeological Resources Protection Act and/or the National Historic Preservation Act. Compliance with U.S. Forest Service regulations may be required. The U.S. Fish and Wildlife Service may require an endangered species consultation. Such steps are required before a permit under SMCRA can be issued. In other words, a great deal of decision-making in SMCRA permitting actually occurs outside of offices authorized to enforce SMCRA. Any chilling effect caused by takings litigation could easily be offset by the requirement of compliance with other regulatory agencies, such as the Army Corps of Engineers or the Forest Service. It would be difficult for an OSM office to weaken its regulatory standards in reaction to a lawsuit when so many of those decisions are made outside of the office.

Bureaucratization was also found internally, with knowledge in the regulatory regime being highly compartmentalized. Given the complex, scientific nature of the requirements placed upon surface mining by SMCRA, employment in OSM or the various state regulatory authorities is based upon some sort of expertise. Although the head of the department has the ultimate authority to approve or deny a permit, and there were occasional stories about the politicization of that decision, by and large, little to no evidence of recommendations consistently ignored was observed. This was particularly true of legal knowledge. Most respondents responded to questions about specific legal standards by saying that they would have to consult with their legal counsel. This does not mean that the respondents were ignorant of changes in legal standards. Frequently, respondents indicated that knowledge about changes in legal standards comes to them in the form of a memo from legal counsel or procedures are changed in writing by directive from above. All in all, the decision-making atmosphere observed was one of compartmentalized ritual. Most respondents indicated that the statute and the regulations are pretty clear as to how things should be done, and if those standards are not met, permits will not be regarded as sufficient, and any legal challenge will be confidently approached with the knowledge that the individual was following the rules.

This observation was particularly apt in relation to regulatory takings litigation. Every respondent was aware of regulatory takings litigation. However, the topic of regulatory takings had to be brought up by the interviewer, as most respondents saw it as a possibility, but stated that its occurrence was rare. Only one respondent offered an unsolicited hesitation that such litigation could increase and could result in a chilling effect. By and large, there appeared to be a strong presence of a culture of obligation within the regulatory agencies. Although the law regarding takings may change to the benefit of property owners, all respondents, without exception, defined their task at hand as one defined by the statute. Most discussions of the threat of litigation involved respondents initially perceiving this threat as being caused by their own deviation from statutory obligation, thus inviting litigation from coal companies or environmental groups, depending on the nature of the deviation.

Furthermore, some of the respondents were, in the past, part of the coal mining industry, and were sympathetic to the degree of regulation faced by mining operators. However, they stated that they must do their job according to the statutory and regulatory requirements, and, if there is going to be a takings challenge, that is a decision that falls out of their hands. Even respondents in offices that had lost a takings challenge and had to pay compensation (or at least perceived they had to pay – frequently, such payments come from the general treasury, not the particular agency) told stories of directives requiring the office to pursue regulation just as before. Interviews made it evident that, for takings litigation to cause a chilling effect, the force of such litigation must overcome this agency culture of statutory obligation and the countervailing threats of litigation that have, historically, helped forge this culture.

Finally, a set of generalizations can be made about the relationship between the various state and federal regulatory offices and the mining operations. These observations point to the presence of factors outside of the legal terrain of SMCRA implementation that shape the expectations held and contexts of meaning used by those involved in such implementation. Like the above bureaucratic decision-making rules, these institutions present likely obstacles to a takings litigation chilling effect on regulatory behavior.

All respondents described their general interactions with permit applicants as cooperative today, but that had not always been the case. The general story that was told by personnel in agencies charged with implementing SMCRA is that the initial resistance of the coal mining community to a new set of regulations was high, and it lasted for several years, but now things are better. A couple of factors could be central to this evolution. First, several respondents indicated that it just took a while for the mining operations to learn about the expectations brought on by the requirements of the law. SMCRA's history appears to be consistent with the general understanding of the development of all the major environmental statutes that developed in the 1970's. Originally, there was a great deal of mistrust as to whether recalcitrant agencies would exercise their newly acquired responsibilities.[161] Scheberle's research on federal/state interactions within SMCRA enforcement indicates that oversight of the state regulatory authorities by the federal OSM has relaxed, partially due to "the development of performance agreements that evaluate states on the basis of 'on-the-ground results' rather than number of inspections and citations issued."[162] Less pressure on the states to produce a simple number of citations can result in more cooperative relationships with the coal mining industry.

Collected data also indicate that there has been a drop in the number of NOVs issued by the states in the last decade. That decline may be caused by several factors. One could be the above described relaxing of federal oversight. Another could be the possible capture of SMCRA enforcing agencies by the coal industry. These are all valid suggestions, but the focus of this book is on the decision-making processes within those agencies. Interviews with those personnel indicate that it could just be the simple passage of time that has resulted in more knowledge on the part of surface miners about the legal requirements of SMCRA. Additionally, the development of mining practices has affected that knowledge. As mining has become more corporate, with more large companies controlling a bigger chunk of surface coal mining in the U.S., knowledge about surface mining regulations has become central to corporate decision-making. Furthermore, large corporations have more legal resources at their disposal, which could lead to more litigation, but as the respondents have indicated, in this case, have lead to more informed decision-making and cost efficient compliance with regulations.

Respondents generally indicated that most takings challenges emerge from poor planning. Agency personnel prefer that potential mining operators consult with the regulatory authority before getting too deeply involved in pursuing mining plans; however, few institutional or informational factors are created by those agencies to inform miners of this preference. Respondents indicated that, when miners do consult with the regulatory authority early in the planning process, the permitting process is done much more smoothly. Larger corporate operations are most likely to have the personnel resources and legal knowledge to be able to seek such information from the beginning. Furthermore, several large operations, particularly those in the West, have more coal estate than they can currently mine. Therefore, current mining practices in those areas are more likely in areas with little reclamation difficulty. Although corporate mining companies are also making their presence felt in the Appalachian and Interior regions, there is still a heavy preponderance of smaller mining operations. These operations are more likely than larger operations to get engaged in situations that could result in takings litigation, as they have less access to the decision-making resources of larger corporations and are, therefore, more likely to enter into situations with expectations to be quashed. They are also more likely to rely on individual, inelastic mining plans, are less likely to have another mining area to fall back on, and may get aggressive if their plans are restricted.[163]

Table 5.5 provides the TSCS regression results when only the Appalachian region is considered. Since this area is less dominated by larger mining corporations, one should expect that takings litigation is not only more likely, for the reasons explained above, but that such litigation would have a greater impact in this region. The results do indicate a positive impact by the presence of each precedent that found a taking, but caution should be applied to these results, as ANOVA testing for panel heteroskedasticity indicated the continued presence of unequal error means; however, serial correlation was less prevalent than in the nationwide regressions, with data for only two of the seven Appalachian states demonstrating serial correlation. The same regression analysis run for the Western states did not produce statistically significant results.

TABLE 5.5: Prais-Winsten PCSE Regression (AR1) Results (Impact of Multiple Regulatory Takings Decisions – Appalachian Region Only)

	Coefficient	Stand. Error	P>|Z|
Surface Coal Tons	-5.932	1.205	0.000
Oversight Visits	-0.138	0.060	0.021
Federal Funds	5.015	0.523	0.000
Notices of Violation	0.130	0.025	0.000
Dem. Governor	-76.450	19.160	0.000
Total Cases	64.02	19.336	0.001
Cons	21.503	30.597	0.482
Y=Permits Issued			R^2=0.7915

Of course, the presence of economic factors mitigating the likelihood of a particular operation seeking compensation through litigation does not mean that operations will never see takings litigation as making economic sense. Shifts in the perceived likelihood of costs and benefits associated with litigation can possibly be shaped by the legal environment. Consider, for example, the Supreme Court's 1992 *Lucas* decision, which established the per se, categorical taking rule, applied when all economic value is lost to regulation.[164] The reaction to this decision from the environmentalist community was one of concern, which "anticipated that a state or local environmental protection agency would reduce its regulatory efforts if it thought that the Supreme Court had dramatically increased the government's obligation to compensate owners of property subject to environmental protection laws."[165] While the case had nothing directly to do with surface coal mining, and there is no obvious evidence that state SMCRA regulatory authorities officially altered their procedures in reaction to the case, *Lucas* was followed by an apparent spike in takings litigations against state surface mining offices in state courts.[166] An increase in litigation, out of heightened expectations on the part of surface coal mining operators, may have stretched the human resources of state regulatory authorities, and may have, albeit indirectly, affected the policy outputs of those agencies.

While such impacts of litigation on regulatory output follow an indirect path (i.e. the agency is pursuing less regulatory activity, not because it fears loss of budgetary revenues through compensation, but because such resources are already tied up in litigation), the ultimate cause and effect are essentially the same. The recognition that the possible widespread impact of regulatory takings cases may occur along multiple pathways may make the analysis of such impact more complex, but it also provides for multiple targets of analysis. If the body of regulatory takings litigation does, in fact, result in a chilling effect on SMCRA implementation, the cause may be changes in decision-making by OSM and state personnel or changes in the behavior of coal mining operations. While the decision-making institutions of SMCRA enforcing agencies have been described as resilient to chilling forces, budgetary concerns were a ubiquitous factor during the interviews, and recognition that litigation restricts the ability of such offices to perform all of their tasks was prevalent. The expectations of legal success or failure, and even the perception of "right" and "wrong" in terms of property expectations, held by surface coal mining operators would certainly be susceptible to changes in the legal environment brought about by regulatory takings cases. That legal environment is actually "unfriendly" to SMCRA-based takings challenges, due to the courts' traditional emphases on the inherent investment risks in coal mining[167] and the established history of coal mining regulation, which predates most lease acquisitions and, thereby, reduces reasonable economic expectations.[168] If larger mining corporations, due to their greater access to legal resources and alternative sources of extraction, are more likely to know and accept this legal position, then one could reasonably assume that takings cases could direct smaller mining corporations to seek compensation of their own.

CONCLUSION

The evidence gathered through TSCS regressions indicates that there is the possibility of regulatory takings litigation having a chilling effect on regulatory outputs by causing an increase in the amount of permits granted by state and federal agencies charged with implementing SMCRA. A couple of concerns, however, should caution against the unquestioned acceptance of this conclusion. First, the possibility for a spurious relationship between the permitting process and the presence of takings precedent is high, given the problems of stationarity faced by TSCS analyses. Second, the interviews conducted with the personnel that make SMCRA permitting decisions produced an image of a regulatory regime that is not particularly susceptible to such direct impacts. The bureaucratization of knowledge, a cultural sense of obligation to the requirements of the statute, and an increase in the knowledge of regulatory requirements by the mining companies, caused in part by the increased corporate nature of coal mining are all factors that make either regulatory takings litigation itself or an observable impact caused by it less likely.

This does not mean that the findings are without merit. Litigation that does stand a chance of altering agency behavior is litigation that confronts the organizational inertia of agencies. Such inertia describes the compartmentalized goals and responsibilities of agency personnel, who see compliance with the statute and regulations defining their agenda. Inertia can also describe the individuals and companies that are regulated. Litigation that could potentially affect the larger operations of SMCRA implementation would have to change the expectations of regulator and regulated. Regulatory takings litigation may have affected policy outputs, not by itself by imposing economic costs and risks upon regulatory decision-makers, but as a part of a larger political context. The property rights expectations of surface coal mining operators, which are central to regulatory takings litigation, are part of a consciousness, either of the public as a whole or of the particular community, in this case, coal mining companies. SMCRA undoubtedly restricts those expectations, but the legitimacy of those restrictions can be changed. Strategic litigation on the part of interest groups can push those expectations one way or the other. The relatively low level of public awareness of SMCRA, however, may insulate the law from social mobilization of property rights to change the law and circumvent the organizational obligation of regulatory personnel to the letter of the law. Whereas other environmental statutes, such as the Endangered Species Act, exist high on the public radar and are more susceptible to public perceptions of a draconian nature, SMCRA is involved with risks that are just as threatening to the property of the public as the statute itself is to the property of those being regulated.

NOTES

[1] Rasband, J, Salzman, J and Squillace, M. 2004. *Natural Resources Law and Policy*. New York: Foundation Press. p. 1136.
[2] Scheberle, D. 2004. *Federalism and Environmental Policy: Trust and the Politics of Implementation.* Washington, D.C.: Georgetown University Press. p. 166.
[3] *Id.*, at 165.
[4] Scheberle, at 164.
[5] Rasband, at 1137.
[6] 30 U.S.C. § 1231-1241
[7] *Id.*, at § 1242-1279
[8] Scheberle, at 155.
[9] 30 U.S.C. § 1253(a)(1)
[10] *Id.*, at § 1211(c)(1)
[11] *Id.*, at § 1254(b)
[12] *Id.*, at § 1202(f)
[13] *Id.*, at § 1265(b)(3)
[14] *Id.*, at § 1265(b)(10)
[15] *Id.*, at § 1265(b)(17)
[16] *Id.*, at § 1265(b)(20)(A)
[17] *Id.*, at § 1265(b)(2)
[18] *Id.*, at § 1265(b)(1)
[19] *Id.*, at § 1259
[20] *Id.*, at § 1267(c)
[21] *Id.*, at § 1271(a)(2)
[22] *Id.*, at § 1271(a)(3)
[23] *Id.*, at § 1272(a)(3)
[24] *Id.*, § 1272(e)
[25] 30 C.F.R. § 761.5 (emphasis added)
[26] *Id.*, § 761.5(b)(1)
[27] *Pennsylvania Coal v. Mahon*, 260 U.S. 393 (1922).
[28] *Id.*, at 412-413.
[29] *Id.*, at 413.
[30] *Id.*, at 415.
[31] *Keystone Bituminous Coal Assn. v. DeBenedictus*, 480 U.S. 470 (1987).
[32] Benjamin, JR, Jr. 2002. "The Best of Both Worlds: Use of Common Law and Statutory Law Together in Applying the Nuisance Exception to Defend a Takings Claim." 11 Fed. Cir. B.J. 855, 862;

Fischel, WA. 1995. *Regulatory Takings: Law, Economics, and Politics*. Cambridge: Harvard University Press. p. 47.
[33] *Keystone*, at 481.
[34] *Id.*, at 476.
[35] *Id.*, at 491.
[36] *Id.*, at 483.
[37] Fischel, at 33.
[38] *Id.*, at 35.
[39] *St. Louis v. Stern*, 3 Mo. App. 48, 53 (1876); see also *Mugler v. Kansas*, 123 U.S. 623, 667 (1887)
[40] *Hodel v. Virginia Surface Mining and Reclamation Association*, 452 U.S. 264 (1981)
[41] *Id.*, at 293.
[42] *Id.*, at 294-295.
[43] *Whitney Benefits, Inc. v. United States*, 18 Cl. Ct. 394, 396 (1989) [*Whitney Benefits* I]
[44] 30 U.S.C. § 1260(b)(5)(A)
[45] *Id.*, § 1260(b)
[46] *Whitney Benefits* I, *supra* note 45 at 398.
[47] *Id.*, at 400.
[48] *Id.*, at 403.
[49] *Whitney Benefits, Inc. v. United States*, 926 F.2d 1169, 1172 (1991) [*Whitney Benefits* II]
[50] *Id.*, at 1178.
[51] Botello-Samson, D. 2008. The Benchmark of Expectations: Regulatory Takings and Surface Coal Mining." *Journal of Natural Resources and Environmental Law*. 22(1). p. 36.
[52] *Rith Energy, Inc. v. United States*, 44 Fed. Cl. 108, 115 (1999) [*Rith* I]; see also *M&J Coal Company v. United States*, 30 Fed. Cl. 360 (1994) [*M&J Coal* I]; *Apollo Fuels, Inc. v. United States*, 54 Fed.Cl. 717 (2002) [*Apollo Fuels* I]
[53] *Wyatt v. United States*, 271 F.3d 1090 (2001); *The Stearns Company, Ltd. v. United States*, 396 F.3d 1354 (2005) [*Stearns* II]
[54] *Penn Central Transp. Co. v. New York City*, 438 U.S. 104, 124 (1978)
[55] 331 F.3d 891 (2003).
[56] *M&J Coal Company v. United States*, 47 F.3d 1148, 1154 (1995) [*M&J Coal* II]; see also, *Chancellor Manor* at 901.

[57] *Lucas v. South Carolina Coastal Council*, 505 U.S. 1003, 1029 (1992)
[58] *M&J Coal* II, at 1154; see also *Chancellor Manor* at 902.
[59] *Lucas*, at 1019.
[60] *Penn Central*, at 124.
[61] *Rith* I, at 113.
[62] *Cane Tennessee, Inc. & Colten, Inc. v. United States*, 57 Fed. Cl. 115, 127 (2003) [*Cane* II]
[63] *M&J* I, at 361-62. The angle of draw is the angle from the vertical line, marking the edge of allowed underground mining, to the edge of an area on the surface where subsidence is to be prevented.
[64] Nyden, P. 1987. "Collapsing Mine Land Still Takes Toll in Homes." *The Charleston Gazette*. Jan. 11. p. 1B.
[65] *M&J* I, at 364.
[66] *Id.*, at 364-65.
[67] *Id.*, at 365-66.
[68] *Id.*, at 363.
[69] *Id.*, at 370.
[70] *M&J* II, at 1154.
[71] *Lucas*, at 1029.
[72] *Apollo Fuels* I, at 734.
[73] *Rith* I, at 115; see also *Apollo Fuels* I, at 735.
[74] *Id.*, at 111.
[75] *Id.*, at 114.
[76] *Apollo Fuels* I, at 720.
[77] *Rith* I, at 114; *Apollo Fuels* I, at 735.
[78] *Rith Energy, Inc. v. United States*, 247 F.3d 1355, 1362 (2001) (*Rith* II); *Apollo Fuels, Inc. v. United States*, 381 F.3d 1338, 1347 (2004) (*Apollo Fuels* II)
[79] *Whitney Benefits* II, at 1177.
[80] *Eastern Minerals International, Inc. v. United States*, 36 Fed. Cl. 541, 551 (1996); overturned by *Wyatt*.
[81] *Id.*, at 545.
[82] *Id.*, at 551.
[83] *Rith* II, at 113.
[84] *Penn Central*, at 124.
[85] *Whitney Benefits* I, at 406.
[86] *Palazzolo v. Rhode Island*, 533 U.S. 606, 631 (2001).
[87] *Cane* II; *Apollo Fuels* I.

[88] *Rith* II.
[89] *Apollo Fuels* I, at 723; citing *Concrete Pipe and Products of California v. Construction Laborers Pension Trust for Southern California*, 508 U.S. 602, 644 (1993)
[90] *Apollo Fuels* II, at 1346; *Tahoe-Sierra Preservation Council v. Tahoe Regional Planning Agency*, 535 U.S. 302, 331 (2002)
[91] *Benchmark Resources Corporation v. United States*, 74 Fed. Cl. 458, 467 (2006).
[92] *Rith* II, at 1362.
[93] *Cane* II, at 121-122, 130.
[94] *Cane Tennessee, Inc. and Colten, Inc. v. United States*, 54 Fed. Cl. 100, 106-108 (2002) (*Cane* I); *Apollo Fuels* I, at 729.
[95] *Whitney Benefits* I, at 405.
[96] *Apollo Fuels* I, at 727; see also *Florida Rock Industries v. United States*, 45 Fed. Cl. 21 (1999)
[97] *Cane* II, at 122.
[98] *Id.*, at 123.
[99] *Id.*
[100] *Id.*, at 127.
[101] *M&J* II, at 1154.
[102] *Rith* I, at 110.
[103] *Rith* II, at 1362.
[104] *Rith* I, at 115.
[105] *M&J* I, at 368.
[106] *Apollo Fuels* II, at 1350.
[107] Burling, JS. 2002. "Private Property Rights and the Environment After *Palazzolo*." 30 B.C. Envtl. L. Rev. 1.
[108] *M&J* I, at 367; see also *Rith* II, at 1364; *Lucas*; *Presault v. Interstate Commerce Commission*, 494 U.S. 1 (1990)
[109] *Whitney Benefits* I, at 396-97.
[110] *Id.*, at 407
[111] *Cane* II, at 119.
[112] *Id.*, at 127.
[113] *Eastern Minerals*, at 549.
[114] *Id.*, at 633. (O'Connor concurring)
[115] *Rith* I, at 1364.
[116] *Rith* II, at 1350.
[117] *Id.*, at 1351.
[118] *Penn Central*, at 124.

[119] *Abbott Laboratories v. Gardner*, 387 U.S. 136, 148 (1967); see also Nichol, GR, Jr. 1987. "Ripeness and the Constitution." 54 U. Chi. L. Rev. 153, 161; Hitchcock, MB. 1998. "*Suitum v. Tahoe Regional Planning Agency*: Applying the Takings Ripeness Rule to Land Use Regulations and Transferable Development Rights." 28 Golden Gate U.L. Rev. 87, 93-94; Mixon, J and Waggoner, J. 1998. "The Role of Variances in Determining Ripeness in Takings Claims Under Zoning Ordinances and Subdivision Regulations of Texas Municipalities." 29 St. Mary's L. J. 765, 773; Hof, at 833-834; Strachan, GC and Strachan, A. 2002. "The Ripeness Doctrine in Regulatory Takings Litigation." 22 J. Land Resources & Envtl. L. 19, 21.
[120] *Williamson County Planning Commission v. Hamilton Bank*, 473 U.S. 172 (1985)
[121] *MacDonald, Sommer & Frates v. Yolo County*, 477 U.S. 340, 359-360 (1986) (White dissenting).
[122] *Boise Cascade Corp. v. United States*, 296 F.3d 1339, 1349-50 (2002); *Tahoe-Sierra*, *supra* note 90 at 332.
[123] *The Stearns Co., Ltd. v. United States*, 53 Fed. Cl. 446, 447 (2002) (*Stearns* I)
[124] *Id.*, at 449.
[125] *Id.*, at 451.
[126] *Id.*, at 447.
[127] *Stearns* II, at 1357.
[128] *Id.*, at 1358.
[129] *Whitney Benefits* II, at 1171-72.
[130] Decision. Petition to Designate Certain Lands in the Rock Creek Watershed, Tennessee as Unsuitable for Surface Coal Mining Operations. Jed D. Christensen, Director, Office of Surface Mining Reclamation and Enforcement. March 24, 1987. 50 Fed. Reg. 10174, March 30, 1987; see also, *Benchmark Resources*, at 461.
[131] *Id.*, at 1173.
[132] *Eastern Minerals*, at 545.
[133] *Id.*, at 550.
[134] *Id.*, at 547.
[135] *Wyatt*, at 1097.
[136] *Id.*
[137] *Id.*, at 1098.
[138] *Cane* II, at 133.
[139] *Wyatt*, at 1098.

[140] *Id.*
[141] *Id.*, at 1098-99.
[142] *Machipongo Land and Coal Co., Inc. v. Commonwealth*, 719 A.2d 19 (Pa. Cmwlth. 1998) [*Machipongo* I]
[143] *Machipongo Land and Coal Co., Inc. v. Commonwealth*, 799 A.2d 751, 760 (Pa. S.C. 2002) [*Machipongo* II]
[144] *Id.*, at 766.
[145] *Id.*, at 768.
[146] *Id.*, at 774.
[147] *Id.*, at 775.
[148] *R.T.G. v. Ohio*, 98 Ohio St. 3d 1 (Oh S.C. 2002)
[149] *Id.*, at 11; see also *Whitney Benefits* I.
[150] *Id.*, at 12; see also *Florida Rock.*
[151] *Concrete Pipe.*
[152] *R.T.G.*, at 12.
[153] *Id.*, at 13.
[154] States selected are as follows: **Appalachian**: Alabama, Kentucky, Maryland, Ohio, Pennsylvania, Tennessee, Virginia and West Virginia; **Interior**: Arkansas, Illinois, Indiana, Iowa, Kansas, Missouri, and Oklahoma; **Western**: Colorado, Montana, New Mexico, Utah, Washington and Wyoming
[155] Scheberle, at 157-61.
[156] One regulatory agent in an Appalachian state enviously characterized the process of removing the overburden from over Western coal as, essentially, involving nothing more than a whisk broom.
[157] Measured in 2005 U.S. Dollars, determined with Bureau of Labor Statistics Consumer Price Index (CPI).
[158] Beck, N and Katz, JN. 2004. "Time-Series—Cross-Section Issues: Dynamics, 2004."
[159] Gujarati, DN. 1995. *Basic Econometrics*, 3rd ed. New York: McGraw-Hill, Inc. pp. 724-26.
[160] Beck and Katz.
[161] Melnick, RS. 1983. *Regulation and the Courts: The Case of the Clean Air Act.* Washington, D.C.: The Brookings Institution.
[162] Scheberle, at 177.
[163] One of the co-owners of the company in *M&J Coal Company v. United States* "suggested that all federal mine inspectors should be shot." See Nyden.

[164] *Lucas*.
[165] Lazarus, RJ. 1993. "Putting the Correct 'Spin' on *Lucas*." 45 Stan. L. Rev. 1411, 1412.
[166] See *Iowa Coal Mining Co. v. Monroe County*, 494 N.W.2d 664 (Iowa S.C. 1993); *Ward v. Harding*, 860 S.W.2d 280 (Ky S.C. 1993); *Natural Resources Commission v. AMAX*, 638 N.E.2d 418 (Ind. S.C. 1994)
[167] *M&J* I, at 368.
[168] *Apollo Fuels* II, at 1350.

CHAPTER 6

The Endangered Species Act

Enacted in 1973, the Endangered Species Act (ESA) originally enjoyed strong political support across party lines and different segments of society. Within a decade, however, positive public imagery of the Act would be diluted by an increased perception of ESA as excessively draconian and damaging to the nation's financial interest. An example of this shift includes recent measures considered by Congress to restrict the scope of ESA by requiring compensation to property owners that must restrict their property usage and removing requirements placed upon the Department of the Interior (DOI) to determine and designate habitats that are critical to endangered and threatened species. Much of the change in the perception of ESA has to do with the Act's seemingly ubiquitous presence within courtrooms. While a key feature of some ESA related litigation seeks stronger enforcement consistent with statutory requirements, much litigation seeks to restrict ESA implementation in order to protect economic interests and property rights.

In this context, regulatory takings litigation could have a high potential to create a chilling effect on the implementation of ESA. This chapter considers that possibility and tests its likelihood and argues that, beyond the particular conflicts between regulatory agencies and property owners that result in regulatory takings litigation, the direct impact of such litigation on the policy outputs related to ESA are negligible. However, such litigation can be a significant part of a larger political strategy to mobilize property rights claims to affect ESA implementation through non-judicial avenues. Additionally, regulatory takings challenges to ESA are currently well positioned to reshape public, political, and regulatory understanding of the purpose of the act in relation to the enjoyed property rights of Americans. Making such an argument requires detailed elaboration of specific components of the regulatory regime which implements ESA, a regime which is already the target of a property rights political agenda. To that end, this chapter begins by discussing the statutory framework of ESA, and then focuses on particular ways in which it is implemented. Then the historical relationship between ESA and the courts is considered in matters both general and specifically related to the question of regulatory takings. Finally, evidence of regulatory takings litigation impact on ESA implementation is consider in the form of statistical analysis of implementation trends and elite interviews conducted with individuals responsible for that implementation.

THE ENDANGERED SPECIES ACT

Congress enacted ESA in 1973 for the stated purpose of "provid[ing] a means whereby the ecosystems upon which endangered species and threatened species depend may be conserved."[1] Through the enactment of the Act, Congress recognized that a diversity of "species of fish, wildlife, and plants are of esthetic, ecological, educational, historical, recreational, and scientific value,"[2] and declared that such threats to biodiversity are "a consequence of economic growth and development untempered by adequate concern and conservation."[3] ESA casts a wide net to promote conversation, focusing on a wide range of targets from individual species to habitats, and from private citizens to the government itself.

In Section 4, Congress authorized the Secretary of the Interior to exercise powers aimed at determining the species and habitats that need government protection. In addition to the power to declare whether a particular species is endangered or threatened,[4] the Secretary is also authorized to declare "critical habitat"[5] and promulgate regulations necessary for the survival of the species. While the Act certainly grants the Secretary of the Interior significant power in the listing of endangered and threatened species, the Act also places upon the Secretary guidelines and restrictions in the use of this power. For instance, the Act establishes a timetable for the declaration of petitioned species and the review of such declarations, making negative declarations open to judicial review.[6] More significantly, while the Act allows the Secretary to take "into consideration the economic impact"[7] of a critical habitat designation, determinations of species listings are to be made "solely on the basis of the best scientific and commercial data available."[8] In addition to these listing powers, in Section 5 of the Act Congress also authorized the Secretaries of Agriculture and the Interior "to acquire by purchase, donation, or otherwise, lands, waters, or interest therein,"[9] as a way to set aside critical habitat.

The acquisition of habitat lands, while deemed by Congress an important part of a larger policy of protecting endangered species, would be cost prohibitive if implemented as the sole means of achieving the goals of ESA. The Act, therefore, also restricts behaviors that further threaten endangered species. The Section 7 provisions of ESA require that all federal agencies "insure that any action authorized, funded, or carried out by such agency...[does not] jeopardize the continued existence of any endangered species or threatened species or result in the destruction or adverse modification of habitat of such species."[10]

In addition to the Section 7 provisions regarding federal agency actions, Section 9 of ESA governs the actions of private individuals. Along with prohibiting the importation, exportation, and interstate sale of endangered species,[11] the Act also prohibits the "taking" of any endangered species within the United States or upon the high seas by anyone under U.S. jurisdiction.[12] While the Section 9 prohibitions against takings can be read as both broad and draconian, Section 10 allows for so-called "incidental takings." In this section of ESA, Congress authorized the Secretary of the Interior to establish Habitat Conservation Plans (HCP), which allow for limited takings of endangered or threatened species, provided that the "taking is incidental to, and not the purpose of, the carrying out of an otherwise lawful activity."[13] To acquire a permit for such a taking, the applicant must demonstrate the incidental nature of the taking, that procedures will be in place to minimize the taking, and that alternatives have been considered but are demonstrably less favorable.[14] These various provisions and components of ESA have been thoroughly examined and interpreted by the courts, thereby heavily embedding the ESA's statutory history within the U.S. judiciary.

HABITAT CONSERVATION PLANS

The above mentioned Section 10 provisions of ESA, namely the issuance of incidental take permits (ITP), which allow the incidental taking of endangered species provided that the permitted action complies with an established and approved Habitat Conservation Plan (HCP), are the central focus of this inquiry into ESA for two reasons. First, the use and availability of HCPs as an implementation tool are a statutory component of ESA that is conceptually antithetical to what is, arguably, the general public perception of the law. On September 9, 2005, the U.S. House of Representatives voted on and approved H.R. 3824, The Threatened and Endangered Species Recovery Act of 2005. The preceding floor debate mirrored so many other reform-oriented legislative debates. Through flowery rhetoric, all sides recognized ESA as "a well-intentioned law," yet portrayed the law as one which "creates an adversarial relationship between landowners and the government."[15] Opponents of the bill described the law as "flawed in many ways" and as having "been abused at the detriment of their constituents' rights."[16] The overall image created throughout the debate was an Act that was burdensome, uncooperative, and superseding of all economic interests,[17] which hides the statutory framework of the Act intended to balance economic and environmental interests. The bill was not taken up by the Senate.[18]

The present focus on HCPs is not intended to disprove these anecdotal accounts of ESA implementation. Attempts to conduct interviews with permit applicants have confronted a number of obstacles, with one applicant refusing an interview because reliving the process would create too much stress for his old age and declining health. At a minimum, one cannot deny that the experience of ESA implementation as adversarial has a factual basis insofar as real people have genuinely perceived it as such. The purpose of this focus is to paint a larger, more inclusive picture of ESA implementation. The origins of HCPs and ITPs lie in the original utilitarian wording of

Section 10, which empowered the Secretary to permit "any action otherwise prohibited by section 9 of this Act...to enhance the propagation or survival of the affected species."[19] Simply put, ESA was originally worded to potentially allow for some harm to individual species to benefit the species population as a whole. ESA was amended in 1982 by establishing the current HCP regime, modeling it on collaborative efforts to protect butterfly habitat on San Bruno Mountain in California (which became the first approved HCP in 1983), and specifying the permitting power of the Secretary by requiring the presence of an HCP, guaranteeing impact minimization and mitigation efforts and the presence of secure funding for such efforts.[20]

Initially viewed as a win-win for both environmental and economic interests, utilization of Section 10 permitting was slow until its high priority adoption by the Clinton Administration.[21] Figure 6.1 demonstrates this trend by showing the number of HCPs approved by the U.S. Fish and Wildlife Service (FWS), the main agency charged with ESA implementation, since the 1982 Amendments. Since HCPs vary greatly, ranging in size from less than an acre to millions of acres, covering one species or up to tens of species, and operating as single omnibus plans or operating as several individual plans for the same species, Figure 6.1 also indicates the number of individual species for which at least one HCP was approved each year. With an increased reliance on HCPs and ITPs, individuals and corporations involved in economic use of habitats on which endangered species rely are brought more into the regulatory regime. Although ESA places the burden of proof on applicants, requiring that they prove that their proposed activity will only result in incidental and acceptable levels of harm to endangered species,[22] ESA's citizen suit provision,[23] which has commonly been used to ensure agency compliance with other requirements of the Act, has rarely been used to ensure proper enforcement of HCPs, leaving open the question of the effectiveness of a reliance on HCPs as a regulatory tool.[24]

FIGURE 6.1: Trends in the Use of Habitat Conservation Plans (1983-2005)

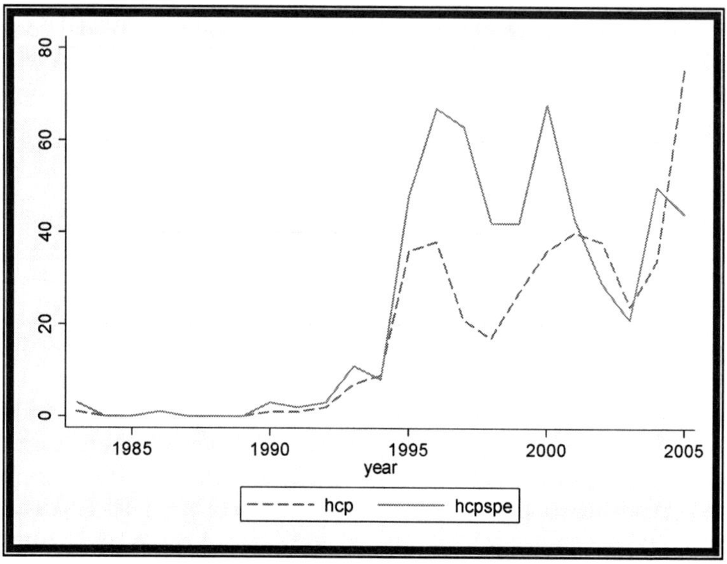

hcp = Habitat Conservation Plans approved
hcpspe = species to which HCPS were dedicated

The second reason for focusing on Section 10 HCPs and ITPs is related to this concern over their effectiveness in protecting threatened and endangered species from economic pressures. The main concern of this book is the measurement of impact, namely, determining the degree to which policy outputs are a function of litigation. The impact of litigation against FWS or the National Marine Fisheries Service (NMFS) could be measured in several of the sections of ESA. Agency decisions on the listing of particular species,[25] determination of critical habitats,[26] or the extent of Section 7 requirements on federal agencies[27] have frequently been subject to litigation, and an impact analysis of any of these types of litigation could provide meaningful and interesting results. Yet all these types of litigation have as their central question the degree to which a particular regulatory action on the part of FWS or NMFS complies with the requirements of ESA. This type of litigation would clearly affect agency decisions on a case-by-case basis, and would likely have larger impacts. More than one interviewed FWS official stated that, although litigation is costly to the agency in terms of time and employees that are monopolized by litigation, litigation also has the positive effect of keeping the agency honest and helping to guarantee stricter compliance with ESA.

However, a different set of questions are raised when the focus is on regulatory takings litigation and its more centrally substantive nature. With the high incidence of endangered species on private lands and the often high costs needed to protect such species, the potential for conflicts between the enforcement of ESA and private property rights is rather great.[28] The HCP and ITP provisions of ESA, like regulatory takings jurisprudence, can likewise be viewed as a balancing act. The purpose of HCPs is "to promote biological conservation along with economic development and the continuation of agriculture."[29] Despite the aforementioned public perception and anecdotal experience of ESA's implementation, the statute itself contains provisions that add a component of balance to the law. This makes the simultaneous attention toward regulatory takings litigation and ITP issuance a potentially fruitful endeavor.

While regulatory takings challenges to ESA are a fairly recent phenomenon, they have not developed within a legal and political environment absent a contextual history. A long observed characteristic of the American judiciary is "that it can only act when it is called upon,... it does not pursue criminals, hunt out wrongs, or examine evidence of its own accord."[30] This means that the very evolving political forces in which ESA was created were also the context in which its challenges occurred. Therefore, regulatory takings challenges arise in a context dependent upon the successes and failures of other challenges pursued for reasons ranging from changes in political climate to changes in the law itself. The next section will briefly chart the history of ESA within the judiciary to provide the legal and political context within which the impact of regulatory takings challenges must be observed.

ESA IN THE COURTS

It has been mentioned above that litigation has played a significant role in agency compliance with the statutory requirements of ESA. While this body of litigation represents an important part of the overall picture of the interactions between agencies, courts, and the public, this section will focus upon cases which challenge, not FWS or NMFS compliance with ESA, but the statute itself. Of course, it is difficult to draw a bright line between these types of cases. One gray area consists of cases which involve statutory interpretation of ESA. Although cases involving FWS listing decisions, for example, involve interpreting the requirements of the statute, some challenges involve larger efforts to interpret ESA in a particular way.

Probably the most famous example of such a case of statutory interpretation involved the well known conflict between the snail darter and the federally funded Tellico Dam in 1978.[31] At question in the case was whether ESA should be interpreted to place such an "incalculable"[32] value on the protection of endangered species that construction on a nearly completed dam should be halted to protect the snail darter, despite the large amount of federal dollars already spent on program and the continued issuance of funds by Congress, which had been made aware of the presence of the snail darter in committee meetings.[33] Relying on the language of the statute, the Supreme Court interpreted ESA as a Congressional statement of the value of endangered species, and therefore stated that the Section 7 provisions on agency actions are a "mandate to protect species notwithstanding economic effects."[34]

Despite the strong protection afforded ESA in the language of *TVA*, this initial case would not prove an insurmountable obstacle to those who would reign in the Act. Congress reacted by amending ESA to incorporate an exemption process, whereby the newly created Endangered Species Committee (ESC, a.k.a. the God Squad, as it was called by its critics), which included several heads of federal agencies and an appointed representative from the governor of the state where a particular project would occur, could exempt a federally funded project from ESA requirements.[35] When the ESC refused to exempt the Tellico Dam project from ESA, due to its perceive status as an unnecessary example of pork-barrel spending, Congress enacted legislation to directly exempt the project.[36] Ultimately, the dam was completed and only relocation efforts and the subsequent discovery of a few other populations of the snail darter spared the fish from extinction. In the end, measuring the impact of *TVA* is challenging and the results of such an endeavor are counterintuitive. A Supreme Court ruling that ordered construction on a dam stopped did not stop the dam. A clearer impact of the case was a change in policy, the creation of the ESC which, likewise, sought to stop construction but failed.

Whereas the Supreme Court was asked to interpret the spirit of ESA in its *TVA* decision, its task with the 1995 *Sweet Home*[37] decision focused on the interpretation of a single word; the implications of that interpretation for the larger spirit of ESA, however, were just as large. The term in question was "harm,"[38] which, plaintiffs alleged, when interpreted by the Secretary to include significant habitat modification and degradation, injured them economically due to reliance on the logging industry.[39] Although the Court acknowledged that the Act's legislative history demonstrates a congressional consideration and removal of habitat modification language from a definition of harm,[40] the Court argued that the actual text of ESA supports the Secretary's definition. The Court stated that "an ordinary understanding"[41] of the word and the Act's stated broad purpose[42] both require an interpretation of harm to include habitat modification "to provide a means whereby the ecosystems upon which endangered species and threatened species depend may be conserved."[43] Furthermore, the 1982 addition of ITP provisions led the Court to argue that Congress must have interpreted ESA to cover indirect, as well as direct, takings because an incidental direct taking would not make sense.[44]

Although litigious attempts to constrain the regulatory power of ESA through statutory interpretation cases have not been successful, those seeking such restrictions were given new life with a sign from the Supreme Court that constitutional efforts to constrain ESA might be more successful. In 1995, the Supreme Court decided *United States v. Lopez*,[45] with *United States v. Morrison* following five years later.[46] Together, these two cases mark a departure from the Court's deference to Congress in its interpretation of the extent of its Commerce Clause powers. In both opinions, Chief Justice Rehnquist characterized the overturned statutes as products of a Congress in the historical moment of exercising "considerably greater latitude in regulatory conduct and transactions under the Commerce Clause than...previous case law permitted."[47] Additionally, the Court indicated that certain wildlife protection statutes "raise significant constitutional questions,"[48] and exist, at least, at the "outer limits of Congress' power."[49]

Within this atmosphere of jurisprudential shifting, a number of lower federal court decisions were made which considered whether Congress' authority to regulate endangered species was limited, at least in particular situations, when the protected species lack an interstate nature.[50] At the center of each conflict was the question whether the federal protection of an intrastate endangered species satisfied the substantial effects test of *Lopez*.[51] These cases did not result in successful challenges, however, as the courts ruled that, even when a species exists fully within the borders of one state, federal regulation of that species is interstate in nature due to the interstate economic nature of the activities threatening the species,[52] the interstate economic potential of the species (i.e. tourism, research, future trade),[53] and the role that the regulation of each individual species plays in a larger regulatory regime, which is economic and interstate in nature.[54]

Within this environment of litigious challenges to the constitutionality of specific implementation of ESA, regulatory takings claims have also provided those experiencing unwanted regulation under the Act, as well as the interest groups that represent them, another tool. Regulatory takings challenges can arise amid the implementation of ESA on numerous grounds, most of which have not had much success before federal judges.[55] For example, the Court of Appeals for the Ninth Circuit rejected the claim that a prohibition against killing endangered species in defense of one's property constitutes a taking.[56] The type of regulatory takings challenge which has had success in federal courtrooms involves challenges to direct regulations of property for the purposes of protecting endangered species; however, this type of challenge has been historically rare.[57]

In 2001, for the first time, a federal court ruled that the implementation of ESA constituted a compensable taking of property.[58] The *Tulare* decision dealt with a conflict over the efforts of NMFS to protect two species of endangered fish, the delta smelt and the winter-run Chinook salmon. These species of fish rely on water supplies that also feed California's private water needs. The State Water Resources Control Board (SWRCB), the Bureau of Reclamations, and the

California state Department of Water Resources (DWR) issue and distribute permits to county water districts.[59] These permits are for specific water entitlement allotments, and are based on the contingency that the state cannot be held liable for shortages beyond its control.[60] Not to threaten the existence of the two endangered fish species, the agencies adopted a "reasonable and prudent alternative" (RPA) to the original permit conditions, which "restricted the time and manner in which water could be pumped..., thereby limiting the water otherwise available to the water distribution systems."[61]

In the end, the Claims Court had to determine what sort of property right was conferred upon the districts by the permits. The defendants considered such rights to be a "usufructuary interest," which "is simply not susceptible to physical possession, much less invasion or occupation,"[62] in which case, the use restrictions would have merely frustrated the plaintiffs' contract instead of appropriating it.[63] The Claims Court, however, sided with the plaintiffs, stating that, "[i]n the context of water rights, a mere restriction on use—the hallmark of a regulatory action—completely eviscerates the right itself since plaintiffs' sole entitlement is to the use of the water."[64] Since "the government has essentially substituted itself as the beneficiary of the contract rights with regard to *that* water and totally displaced the contract holder,"[65] the Claims Court determined that, since the individual districts were being forced to solely bear the costs of public good,[66] they are due compensation.

In its *Tulare* assessment, the Claims Court regarded the reduction in water access as a physical taking of property.[67] A ruling that a reduction in property use to be ESA-compliant could be regarded as a physical confiscation of property has tremendous potential to affect ESA implementation, since such confiscations have been understood to constitute a per se taking.[68] After *Tulare*, the federal judiciary heard takings claims similar to those in *Tulare*, and ruled with mixed results. In *Klamath Irrigation District v. U.S.*, the Claims Court criticized the *Tulare* decision for regarding the contractual water rights absolutely, without considering whether they may have been legitimately conditioned by shortages which ESA would require the government to prevent.[69] In *Casitas Municipal Water District v. U.S.*, however, the Court of Appeals for the Federal Circuit, in a case it remanded back to the Claims Court, required a physical taking analysis be applied to a reduction in water access rights due to ESA implementation.[70] It should be noted that, while the nature of the restriction was similar in *Tulare* and *Klamath*, the Court of Appeals for the Federal Circuit, in *Casitas*, relied heavily on the fact that water was diverted from the original channel to maintain a fish ladder and is, therefore, "forever gone."[71]

The federal judiciary has also heard regulatory takings challenges against ESA in situations distinct from those involving restrictions on water access rights. In the majority of these cases, the courts did not rule that a taking occurred, for a variety of reasons. While a number of these decisions were on ripeness grounds, which allow for the possibility that ESA restrictions could ultimately result in a taking, some components of those ripeness rulings illuminate the working reality of ESA implementation, a reality that draws the public portrayals of ESA as overly-draconian into question. By adhering to its final decision requirement,[72] the courts have emphasized that FWS has the discretionary power to suggest and/or accept alternative ITP applications after an initial rejection, meaning that there still may be legal uses of the property under ESA, and the property owner cannot challenge the initial denial until such alternatives are considered (or FWS declines to consider them).[73] Likewise, ESA-implementing agencies generally have the discretion to provide technical assistance in the formulating of an ITP application, and property owners cannot challenge property restrictions if they have not availed themselves of such service, if available.[74]

Some claimants have argued that the regulatory process, while necessary to make a claim ripe, can be a source of a taking. Such claims argue that the mere presence of regulatory authority, with inevitable delays, can constitute a temporary taking, causing property owners to go without the use of their property temporarily, and justifying compensation for that time. The federal courts, however, have been suspicious of such claims, stating that "the mere assertion of regulatory jurisdiction by a governmental body does not constitute a regulatory taking."[75] Since a "reasonable permitting process is an incident of ownership,"[76] and "delays are inherent in complex regulatory permitting processes..., government agencies dealing with the complex regulatory schemes should be afforded *significant deference* in determining what additional information is required to satisfy statutorily imposed obligations."[77]

These decisions might couch and limit the *Tulare* ruling in other ways. In *Tulare*, the Claims Court severed the interest in the limited water rights from the rest of the water rights, and ruled that a total taking of those water rights had occurred.[78] A similar argument was made in *Casitas*,[79] indicating that this ruling may be due to the unique nature of water rights. When the property in question has been something more permanent and stationary, calls to sever the regulated property from the remainder have been less successful. The Claims Court rejected an argument to sever the rights in 40 acres of timber from the remaining 160 acres owned, thus avoiding a total taking.[80]

Furthermore, the more stable nature of property in land and forests also make it more difficult for claimants to prove a per se, physical taking through physical invasion and occupation. In some cases involving efforts by FWS to protect the spotted owl, property owners have argued that their rights to exclude others from their property were taken, either by requirements to allow FWS employees to enter their property to conduct owl surveys,[81] or by prohibiting the owners from excluding the owls from the property via logging.[82] The Courts have rejected these arguments, classifying the government's actions as "a restriction on private use of the land and not a per se taking by the government,"[83] and that such actions do not deprive the owners "of their right to possess the property themselves" or to exclude others.[84]

Despite what might appear to be an insulation of land-based ESA restrictions from the water-based ruling in *Tulare*, one needs to cautious in any such assessment. Ongoing litigation has been remanded to the Claims Court, altering that lower court's ruling to provide for a cognizable right in property where the Claims Court had earlier ruled one did not exist.[85] In the case, the federal government conditioned the purchase of property for the purpose of development on the sale of additional land to the government from the same owner for the purpose of mitigating the loss of critical habitat caused by the development.[86] The Claims Court interpreted the claimed right lost by the owner as the non-cognizable right to sell property without conditions.[87] The Court of Appeals ruled that the case must decide whether the owner's development rights were taken by the regulations, thus lowering the value of the property and the purchase price.[88] This ruling reiterates that basic diminutions in property value caused by ESA can be the basis of a takings claim. However, it should be noted that dicta from the Court of Appeals indicates that ripeness, the reasonableness of expectations, and the timing of property acquisition and critical habitat designation could still affect a *Penn Central* analysis and result in a ruling of no taking.[89]

The question that then arises is to what degree, if any, such litigation affects the implementation of ESA. Several political concerns are central to such an inquiry. Considering the effectiveness of ESA, Section 5 does provide agencies with the power to acquire through purchase properties needed for the protection of species,[90] but could ESA effectively operate if FWS and NMFS were effectively required to "purchase" all or most necessary habitats through compensation? There is also a question of justice. Granted, one individual should not be forced to bear the burden of a good enjoyed by all, but to what degree do private property rights include the right to destroy something in which the public has a legitimate interest?[91] Beyond the questions of efficiency and ethics, one must also ask whether such an impact is likely to occur. The next sections consider that question.

BEHAVIORAL ADJUSTMENTS

To test the hypothesis that the aforementioned regulatory takings challenges to ESA implementation affected the policy outputs of FWS, cross-sectional time-series analyses were conducted to assess regulatory output trends before and after the *Tulare* decision, as was done with SMCRA cases in Chapter Five. Data was collected from 1983, the year of the first approved HCP, to 2005 from the U.S. Fish and Wildlife Service's Conservation Plans and Agreements Database. Panels were comprised of the eight FWS regions, although, since Region 7, which consists of the state of Alaska, has never approved a HCP, it was not included in the dataset. Inclusion and awareness of the various FWS regions is important for a number of reasons. Dividing the data into regions provides for more observations, but it also allows one to control for the unique characteristics of particular regions. This is crucial for ESA studies, given the high degree of variance between regions on such issues as number of listed species, amount of development threat, and ecological characteristics.

FIGURE 6.2: U.S. Fish and Wildlife Service Regions

Region 1 (Pacific): Hawai'i, Idaho, Oregon, Pacific Islands, Washington
Region 2 (Southwest): Arizona, Oklahoma, New Mexico, Texas
Region 3 (Great Lakes-Big Rivers): Illinois, Indiana, Iowa, Michigan, Minnesota, Missouri, Ohio, Wisconsin
Region 4 (Southeast): Alabama, Arkansas, Florida, Georgia, Kentucky, Louisiana, Mississippi, North Carolina, Puerto Rico, South Carolina, Tennessee, Virgin Islands
Region 5 (Northeast): Connecticut, Delaware, Maine, Maryland, Massachusetts, New Hampshire, New Jersey, New York, Pennsylvania, Rhode Island, Vermont, Virginia, West Virginia
Region 6 (Mountain-Prairie): Colorado, Kansas, Montana, North Dakota, Nebraska, South Dakota, Utah, Wyoming
Region 7 (Alaska): Alaska
Region 8 (California and Nevada): California, Nevada, the Klamath Basin of Oregon

For this particular study, the issuance of the 2001 Claims Court decision, *Tulare*, which was significant as it was the first time a federal court ruled that enactment of ESA constituted a taking of private property and compensation was, therefore, constitutionally required, will operate as the interruption. The dependent variable to be measured is the level of HCP activity in each region. HCPs, however, present particular problems for the theoretical assumptions underlying the study. In particular, one must consider what sort of impact would represent a chilling effect caused by regulatory takings litigation. Since the ITP provisions of Sec. 10 were added to create a balance between economic and environmental interests, an agency might react by either decreasing or increasing its activities, since ITPs simultaneously permit development yet subject it to restrictions. Having conducted interviews with FWS personnel, it is my impression that most challenges to ITP issuance seek issuance, and the threat of non-issuance or retraction is present. However, it was also made clear that the beginning of an HCP process relies heavily on the willingness of regulatory agencies to impose restrictions on property development in the first place. In the aforementioned post-*Tulare* ESA litigation which involved Sec. 10 (as opposed to Sec. 7 restrictions on other federal government permitting[92]), the suit was generally sparked by a denial of an ITP.[93] Even when the claimant had not filed an ITP, the federal courts have generally maintained that a rejection of an ITP is a necessary component of a ripe taking claim.[94] Therefore, it is assumed that a chilling effect will be characterized by a decrease in HCP activity.

A further difficulty caused by the nuances of HCPs is their wide diversity. HCP activity can be measured in different ways. Some regions have issued permits for several small HCPs; others for a few very large ones. The FWS Southeast Region (Region 4), for example, has approved 169 HCPs, 81 of which are single-species HCPs for the Alabama Beach Mouse. Region 8, consisting mainly of California and Nevada, on the other hand, has approved ten HCPs for ten or more species, ranging in size from 124 acres to 1.3 million acres,[95] demonstrating how geographic, climatological, and biotic diversity across regions could make any individual measure of HCP activity misleading. For that reason, FWS databases were examined and data was gathered for each region that measured the number of each HCP permitted, the number of species for which at least one HCP was permitted, and the total acreage under HCP regulation for each year.

Various measures of HCP activity were created to provide for the opportunity of more robust measurement. In particular, HCP activity was measured by the number of HCPs permitted in a given year, the number of acres protected under those new HCPs, and the number of individual endangered species brought under the protection of at least one of those HCPs. Other independent variables were considered and measured to provide an explanation for the variance in HCP activity outside of that which might be explained by the *Tulare* decision. One could reasonably expect factors such as the budget of the Interior Department, as well as the number of employees of that agency, to affect the amount of HCP activity positively. Likewise, an increase in the number of species on the endangered species list would likely cause in increase in such activity. Finally, it is also important to control for the uniqueness of different FWS regions, some of which are simply more reliant on HCPs, as well as the agendas of particular presidential administrations. For example, given that Bill Clinton made the use of HCPs a central part of his plan for FWS, one would expect a general increase in such activity, regardless of the impact of other variables.

TABLE 6.1: Prais-Winsten PCSE Regression (AR1) Results (Habitat Conservation Plan Activity)

	Coefficient	**Stand. Error**	**P>|Z|**
ESA List	0.007	0.001	0.000
Region 2	4.250	1.241	0.001
Region 4	5.728	2.582	0.026
Region 8	4.076	0.803	0.000
Cons	-5.116	0.926	0.000
Y=HCPs			R^2=0.2890

	Coefficient	**Stand. Error**	**P>|Z|**
ESA List	0.007	0.001	0.000
Region 2	4.226	1.267	0.001
Region 4	5.704	1.093	0.000
Region 8	4.052	0.820	0.000
Cons	-5.131	0.715	0.000
Y=HCP Acres			R^2=0.2896

	Coefficient	**Stand. Error**	**P>|Z|**
Interior Employees	-0.441	0.118	0.000
ESA List	0.006	0.001	0.000
Clinton Admin.	2.246	0.726	0.002
Region 2	1.793	0.490	0.000
Region 4	1.750	0.390	0.000
Region 8	14.576	3.275	0.000
Cons	26.662	8.777	0.002
Y= Species w/ HCP			R^2=0.5132

Efforts to establish a baseline for HCP activity, independent of any effect caused by the *Tulare* decision, identified different explanatory variables depending on the way in which HCP activity was measured. The number of HCPs and the acreage protected were determined to be a function of the number of species on the endangered species list and the uniqueness of FWS Regions 2 (Southwest), 4 (Southeast), and 8 (California/Nevada). When HCP activity was measured as the number of species protected, the number of Interior employees (measured in 100 employees) and the Clinton administration became significant independent variables and the model, as a whole, explained more of the variance. The results of these PCSE regressions can be found in Table 6.1. When the *Tulare* interruption was added to the models, very little effect was observed. There was no significant impact of the *Tulare* decision on the number of HCPs or the number of species protected. There was a statistically significant impact on the HCP acres dependent variable, but the impact was small and the addition of the *Tulare* variable did little to affect the explanatory power of the overall model. The effects of the *Tulare* decision on the HCP acres variable can be seen in Table 6.3.

There are a number of reasons why these results may not tell us very much. To begin, the R^2 values are rather low for the HCP and HCP acres dependent variables, which indicate that much of the variance in those dependent variables is a product of unidentified independent variables. Second, the overall reliability of the data could still be at issue. Table 6.3 indicates that, while there is greater stationarity with the ESA data than with the SMCRA data, as observed in Chapter Five, there are still observable incidents of non-stationary data (See, for example, Z(t) for Region 4 for the HCP acres variable, and Q(L1) for Region 8 for the species with an HCP variable). Error variance testing that was run after the regressions did, however, demonstrate that the PCSE regression did correct for problems associated with stationarity. However, while ANOVA testing did demonstrate a low likelihood of continued panel heteroskedasticity, error variance testing also demonstrated a high degree of serial correlation of the errors within the regional data panels. For the species with an HCP variable, four of the seven panels contained serial correlation; for the remaining two dependent variables, all panels were serially correlated.

TABLE 6.2: Results of Dickey-Fuller and Correlogram Testing for Stationarity

Region	Z(t)*	Q(L1)	Prob>Q
Y= HCP Acres			
1	-4.374	0.00469	0.9454
2	-3.424	0.05523	0.8142
3	-4.633	0.06245	0.8027
4	-3.165	3.054	0.0805
5	-3.894	2.3034	0.1291
6	-5.223	0.20889	0.6476
8	-5.547	0.31681	0.5735
Y= Species w/ HCP			
1	-3.678	2.8208	0.0931
2	-4.023	5.8164	0.0159
3	-5.443	0.38844	0.5331
4	-2.598	15.761	0.0001
5	-6.143	0.17984	0.6715
6	-4.825	0.02558	0.8729
8	-2.213	14.85	0.0001

	***Interpolated Dickey-Fuller**	
1% C.V.	**5% C.V.**	**10% C.V.**
-4.38	**-3.60**	**-3.24**

Finally, while the presence of the *Tulare* decision does demonstrate a statistically significant impact on the amount of acres dedicated to HCP plans, little of the overall variance in acreage is explained. Although that impact is positive, as would be expected, the impact is small, especially when one considers that the HCP acres variable is measured in single acres.

TABLE 6.3: Prais-Winsten PCSE Regression (AR1) Results (Impact of *Tulare* Decision)

	Coefficient	Stand. Error	P>|Z|
ESA List	0.006	0.001	0.000
Region 2	4.214	1.267	0.001
Region 4	5.692	1.092	0.000
Region 8	4.040	0.820	0.000
Tulare Decision	1.747	0.827	0.035
Cons	-4.576	0.793	0.000
Y= HCP Acres			R^2=0.2978

ASSESSING THE IMPACT

To develop a better understanding of the internal workings of FWS and how the *Tulare* decision, and possible future regulatory takings challenges, could affect HCP activities, elite interviews were conducted with key personnel in FWS regional offices. Subjects for interviewing were selected based on responsibilities held within FWS. While regional directors bear ultimate responsibility for signing off on HCP permits, their varied responsibilities made them both generally inaccessible and not ideal interview subjects. Therefore, interview solicitations focused on personnel directly involved in HCP permitting. These individuals were coordinators and biologists within the endangered species offices of regional FWS offices. Additionally, when available, an individual from the office's legal counsel was interviewed. As there are only eight FWS regional offices, and HCP activity varies among them, variance in representation exists, as levels of responsiveness to interview requests varied.

In a manner similar to what was observed with SMCRA implementing agencies, a high degree of bureaucratization, both internal and external, was observed. Internally, many decisions in the HCP process are made outside of the regional office. Field offices interact with applicants far more than do the regional offices, although the responsibility of HCP approval falls on the shoulders of the regional offices. By the time a permit application finds its way to the regional office, a great deal of communication has occurred between the applicant and experts in field offices, who can generally steer applicants away from application errors. More significantly, the HCP process is usually triggered by agencies other than FWS. Agencies ranging from local zoning and planning boards to state and federal departments of agriculture, wildlife, natural resources, etc. have their own regulations keeping them ESA compliant, and these agencies are usually the applicants' first contact. One could reasonably predict that a chilling effect caused by regulatory takings litigation would be hampered by this characteristic. Key decision makers within FWS would be less likely to alter their behavior in anticipation of a takings lawsuit if there are more agencies involved in the permitting process, and the onus of takings requirements could be passed on to them.

Furthermore, FWS decision-making processes were also internally bureaucratized, again, in a way similar to the internal bureaucratization witnessed in SMCRA implementing agencies. Inquiries about legal standards usually received a response indicating that the individual would have to check with legal counsel. One effect of this system is that individuals charged with particular decision-making responsibilities, whether those responsibilities are biological, financial, or procedural, did not appear overly concerned with legal standards. This does not mean that these individuals were unaware of legal standards. In fact, every respondent indicated that knowledge about changes in legal standards flows fairly efficiently, and if a new case changes the way they need to do things, such information usually comes to them in the form of a memo from legal counsel or procedures are changed in writing by a directive from above. All in all, the decision-making atmosphere observed was one of compartmentalized ritual, and the interview respondents most frequently described their tasks and roles as defined by statutory requirements. Most respondents believed that the statute and the regulations are pretty clear as to how things should be done, and if those standards are not met, permits will not be regarded as sufficient, and any legal challenge will be confidently approached with the knowledge that the individual was following the rules.

This feature was readily observed in responses to questions on regulatory takings litigation. Every respondent from a FWS regional office was aware of regulatory takings litigation, was aware of the *Tulare* decision, and no one needed the term "regulatory takings" to be defined for them. However, almost without fail, the interviewees never brought up regulatory takings on their own, despite efforts by the interviewer to direct conversation in that direction. There was an acute awareness of the constant threat of litigation, and an equally acute awareness of budgetary constraints, but that litigious threat was generally described as springing from deviation from the statute, and not from constitutional sources. In fact, while a few interviewed personnel described debating factions that arise within discussions on particular HCP decisions, those debates are generally over whether particular proposed activities or precautions associated with an HCP would sufficiently mitigate potential harm to endangered species. Additionally, there appears to be a faction within FWS, or perhaps more accurately a commonly (although not monolithically) held opinion that the *Tulare* decision was wrongly decided and should have been appealed.

Finally, and most surprisingly, all respondents described their general interactions with permit applicants as cooperative, as opposed to confrontational. On its own, this set of responses merely acts as a single counterpoint to the larger public image of ESA as a draconian, unyielding policy. Confrontations clearly exist, and several HCP application processes involve litigation. However, most development groups have developed within a large regulatory context, and well financed development projects usually are organized to take advantage of expertise that directs development most efficiently through regulatory requirements. Interview respondents have generally indicated that this is becoming more the case through time as industries come to accept ESA as the cost of doing business. Stories were told of particular industries developing drafts of regulations that eventually were put in place. Such anecdotes may raise the specter of agency capture, and this book is not intended to prove or disprove such a phenomenon. However, it does indicate that, within the ESA program, the regulated/regulator relationship is not as confrontational as external images present it; bargaining plays a larger role in the relationship, which is generally changing as political, economic, and informational contexts change.[96] The end result is a regulatory history of ESA similar to the one described in the chapter on SMCRA. Those regulated by SMCRA, i.e. surface coal mining operators, are a more homogenous group, than the numerous interests that may find themselves regulated under ESA, and characteristics such as "corporatized" may be more readily applied to coal companies, as a group, than those other interests. However, the availability of expertise and the presence of an institutionalized expectation of and preparation for regulation within development corporations, for both SMCRA and ESA implementing agencies, are generally seen as a source of cooperative relationships.

CONCLUSION

Data collected on the policy outputs of FWS implementation of ESA, like the data collected for SMCRA implementing agencies, failed to demonstrate, with trustworthy results, an impact of the *Tulare* decision on regulatory outputs. Interviews with FWS personnel demonstrated the presence of similar decision-making characteristics within the regulatory institutions surrounding both ESA and SMCRA implementation. In general, internal and external bureaucratization of decision-making, an agency culture define by statutory obligation, and an increase in the cooperative nature between regulators and those they regulate, all function to resist, albeit certainly not prevent, the likelihood of regulatory takings litigation and a subsequent chilling effect.

Although one cannot discount the possibility of individual litigants bringing regulatory takings cases against FWS or NMFS, especially when potential plaintiffs are well financed and possess expertise in property law, the likelihood of such cases occurring increases with external influence. Despite the frequent cost effectiveness of non-litigious interactions with ESA implementing agencies, coupled with the risk of pursuing litigation under an ad hoc jurisprudence, one cannot outright dismiss predictions that ESA enforcement will attract litigation. Plaintiffs in the *Rancho Viejo* case challenging ESA implementation of Commerce Clause grounds, were proposed alternative options for construction that, as described by the D.C. Appeals Court, appeared fairly minimal,[97] yet litigation resulted. Economic explanations alone cannot explain all litigious challenges, although the payoffs can be high, as can the costs of compliance.

Interviews with agency personnel indicate a suspicion on behalf of at least some interviewees that the intervention of interest groups is a key component in regulatory takings litigation. At least one story was told of high levels of agency participation with an applicant, participation that should be characterized as service oriented, only to result in a regulatory takings challenge. The suspicion was, on the part of the subject, that it was the intervention of a public interest, property rights law firm that convinced the applicant to sue.

Efforts on the part of litigation-based interest groups go beyond seeking justice for particular individuals and, as such, are less hampered by economic disincentives and less motivated by paths of least resistance; the ultimate goal is a shift in policy. This goal can be achieved by raising public interest in an issue, and shifting how such issues are viewed. The *TVA* decision has already demonstrated that ESA could be susceptible to changes in public attitude, given not only the Congressional reaction to the decision, but also a subsequent concern from the public that ESA was overly restrictive on economic development.[98] While interviews may indicate that ESA may already shape the expectations of property developers, such expectations can be altered, and the high profile nature of ESA may make the use of litigation against the act an effective tool to mobilize property rights.

In this regard, the social mobilization of property rights via regulatory takings litigation against ESA implementation may chill regulatory outputs, not by altering the attention individual regulators give to property rights, but by altering the legislation through which regulators define their roles. While legislative change is dependent on a number of circumstances, ESA has already proven itself to be a popular target for reform. In 2005, during efforts to pass H.R. 3824, The Threatened and Endangered Species Recovery Act, which sought to require payment of compensation to property owners for value lost due to endangered species protection, property rights litigation figured prominently in legislative discussions. During debate on the House floor the supporters of the bill referenced *Kelo* as a decision consistent with the abuses of power under King George[99] and applauded Congressional efforts "to stop the government from being able to use eminent [domain] to take away somebody's house and give it to somebody else."[100] These sorts of decisions, decisions that experience a public life in the way that *Tulare* did not, have the potential to shift public attitudes and expectations regarding the relationship between property rights and public interest regulations, and possibly spur legislative adjustments toward those attitudes.

NOTES

[1] 16 U.S.C. § 1531(b) (2000).
[2] *Id.* § 1531(a)(3).
[3] *Id.* § 1531(a)(1).
[4] *Id.* § 1533(a)(1).
[5] *Id.* § 1533(a)(3).
[6] *Id.* § 1533(b)(3).
[7] *Id.* § 1533(b)(2).
[8] *Id.* § 1533(b)(1).
[9] *Id.* § 1534(a)(2).
[10] *Id.* § 1536(a)(2).
[11] *Id.* § 1538(a)(1)(A, E-F).
[12] *Id.* § 1538(a)(1)(B-C).
[13] *Id.* § 1539(a)(1)(B).
[14] *Id.* § 1539(a)(2)(A-B).
[15] Comments of Rep. Aderholt (R-AL). *Congressional Record*, September 29, 2005. pp. H8546-H8584.
[16] Comments of Rep. Holt (D-NJ). *Congressional Record*, September 29, 2005. pp. H8546-H8584.
[17] See Comments of Rep. Graves (R-MO). *Congressional Record*, September 29, 2005. pp. H8546-H8584.
[18] http://www.govtrack.us/congress/bill.xpd?bill=h109-3824
[19] See Goble, DD and Freyfogle, ET. 2002. *Wildlife Law*. New York: Foundation Press. p. 1316.
[20] *Id.*
[21] Kostyack, J. 2001. "*NWF v. Babbitt*: Victory for Smart Growth and Imperiled Wildlife," 31 Envtl. L. Rep. 10712. See also Goble, at 19.
[22] *Nebraska v. Rural Electrification Admin.*, 12 Env't Rep. Cas (BNA) 1156 (1978); Goble, at 1312.
[23] 16 U.S.C. § 1540(g) (2000).
[24] Kostyack; See also *Friends of Endangered Species v. Jantzen*, 760 F.2d 976 (1985); *Sierra Club v. Babbitt*, 15 F.Supp.2d 1274 (1998); *Loggerhead Turtle v. County Council of Volusia County, Florida*, 120 F.Supp.2d 1005 (2000); *National Wildlife Federation v. Babbitt*, 128 F.Supp.2d 1274 (2000)
[25] See, e.g., *Center for Biological Diversity v. Norton*, 254 F.3d 833 (2001); *Defenders of Wildlife v. Norton*, 258 F.3d 1136 (2001); See Goble, at 1184-1205 for a more exhaustive list.
[26] See, e.g., *Catron County Board of Commissioners v. U.S. Fish and Wildlife Service,* 75 F.3d 1429 (1996); *New Mexico Cattle Growers Association v. U.S. Fish and Wildlife Service*, 248 F.3d 1277 (2001); See Goble, at 1205-1216 for a more exhaustive list.

[27] See, e.g., *Thomas v. Peterson*, 753 F.2d 754 (1985); *Defenders of Wildlife v. Babbitt*, 130 F.Supp.2d 121 (2001); See Goble, at 1216-1251 for a more exhaustive list.
[28] Innes, R, et al. 1998. *Takings, Compensation and Endangered Species Protection on Private Lands*, 12 J.Econ. Persp. 35, 52.
[29] *National Wildlife Federation v. Babbitt*, 128 F.Supp.2d 1274, 1279-1280 (2000)
[30] De Tocqueville, A. 1956. *Democracy in America*. Richard D. Heffner, ed. Penguin Books. p. 73.
[31] *TVA v. Hill*, 437 U.S. 153 (1978)
[32] *Id.*, at 187.
[33] *Id.*, at 163-167.
[34] Dwyer, L, et al. 1995. "Property Rights Case Law and the Challenge to the Endangered Species Act." *Conservation Biology*. Vol. 9. p. 728
[35] Peterson, S. 2002. *Acting for Endangered Species: The Statutory Ark*. Lawrence: University Press of Kansas. pp. 63-64.
[36] *Id.*, at 65-68.
[37] *Babbitt v. Sweet Home Chapter of Community for a Great Oregon*, 515 U.S. 687 (1995).
[38] 16 U.S.C. § 1532(19) (2000).
[39] *Sweet Home*, at 691.
[40] *Id.*, at 691-692.
[41] *Id.*, at 695.
[42] *Id.*, at 698.
[43] *Id.*; 16 U.S.C. § 1531(b) (2000).
[44] *Id.*, at 698-699.
[45] 514 U.S. 549 (1995).
[46] 529 U.S. 598 (2000).
[47] *Id.*, at 608; see also *U.S. v. Lopez*, 514 U.S. 549, 556 (1995).
[48] *Solid Waste Agency of Northern Cook County v. Army Corps of Engineers*, 531 U.S. 159, 173 (2001)
[49] *Id.*, at 172.
[50] *National Ass'n of Home Builders v. Babbitt*, 130 F.3d 1041 (D.C. Cir. 1997); *Gibbs v. Babbitt*, 214 F.3d 483 (4th Cir. 2000); *Rancho Viejo v. Norton*, 323 F.3d 1062 (D.C. Cir. 2003); *GDF Realty Investments, Ltd. v. Norton*, 236 F.3d 622 (5th Cir. 2003). See Botello-Samson, D. 2006. "You Say Takings, and I Say Takings: The History and Potential of Regulatory Takings Challenges to the Endangered Species Act." 16 Duke Env. L. & Pol'y Forum 293, 301-309.
[51] *Lopez*, at 561-562.
[52] *National Ass'n of Home Builders*, *supra* note 54 at 1054; *Gibbs*, at 492; *Rancho Viejo*, at 1069-1070.
[53] *Gibbs*, at 492; *GDF Realty*, at 637-638.

[54] *GDF Realty*, at 640; See also Van Loh, SD. 2004. "The Latest and Greatest Commerce Clause Challenges to the Endangered Species Act: *Rancho Viejo* and *GDF Realty*," 31 Ecology L.Q. 459.
[55] Botello-Samson (2006), at 320-325.
[56] *Christy v. Hodel,* 857 F.2d 1324, 1330 (1988); see also *Mountain States Legal Foundation v. Hodel*, 799 F.2d 1423 (1986).
[57] Babbit, B. 1994. "ESA and Private Property: The Endangered Species Act and 'Takings': A Call for Innovation Within the Terms of the Act," 24 Envtl. L. 355, 360. (Former Secretary of the Interior Bruce Babbitt, reacting to allegations of "egregious abuse" under ESA, expressed some surprise that as of 1994 "there has not been a single case filed in that [Federal Claims] court alleging a taking under the ESA.")
[58] *Tulare Lake Basin Water District v. United States*, 49 Fed. Cl. 313 (2001)
[59] *Id.*, at 314-315.
[60] *Id.*, at 315.
[61] *Id.*, at 316.
[62] Brief of the Natural Heritage Institute & the Environmental Law Foundation as Amici Curiae Supporting Defendants at 31, *Tulare Lake*, 49 Fed. Cl. 313 (No. 98-101L)
[63] *Tulare*, at 316-317.
[64] *Id.*, at 319.
[65] *Id.* (emphasis added)
[66] *Armstrong v. United States*, 364 U.S. 40, 49 (1960).
[67] *Tulare*, at 319.
[68] *Loretto v. Teleprompter Manhattan CATV Corp.*, 458 U.S. 419 (1982).
[69] 67 Fed. Cl. 504, 508 (2005).
[70] 543 F.3d 1276, 1296 (2008).
[71] *Id.*
[72] *Williamson County Planning Comm'n v. Hamilton Bank*, 473 U.S. 172 (1985).
[73] *Seiber v. United States*, 53 Fed. Cl. 570, 575 (2002).
[74] *Morris v. United States*, 392 F.3d 1372, 1377 (2004).
[75] *Boise Cascade Corporation v. United States*, 296 F.3d 1339, 1346 (2002); *United States v. Riverside Bayview Homes*, 474 U.S. 121, 126 (1985).
[76] *Seiber*, at 579.
[77] *Aloisi v. United States*, 85 Fed. Cl. 84 (2008).
[78] *Tulare*, at 319.
[79] *Casitas*, at 1296.
[80] *Seiber*, at 577.
[81] *Boise Cascade*, at 1353.

[82] *Id.*; *Seiber*, at 576.
[83] *Boise Cascade*, at 1354.
[84] *Seiber*, at 576.
[85] *Schooner Harbor Ventures v. United States*, 569 F.3d 1359 (2009).
[86] *Id.*, at 1360-1361.
[87] *Id.*, at 1363.
[88] *Id.*
[89] *Id.*, at 1366.
[90] 16 U.S.C. § 1534(a)(2) (2000).
[91] See Sax, JL. 1999. *Playing Darts with a Rembrandt: Public and Private Rights in Cultural Treasures.* Ann Arbor: University of Michigan Press.
[92] *Aloisi.*
[93] *Seiber.*
[94] *Morris.*
[95] United States Fish and Wildlife Service. Conservation Plans and Agreements Database.
[96] Rossi, J. 2005. *Regulatory Bargaining and Public Law.* New York: Cambridge University Press. pp. 12-13.
[97] *Rancho Viejo*, at 1065.
[98] Peterson, S., at 60; See also Kellert, SR. 1996. *The Value of Life: Biological Diversity and Human Society*, Washington, D.C.: Island Press. pp. 164-166. (discussing public opinion survey results on attitudes toward the values of lesser known endangered species and hydroelectric power).
[99] Comments of Rep. Gohmert (R-TX). *Congressional Record*, September 29, 2005. pp. H8546-H8584.
[100] Comments of Rep. Pombo (R-CA). *Congressional Record*, September 29, 2005. pp. H8546-H8584.

CHAPTER 7

Conclusion

Throughout the chapters in this book, regulatory takings litigation and the possibility of a chilling effect on policy outputs were considered through theoretical, legal, quantitative, and qualitative approaches. This approach was taken under the assumption that, by avoiding a reliance on a single research approach, a wider array of significant factors present with the legal phenomenon of regulatory takings litigation could be considered and portrayed in the most robust manner possible. This final chapter reviews the conclusions derived from these inquiries through each of these approaches by highlighting and reviewing the various institutions within the regulatory environment surrounding regulatory takings litigation which can affect the likelihood or possibility of a chilling effect in regulatory output by shifting and shaping the reasonable expectations of property use held by actors involved in the process.

THEORETICAL ANALYSIS

The primary account of a chilling effect caused by takings litigation rests on the assumptions central to the law and economics school of thought. Beginning from the assumption that "(t)he influence of legal rules on behavior is mediated through the rational calculations of agents seeking to maximize their preferences,"[1] a chilling effect is predicted as a result of regulatory takings litigation due to the manner in which such litigation shapes the economic calculations of a potentially affected regulator. In this situation, a regulatory actor is governed by the dictates of a statute to which he or she is beholden and the threat of having such obedience be more costly than originally anticipated. "When public officials face resource constraints and cannot meet *all* their legal obligations, or when their legal obligations are ambiguous or otherwise unclear..., they act to maximize social welfare."[2] In the case of a key regulatory actor, social welfare maximization involves a reduction in overall regulatory output to reserve resources for instances and issues that most legitimate the increased costs.

Undoubtedly, this sequence of events is within the realm of possibility, and the purpose of the preceding chapters is not to deny that a particular agency may confine its regulatory reach in reaction to past or predicted future litigation. However, a conclusion has been drawn that the potential of regulatory takings litigation to form an overarching impediment to environmental regulatory regimes, the concern of environmentalists and the hope of active pursuers of insulated property rights, is unlikely. While much of that conclusion has been drawn in the context of specific observations made on two particular environmental regulatory programs, implications also exist for the theoretical foundations of chilling effect prediction. Specifically, the economic framework on which such predictions rest fails to fully understand regulatory takings litigation.

By utilizing an individual level of analysis which has resource maximization efficiency as its primary motivator, the classical story of the takings chilling effect assumes that individuals will be situated within a regulatory environment in a manner conducive to behavior consistent with observations of a chilling effect. However, observations of regulatory behavior indicate that such motivators of action, while present, are surrounded by institutional constraints which reduce their significance in the final analysis. These empirical observations demonstrate the inability of economic models to fully articulate the manner in which takings litigation functions within a regulatory environment. While the observations do not disprove the possibility of instances of key regulatory personnel assessing the likelihood and potential costs of takings litigation and, therefore, reducing the strength or frequency of regulations, these observations do indicate that several institutional structures obstruct against such considerations.

This conclusion not only demonstrates the problem of so many predictions about the effects of regulatory takings litigation based upon law and economics assumptions, but it also draws into question the jurisprudence at the heart of those analyses. At the heart of the law and economics school of thought are normative and descriptive concepts of the law as fundamentally guided by intrinsic notions of economic efficiency.[3] In other words, chilling effect predictions based on economic legal thought see the law of regulatory takings as doing nothing more than reflecting calculations of cost minimization[4] and Rawlsian utility maximization.[5] If this is one's understanding of the law of takings, then the leap to economic predictability in the effects of takings litigation is not far. However, by looking more closely at the development of the law of takings, one sees not a rigid calculus but a pluralistic shifting of legal values and foci. The inherent flux of takings law is problematic for economic analyses, as unpredictability makes cost-minimizing activity less likely. This makes the status of the law itself, and the legal values brought into it by judges, an important factor in understanding takings, as the impact of regulatory takings law is going to be more of a product of the status of the law and less about economic calculations. At this point, the theoretical implications being discussed bleed into legal discussions. The two may be difficult to parse apart; therefore, while the analysis of the theoretical implications is incomplete, it is necessary at this point to discuss the law itself.

LEGAL ANALYSIS

A key conclusion here is that the law itself does matter; the status of takings law, as interpreted by the courts, can affect the manner in which actors behave in a regulatory environment. This statement not only makes economic predictors of post-litigation regulatory strategies less reliable, but it is also antithetical to economic foundations of the law as based on unwavering calculi. Caution must be exercised, however, when rejecting economic understandings of takings law that one does not adopt a purely legalistic interpretation. A growing consensus is developing with the legal field that the sporadic, ad hoc nature of takings law did exist, but those questions have been asked and answered and that regulatory takings as a component of the law is essentially dead.[6] While a review of regulatory takings jurisprudence does reveal that governmental incursions into private property for the public good enjoy significant insulation from compensation, and the courts' rules for determining the balance between permissible and impermissible governmental intrusion are significantly clearer,[7] the pluralistic nature of takings law provides avenues of change to the law, allowing for alterations to the law and, at least, the possibility of a chilling effect caused by the law.

In Chapter Three, the lens of legal pluralism was used to shed light on the doctrine of regulatory takings, a doctrine frequently described through recitation of the Supreme Court's own description in *Penn Central* as ad hoc[8] and, therefore, unpredictable. An analysis of the doctrine in the prior chapter demonstrated that, while the Court has indeed issued rulings at seeming odds with other rulings, a series of key factors/questions are discernable, and provide a general framework for approaching such questions. Generally, the Court has approached regulatory takings cases with an eye toward alleged takings that involve physical appropriation of property,[9] governmental efforts to regulate nuisances,[10] and alleged takings that remove all economic use,[11] in that order. When each of those questions is answered in the negative, then the Court proceeds to a *Penn Central* analysis. Previous chapters also demonstrated consistency in the application of rules on issues that arise with *Penn Central* analyses, such as ripeness and relevant parcel questions. The end result is that governmental efforts at nuisance prevention, such as in the area of environmental regulation, enjoy a strong rate of success against takings challenges.[12]

The development of the regulatory takings doctrine has followed the hand played by Holmes in *Pennsylvania Coal*. Confronted by a constitutional restriction on governmental regulatory authority and a common law nuisance tradition restricting use and enjoyment of private property, Holmes utilized a balancing test, acknowledging "that while property may be regulated to a certain extent, if regulation goes too far it will be recognized as a taking."[13] It is the omnipresence of balancing within takings jurisprudence, i.e. the presence of conflicting constitutional and common law traditions, which makes legal pluralism a useful analytic tool. Instead of searching for a perfect balance between divergent sources of law and conflicting values, legal pluralism highlights their hermeneutic and evolutionary relationship.

The problem that legal pluralism poses for both economic and legalistic explanations of regulatory takings is that the law and/or the meaning of the law changes over time and such change is frequently the result of something external to the law. As contexts, histories, perceptions, and environments change, the meaning of terms within the law change with them. Key to regulatory takings jurisprudence is the reasonableness of use expectations held by the property owner absent and under regulation, a central component of the Court's *Penn Central* test.[14] Empirical observations indicated that the expectations of property owners, and the regulators' perceptions of the reasonableness of those expectations, are susceptible to change and such changes can affect the state of the law and regulations.

In particular, the qualitative interviews conducted illuminated various institutional factors which, in general, operate to make a chilling effect less likely. Most of these factors are external to the law. These non-legal institutions operate by shaping what expectations for property use key actors in a regulatory takings dispute find to be reasonable. Additionally, there is nothing to prevent the law itself from also playing a participating role in such expectation shaping. A key feature that cannot be forgotten, though, is that none of these institutions are necessarily static. While observations of regulatory behavior and legal decisions may indicate a strong preference for the non-compensatory status of environmental regulation, making that observation through the lens of legal pluralism allows one to see that preference but also allows one to anticipate and/or explain change. Although the observations detailed in the previous chapters indicate a strong institutional resistance to takings litigation induced chilling effects, those institutions are, at least potentially, susceptible to incursion by forces of change, including the law itself.

The remainder of this concluding chapter discusses that regulatory resistance to the takings litigation chilling effect. This discussion will focus on the factors unveiled by empirical observation which, at least in the current context, make a broad chilling effect unlikely. Furthermore, this chapter will conclude with a consideration of the ways in which the law itself, while currently a factor in resisting a chilling effect, can play a role in overcoming those current institutional impediments.

QUANTITATIVE ANALYSIS

Beginning from the position of legal pluralism, with its emphasis on shifting between opposing values, one should expect changes in regulatory behavior brought about by litigation to occur over time and at the edges. After all, an impact caused by litigation that reshapes the ways in which actors think about and perceive the problem itself is less likely to be as immediate and obvious as a case which, more simply and clearly, alters the agreed upon rules of behavior. Therefore, analyses of such changes will generally be thickly descriptive and reliant upon historical, cultural, and psychological dimensions and less on rigid numeric indicators which may have difficulty elucidating such complex phenomena. However, the numbers are a good place to start. The complexity of the regulatory environment, especially in its interactions with the legal world, may make quantification difficult and even counterproductive, and the absence of quantifiable observations of a chilling effect may not be sufficient to rule such an effect as nonexistent. The presence of significant statistical evidence of such an effect, however, should certainly not be ignored if present. Such evidence validates and directs needed qualitative research and may indicate situations in which the institutional relations within a regulatory environment are so specifically ordered and understood that the presence or absence of a chilling effect, in that situation, can be verified, and lessons learned can be applied to more slippery situations. While shifts in meanings and contexts are the impact ultimately pursued, the possibility of more immediately observable changes in rules, procedures, and outputs should not be ignored.

In Chapters Five and Six, interrupted cross-sectional time-series quasi-experiments were conducted on the regulatory outputs of Fish and Wildlife Service implementation of the Habitat Conservation Plan component of the Endangered Species Act (ESA) and the Surface Mining Control and Reclamation Act (SMCRA) permitting activities of the federal Office of Surface Mining and authorized state coal mining regulatory agencies. Unfortunately, the results of these analyses were inconclusive due to concerns over significance brought about by issues of stationarity and correlated variance. Nonetheless, some observations are worth highlighting.

For both regulatory programs, the baselines of regulatory output, i.e. the identification of independent variables other than takings litigation that affect regulatory behavior, were similar. Both baselines are the product of budgetary resource and regional elements. Implementation of ESA was a function of personnel resources (full time employees) and the federal budgetary allotment, controlling for the unique regulatory environment of the California-Nevada region. Implementation of SMCRA was a function of the availability of federal funds, coal productivity, and the unique coal mining aspects of Wyoming and the Appalachian region.

Beyond these baseline similarities, however, the data go in two different directions for the two programs. Once the litigation variable was entered into the ESA analysis, explanatory power diminished. Across different measures of regulatory output, the inclusion of the *Tulare* decision resulted in low R^2 scores for the models. In fact, the strongest explanatory power was reached when the *Tulare* variable was omitted and the number of species protected by HCPs was measured. In that instance, the independent variable of the administration's political party became significant. One possible explanation for the weak predictive ability of the takings variable under ESA is the short period of time after the decision available for observation.

More promising results were found in the analysis of SMCRA implementation. A more robust set of significant explanatory variables, such as mining efficiency and coal prices, were discovered with the inclusion of takings variables, which were themselves more numerous than in the ESA data, and the explanatory power of the models as a whole was high. In general, the presence of a judicial precedent finding a compensable taking for SMCRA implementation within that office's jurisdiction, i.e. a state court ruling in that state or an across-the-board federal ruling, was correlated with an increase in the number of surface coal mining permits issued. That relationship was stronger in the Appalachian region, a region characterized by the presence of numerous small mines. While the SMCRA results were more definitive than the ESA results, caution must still be exercised in acceptance of the data, as issues of stationarity, serial correlation, and panel heteroskedasticity were present in both analyses.

QUALITATIVE ANALYSIS

Despite the inconclusive nature of the quantifiable observations made in this research, conclusions can be drawn regarding the potential for a chilling effect caused by regulatory takings litigation. The starting point is that the conditions of takings litigation is best described as legally pluralistic, as a dialectic and hermeneutic product of constitutionalism and the common law, of rules and standards. Therefore, the significant changes that occur within takings litigation, and the surrounding regulatory environment, are changes in the meanings and contexts of the expectations of property usage. Such shifts can be quite difficult to measure over time, but it is feasible to develop an understanding of the institutions in which such meanings develop and, thereby, understand the potential that exists for change and the existence of obstacles against such change. As described earlier, interviews were conducted with key regulatory personnel in the federal offices of the Fish and Wildlife Service and the Office of Surface Mining, as well as within state regulatory offices authorized to implement SMCRA. While the results of those interviews are detailed in previous chapters, this chapter can serve to highlight some general observations. These observations focus on the presence of institutional structures which confine regulatory decision-making, structures which, if a chilling effect is going to occur, would have to be overcome by takings litigation.

Centralization of Decision-Making

The idea of a chilling effect caused by regulatory takings litigation assumes a rational and economic actor, relatively aware of his/her options and the consequences of his/her actions. Such assumptions may be permissible if the regulatory body is a small town zoning board or a body of similar scale, but at the level of federal regulation, such assumptions are risky. Both sets of interviews revealed a decision-making process characterized by a high level of decentralization and bureaucratization, both internally and externally. Internally, permitting decisions were rarely, if ever, the product of a single individual. While final decisions were disproportionately affected by a single individual, in the form of a director, those decisions were the product of information obtained and developed through various compartmentalized segments of the regulatory office. A key compartment of this internal decentralization of knowledge is the office of legal counsel. General observations indicated that, while key decision-makers within regulatory offices knew of takings cases related to their field, few were willing to claim sufficient knowledge of the cases without consulting legal counsel. While such avenues for discussion are frequently open, providing an avenue of knowledge of takings cases, a prerequisite for a chilling effect, the voice of legal counsel is one voice among many. In particular, the scientific voices outnumbered the legal voices, as both observed programs' permitting processes involved information gathering from multiple scientific disciplines. Generally speaking, environmental regulatory regimes are characterized by a high level of decision-making compartmentalization, which acts as an obstacle to takings litigation forging a chilling effect within such offices.

Externally, such compartmentalization of knowledge is compounded. Just as permitting decisions are very seldom the product of single decision-makers within an agency, such decisions are also, very seldom, the product of a single agency. The two studied regulatory programs, HCP permitting under ESA and surface mining permitting under SMCRA, provide strong examples of this characteristic. Both permitting programs generally require compliance with other applicable environmental and public interest regulations as a condition of permitting. A SMCRA permit, for example, can be interpreted as a sign of compliance, at least in the planning and design stage, with such laws as the Clean Water Act, the Archeological Resources Protection Act, and ESA. The end result is that permitting decisions are just as much a product of other agency decisions as the particular agency charged with implementation.

The presence of decentralization and compartmentalization of decision-making with environmental regulatory agencies is a key factor in explaining whether a chilling effect could be caused by regulatory takings litigation. The assumption of such an effect presumes a decision-making environment in which key actors can make the economic calculations that are necessitated by reductions in regulatory output for the purpose of cost avoidance. The presence of decision-making fragmentation, among personnel within agencies and between agencies themselves, is not conducive to that sort of economic decision-making environment. Individual decision-makers are likely to view the possibilities of regulatory chilling as outside their decision-making capabilities. Key decision-makers are likely to view compliance with a "takings precedent" as one factor among many for their consideration, and possess the ability to "pass the buck" of such responsibility onto other agencies or departments.

Agency Culture

The above-described fragmentation of environmental regulatory decision-making is related to another aspect of regulation that can work to hinder the ability of takings litigation to cool regulatory outputs, namely, an agency culture which may need to be overcome if a chilling effect is to come to fruition. The two are related because the compartmentalization and decentralization of regulatory decision-making produces a ritualization of responsibilities within agencies. When regulators must choose between the options of strong enactment of regulatory responsibilities and the compensatory dictates of a court, a mechanism of rationalization can be the definition of one's role as a responsibility toward one of those two options. In the case of fragmentation, that rationalization is more easily accomplished, as tasks and roles are defined specifically, and the responsibility to property owners created by takings litigation may likely be perceived as being someone else's responsibility.

While explanatory references to culture may be easy to elide, the impacts of a culture within the observed agencies was discernable. It is important to remember that the presence of a culture within an agency can be explained. As agencies have found themselves, historically, in an increasing number of conflicts with the judicial system, the developed path of least resistance has become an evasion from such conflict through a satisfaction of the courts' concerns; agencies have learned they can justify behavior through adherence to the relevant statute.[15] Observed within the agencies is an enforcement culture, paraphrased by the statement, "If I stick to the statute, I'm doing my job." Litigious pressure under takings law is confronted by litigious pressure from cases of statutory interpretation.

The end result of an agency culture of enforcement is that regulatory decision-makers tend to define their roles and tasks through compliance with statutory requirements, not judicial precedent, especially when courts have historically been satisfied by adherence to the letter of the statute. Both the demands of the statute authorizing environmental regulation and the decisions of courts placing compensatory requirements on the implementation of such statutes impose responsibilities on regulators under the law; however, when such demands conflict, the discretion of regulatory personnel come into play. The demands of a statute are clear. The statute forms the very *raison d'être* of an agency. As the purpose of the agency is so intertwined with the letter of the statute, its content, definitions, meanings, applications, etc. are generally well understood. Court rulings on regulatory takings lack this certainty, giving the agency personnel ample opportunities to rationalize adherence to the statute, even at the risk of defying takings precedent. While the court decision may be clear to the parties directly involved, similarly situated agencies can always argue that the facts of a particular case were unique. Whether regulatory personnel see takings law as not specifically applied to their actions or as a secondary concern outweighed by the more pressing demands of statutory compliance, the resulting lesson is clear: for regulatory takings litigation to have a chilling effect on regulatory output, the litigious pressure must overcome an agency culture of enforcement that directs personnel to statutory compliance, regardless of threats of compensation.

Time and Relationships

The interviews revealed that the likelihood of a chilling of regulatory output caused by takings litigation is shaped by more than just the characteristics of agencies; external factors also shape the regulatory landscape and agency reactions to litigation. Various factors, all relating more to the nature of the specific regulatory program than the agencies, were identified by insiders as affecting that office's reaction to takings pressure. The unique histories of SMCRA and ESA each are important points for understanding how they react to the pressures of takings litigation, and understanding the effect of such litigation necessitates a specification of the environmental program potentially affect. This section details a few general categories of external factors that will likely shape a regulatory program's reaction to takings litigation.

A factor clearly beyond the control of decision-makers within agencies, but one which was nearly omnipresent in the interview responses, was the simple factor of time. Interview respondents charged with the implementation of SMCRA, in particular, universally referred to the manner in which time has changed the relationship between regulators and the regulated, thus shaping the manner in which the agency would react to takings litigation. Many time-based factors are only tangentially related to time. Consider, for example, the previous discussion on SMCRA and takings litigation. Factors such as the price of coal and changes in mining technology or coal availability affect the desire of particular mining operations to access particular coal resources, thus affecting the likelihood that any individual operation will pursue litigation in reaction to inaccessible property in coal. These factors are understood as changing over time, yet they are not, specifically, time-based factors. Nevertheless, they serve as reminders of another important lesson: the ability of regulatory takings litigation to overcome the obstacles in the way of the creation of a chilling effect is going to be, at least partially, contingent upon temporal circumstances.

This lesson is made clearer when the concept of time is considered on its own. Beyond the exogenous variables identified by respondents, variables which are understood in terms of time, interview respondents also identified time itself as a factor affecting their reactions to takings litigation. Generally, respondents appeared to be claiming that, as time goes on, takings litigation becomes less likely. If litigation is less likely, then a chilling effect is also less likely for two reasons. First, an agency is simply less likely to find itself the subject of takings litigation and, second, takings litigation is seen as a less realistic threat on the status quo ability of agencies to perform necessary duties.

Such explanations almost seem to embody takings litigation and agency actions with an organic nature, a nature which evolves and changes in a predictable manner through the explanation of no other factor than time. Such claims come with risks, and it is highly unlikely that conceptualizing regulatory and litigious behavior in this manner will result in fruitful and valid conclusions. After all, one of the conclusions of this research, discussed below, is that the obstacles to a chilling effect, including the time-based ones, can be overcome; despite the fact that ESA predates SMCRA and takings challenges against ESA were non-existent for the vast majority of the statute's history, ESA is positioned in a manner that makes it more susceptible to a future chilling effect, which is discussed in the next two sections.

Interviewees indicating that time has shaped their agency's reaction to takings litigation against their implementation of SMCRA were able to detail events and changes that indicate that time must still be considered an important factor in understanding takings litigation and agency reaction. Responses about agency/miner relations in the early years of SMCRA focused on the hesitance on the part of mining operations to be regulated on issues over which they had not been regulated in the past. As time passed, mining operations saw SMCRA compliance, more and more, as a "part of doing business." Regulators indicated that, as time passed, mine operators became more receptive to prescribed changes, became more inquisitive and assistance-seeking during mine planning, and took measures during the planning stages to avoid conflicts with SMCRA. This behavior indicates a shift in what has been described above as the expectations of property use. The rationality of these expectations is shaped by, among other things the presence of statutes and regulations proscribing and/or qualifying certain property uses. The more a particular statute, and its corresponding regulatory regime(s), become part of the accepted set of norms governing property use, the less likely enactment of that statute will violate the reasonable expectations of property use held by the owner. It is reasonable to expect that such expectations will be more in tune with the statute when that statute is well established than when the statute is freshly enacted after a contentious adoption process.

Popularity

While a long standing statute may enjoy more recognition as a legitimate limitation on reasonable property expectations than a freshly legislated statute, that relationship is certainly not a product of a deterministic evolution. The reason time functions as an obstacle to a chilling effect caused by takings litigation is that it allows for the public's expectations of property use to be shaped by the presence of the enabling statute and the corresponding regulatory regime. Other factors exist that can affect the ability of environmental regulations on property use to alter such expectations. The manner in which an environmental law alters property expectations, and the degree to which it does so, may make significant acceptance of shifts in expectation more immediate or more prolonged. Ultimately, the popularity of the regulatory program may have more impact on the ability of takings litigation to chill regulatory outputs than basic economic calculations of costs and benefits.

The manner in which statutory popularity can be a result of the nature of the statute and the nature of the regulated entity is demonstrated by a comparison between ESA and SMCRA. ESA is a far more well-known regulatory program. Its scope is broad, potentially bringing everyone from multi-million dollar developments to small individual home improvements under its reach. SMCRA is far more innocuous in that regard, regulating only one specific entity. Conflicts arising under ESA, which may reach the level of takings litigation, are frequently characterized as burdening single individuals for a public benefit, which may not be regarded as important by the public in the first place. SMCRA conflicts, on the other hand, frequently involve more immediately recognizable costs, such as threats to public safety. Of most immediate concern to the present discussion, those threats are frequently to values more easily conceptualized as property. In other words, while ESA conflicts frequently pit private property interests against the public interests in biodiversity, SMCRA conflicts pit one individual's access to resource property against another individual or community's resource property. Restrictions on coal mining under SMCRA are more immediately in tune with commonly held American perceptions of property rights and their limitations. Restrictions imposed by ESA more fundamentally redesign and challenge commonly held beliefs, and do so in a more conspicuous manner than SMCRA restrictions.

Subsequent considerations of the potential for a chilling effect caused by takings litigation must ask the same type of question raised by this comparison between ESA and SMCRA. Inquiries into the potential for a chilling effect cannot be made generally; they must be made with an awareness of the type of regulation being challenged. Some regulations fundamentally challenge commonly held notions of legitimate property use while some regulations work to strengthen such perceptions. As courts continue to use the reasonableness of use expectations in their takings analyses, the answer to this question will likely affect the immediate outcome of particular regulatory takings cases. Additionally, the ability of such litigation to affect similarly situated regulatory entities also hinges on the degree to which takings rulings reify the declarations of legitimate uses of and restrictions on property made by various regulations.

Statutory and Judicial History

It has been argued, to this point, that the basic economic analysis of takings litigation, and its conclusion that significant litigation of this nature against executive agencies implementing environmental regulations can produce a chilling effect on regulatory outputs, misses fundamental points of analysis that highlight factors which can mitigate such an effect. Elements of decision-making processes common in regulatory institutions, for example, may prevent any one individual or office from conducting the cost/benefit analysis central to such predictions. An effective chilling effect must do more than impose additional costs on regulation; it must overcome the contexts of meaning that define reasonable property use expectations found in such institutions as an agency's enforcement culture, the regulated entities general business practices, and public perceptions of legitimate property use and restriction. "Popular" regulatory programs reify commonly held perceptions of property; structures exist within agencies that allow regulators to continue adherence to statutory requirements even in the face of potential compensatory costs. This final section considers what factors may indicate a popular, and therefore, chilling effect resistant, regulatory program and, in the process, analyzes manners in which takings litigation can be a part of a process of changing public and regulatory perceptions of reasonable property expectations, thus creating a chilling effect.

It was observed, above, that long standing statutes form their own legitimization through time by becoming a component of the "cost of doing business." While this observation was most prevalent in interviews conducted with regulators implementing SMCRA, it was not foreign to ESA interviews. Any entity that has a history of interaction with land use agencies is generally nominally familiar with endangered species protection requirements. Furthermore, as with SMCRA, some ESA implementing personnel indicated that more institutionalized and corporatized entities were generally better equipped and more informed about ESA requirements, which may prepare them to avoid the necessity of even considering a takings challenge by avoiding contestable projects. In both cases, time has worked to shape property use expectations in a manner counter to the claims inherent in regulatory takings cases.

While this similarity in statutory history exists, significant differences exist in their judicial histories, especially under takings law. The history of SMCRA in the courts is riddled with cases involving claims of regulatory takings. Such claims against ESA implementation have been, by contrast, historically rare. One might expect this situation to result in SMCRA implementing decision-makers to be more wary of takings litigation than their ESA counterparts. That is not the case. SMCRA-based takings litigation, while numerous, is generally unsuccessful. While occasional mining operators are successful[16], and SMCRA personnel were well aware of such cases, federal case law almost unanimously justifies SMCRA restrictions on coal mining without compensation.

The judicial history of ESA, in cases involving regulatory takings claims, is different. This history of ESA contains a long initial era absent any regulatory takings litigation against property restrictions enforced under the act. Relatively recently, the first major case litigated under those conditions resulted in a ruling for compensation. After that decision, several more takings suits were filed, and while most of those decisions protected ESA implementation from compensatory claims, this has occurred over a relatively short time span, and the federal judiciary has identified certain conditions which have been interpreted as compensable takings.

Neither regulatory program demonstrated any sort of consideration for the risk of compensation in its decision-making process. Both sets of interviews, upon further pressing, were knowledgeable about takings cases, but did not see such cases as the source of legitimate consideration in the permitting process. With substantially different judicial histories, however, a radical shift in takings decisions would have much less ESA-history to overcome to produce a wider chilling effect than SMCRA-history. Such a radical shift, however, would still need to alter assumptions of reasonable property expectations, embedded in the role perceptions of agency personnel, to create such an impact. The question remains whether litigation can have such an impact. The answer to such a question must move beyond answers based upon economic modeling of decision-making and to political answers that use power to shape the role perceptions of individuals charged with the implementation of environmental laws.

As property rights and small government advocates have not accomplished their larger expectations through takings litigation, they have shifted strategies to the reshaping of legislation.[17] Such a strategy makes sense, given the above observations on the presence of an enforcement culture within executive agencies, which defines executive roles and responsibilities through statutes. Such statutes change the role perception of regulatory personnel by redefining the decision-making process. Statutes may require administrative assessment of property impact along side of general scientific inquiries, they may define dispute resolution procedures favorable to property owners, or they may make compensation a required action for specified regulatory actions.[18] These statutory efforts, while the product of litigious failures, are still connected to litigious activity.

One manner in which litigation serves activist goals is through the circumvention of "barriers to activist government posed by the structures of the Constitution. The Constitution's dispersion of power...makes it difficult for activists to control the implementation of their schemes and easy for enemies to derail them. Courts offer a way around these problems."[19] Statutory efforts to chill environmental regulatory output through procedural or compensatory requirements have been less successful at the federal level than lower levels. A continued litigious strategy may ultimately address the perceived shortcomings of state-based legislative efforts to insulate property rights from responsibilities imposed by environmental laws.

Second, "courts offer activists a way to address social problems without seeming to augment the power of the state."[20] By donning the mantle of legal objectivity and neutrality, takings rulings lend credence and legitimacy to one interpretation of the reasonableness of property use expectations. In this way, advocates of strict, rule-based protections for property rights view judicial decisions for compensation as unveiling a *de facto* proper interpretation of the balance between property rights and responsibilities based upon an underlying calculus within the law, as espoused by advocates of the law and economics school of thought.[21] This activity has potential to act as a strong force shaping the cultural perceptions of the public, regulators, property owners, etc. as to the reasonableness of property use expectations.

However, that type of impact is substantially different from a prediction of a chilling effect caused by takings litigation based upon economic calculations of costs and benefits. The root of such an impact is the manner in which litigation may act to change social and cultural expectations regarding property. The key difference is, that while this explanation does not deny the possibility that general cost increases incurred, or thought to potentially be incurred, by regulatory agencies may reduce regulatory outputs, it recognizes the degree to which perceptions of right and wrong, in terms of property rights and responsibilities, are instilled in the institutions of regulations and the manner in which institutionalized obstacles to a chilling effect are present. By focusing on the potential for judicial rulings to shape the way key decision-makers understand the proper balance between property rights and responsibilities, this explanation focuses on an oft ignored but important avenue for change. Furthermore, while judicial rulings may shape the way we understand property, if a chilling effect is to be caused by such rulings, those rulings, like economic pressure, must overcome the institutional presence of forces within agencies directing their activities toward compliance with the statutory letter of the law.

NOTES

[1] Kornhauser, LA. 2005. "Economic Rationality in the Analysis of Legal Rules and Institutions." *Philosophy of Law and Legal Theory*. Martin P. Golding & William A. Edmundson, eds. Malden: Blackwell Publishing. p. 69.

[2] *Id.*, at 70

[3] Kronman, AT. 1993. *The Last Lawyer: Failing Ideals of the Legal Profession*. Cambridge: The Belknap Press of Harvard University Press. pp. 226-227.

[4] Michelman, F. 1967. "Property, Utility, and Fairness: Comments on the Ethical Foundations of 'Just Compensation' Law." 80 Harv. L.R. 1165, 1215.

[5] *Id.*, at 1220.

[6] Echevarria, JD. 2007. "The Death of Regulatory Takings." 34 Ecology L.Q. 291.
[7] Meltz, R. 2007. "Takings Law Today: A Primer for the Perplexed." 34 Ecology L.Q. 307, 370.
[8] *Penn Central Transportation Co. v. New York City*, 438 U.S. 104, 124 (1978).
[9] *Loretto v. Teleprompter Manhattan CATV Corp.*, 458 U.S. 419 (1982).
[10] *Lucas v. South Carolina Coastal Council*, 505 U.S. 1003, 1030 (1992).
[11] *Id.*, at 1020.
[12] Alexander, GS. 2006. *The Global Debate of Constitutional Property: Lessons for American Takings Jurisprudence*. Chicago: University of Chicago Press. p. 206.
[13] *Pennsylvania Coal v. Mahon*, 260 U.S. 393, 415 (1922).
[14] *Penn Central*, at 124.
[15] Nakamura, RT and Church, TW. 2003. *Taming Regulation: Superfund and the Challenges of Regulatory Reform*. Washington, D.C.: Brookings Institution Press. p. 7.
[16] *R.T.G. v. Ohio*, 98 Ohio St. 3d 1 (Oh S.C. 2002)
[17] Jacobs, HM and Ohm, BW. 1995. "Statutory Takings Legislation: The National Context, the Wisconsin and Minnesota Proposals." 2 Wis. Envtl. L.J. 173.
[18] Sabath, ME. 2004. "The Perils of the Property Rights Initiative: Taking Stock of Nevada County's Measure D." 28 Harvard Envtl. L. Rev. 249, 255.
[19] Burke, TF. 2002. *Lawyers, Litigants, and Legal Rights: The Battle over Litigation in American Society*. Berkeley: University of California Press. p. 7.
[20] *Id.*
[21] Kronman, at 233.

REFERENCES

BOOKS AND ARTICLES

Agrawal, Arun. 2002. "Common Resources and Institutional Sustainability." *The Drama of the Commons*. Ostrom, Elinor, et al., eds. Washington, D.C.: National Academy Press.

Alexander, Gregory S. 2006. *The Global Debate over Constitutional Property: Lessons for American Takings Jurisprudence*. Chicago: University of Chicago Press.

Altman, Andrew. 1990. *Critical Legal Studies: A Liberal Critique*. Princeton: Princeton University Press.

Arizona Secretary of State. "Arizona 2006 Ballot Propositions; General Election, November 7, 2006." p. 178.

Babbit, Bruce. 1994. "ESA and Private Property: The Endangered Species Act and 'Takings': A Call for Innovation Within the Terms of the Act," *Environmental Law*, 24: 355.

Balko, Radley. 2004. "Property Rights Form Foundation of Freedom." *Fox News*, March 25.

Baum, Lawrence. 1998. *The Puzzle of Judicial Behavior*. Ann Arbor: University of Michigan Press.

Bayne, Katherine A. 1993. "*Lucas v. South Carolina Coastal Council*: Drawing a Line in the Sand." *Catholic University Law Review*, 42: 1063.

Beck, Nathaniel, and Jonathan N. Katz. 2004. "Time-Series—Cross-Section Issues: Dynamics, 2004."

Belsky, Martin H. 1994. "The Public Trust Doctrine and Takings: A Post-Lucas View." *Albany Law Journal of Science and Technology*, 4: 17.

Benjamin, James Reginald, Jr. 2002. "The Best of Both Worlds: Use of Common Law and Statutory Law Together in Applying the

Nuisance Exception to Defend a Takings Claim." *Federal Circuit Bar Journal*, 11: 855.
Berger, Lawrence. 1978. "The Public Use Requirement in Eminent Domain." *Oregon Law Review*, 57: 203.
Bickel, Alexander M. 1962. *The Least Dangerous Branch*. New Haven: Yale University Press.
Blackstone, William. 1979. *Commentaries on the Laws of England*, Vol. 1. Chicago: University of Chicago Press.
Bogus, Carl T. 2001. *Why Lawsuits are Good for America: Disciplined Democracy, Big Business, and the Common Law*. New York: New York University Press.
Bone, Robert G. 1986. "Normative Theory and Legal Doctrine in American Nuisance Law: 1850-1920," *Southern California Law Review*, 59: 1101.
Botello-Samson, Darren. 2006. "You Say Takings, and I Say Takings: The History and Potential of Regulatory Takings Challenges to the Endangered Species Act." *Duke Environmental Law and Policy Forum*, 16: 293.
__________. 2008. "The Benchmark of Expectations: Regulatory Takings and Surface Coal Mining." *Journal of Natural Resources and Environmental Law*, 22: 1.
Boudreaux, Karol, and Bruce Yandle. 2002. "Public Bads and Public Nuisance: Common Law Remedies for Environmental Decline." *Fordham Environmental Law Journal*, 14: 55.
Brisbin, Richard A., Jr. 1990. "The Conservatism of Antonin Scalia." *Political Science Quarterly*, Vol. 105, No. 1.
Burke, Thomas F. 2002. *Lawyers, Litigants, and Legal Rights: The Battle over Litigation in American Society*. Berkeley: University of California Press.
Burling, James S. 2002. "Private Property Rights and the Environment After *Palazzolo*." *Boston College Environmental Affairs Law Review*, 30: 1.
Butler, Henry N., and Jonathan R. Macey. 1996. "Externalities and the Matching Principle: The Case for Reallocating Environmental Regulatory Authority." *Yale Journal on Regulation*, 14: 23.
Byrne, J. Peter. 2005. "Can Your Town Take Your Home? Richard A. Epstein and J. Peter Byrne Debate." *Legal Affairs*, Feb. 21.

Cane, Peter. 2004. "Understanding Judicial Review and Its Impact." *Judicial Review and Bureaucratic Impact: International and Interdisciplinary Perspectives*, Marc Hertogh and Simon Halliday, eds. New York: Cambridge University Press.

Canon, Bradley C. 2004. "Studying Bureaucratic Implementation of Judicial Policies in the United States: Conceptual and Methodological Approaches." *Judicial Review and Bureaucratic Impact: International and Interdisciplinary Perspectives*. New York: Cambridge University Press.

Canon, Bradley C. and Charles A. Johnson. 1999. *Judicial Policies: Implementation and Impact*. Washington, D.C.: Congressional Quarterly Inc.

Carter, Leif H. and Burke, Thomas F. 2010. *Reason in Law*, 8th ed. New York: Longman Classics in Political Science.

Clayton, Cornell W. 1999. "The Supreme Court and Political Jurisprudence: New and Old Institutionalisms." *Supreme Court Decision-Making*. Cornell W. Clayton and Howard Gillman, eds. Chicago: University of Chicago Press.

Cole, Daniel H. 2002. *Pollution and Property: Comparing Ownership Institutions for Environmental Protection*. New York: Cambridge University Press.

Comments of Rep. Aderholt (R-AL). *Congressional Record*, September 29, 2005. pp. H8546-H8584.

Comments of Rep. Gohmert (R-TX). *Congressional Record*, September 29, 2005. pp. H8546-H8584.

Comments of Rep. Graves (R-MO). *Congressional Record*, September 29, 2005. pp. H8546-H8584.

Comments of Rep. Holt (D-NJ). *Congressional Record*, September 29, 2005. pp. H8546-H8584.

Comments of Rep. Pombo (R-CA). *Congressional Record*, September 29, 2005. pp. H8546-H8584.

Cook, Thomas D., and Donald T. Campbell. 1979. *Quasi-Experimentation: Design & Analysis for Field Setting*. Boston: Houghton Mifflin Company.

Coursen, David F. 1999. "The Takings Jurisprudence of the Court of Federal Claims and the Federal Circuit." *Environmental Law*, 29: 821.

Davis, Sue. 1986. "Federalism and Property Rights: An Examination of Justice Rehnquist's Legal Positivism." *The Western Political Science Quarterly*. Vol. 39, No. 2.

_________. 1992. "Rehnquist and State Courts: Federalism Revisited." *The Western Political Quarterly*. Vol. 45, No. 3.

De Tocqueville, Alexis. 1956. *Democracy in America*. Richard D. Heffner, ed. Penguin Books.

Dietz, Thomas, et al. 2002. "The Drama of the Commons." *The Drama of the Commons*. Ostrom, Elinor, et al., eds. Washington, D.C.: National Academy Press.

Dowling, Timothy J. 2002. "On History, Takings Jurisprudence, and *Palazzolo*: A Reply to James Burling." *Boston College Environmental Affairs Law Review*, 30: 65.

Dukeminier, Jesse and James E. Krier. 1998. *Property*, 4th ed. Aspen: Aspen Law and Publishers.

Dwyer, Lynn, et al. 1995. "Property Rights Case Law and the Challenge to the Endangered Species Act." *Conservation Biology*. Vol. 9.

Echevarria, John D. 2007. "The Death of Regulatory Takings." *Ecology Law Quarterly*, 34: 291.

Ely, James W., Jr. 1992. *The Guardian of Every Other Right: A Constitutional History of Property Rights*. New York: Oxford University Press.

Ely, John Hart. 1980. "Democracy and Distrust: A Theory of Judicial Review." Cambridge: Harvard University Press.

Engel, Kirsten H., and Scott R. Saleska. 2005. "Subglobal Regulation of the Global Commons: The Case of Climate Change." *Ecology Law Quarterly*, 32: 183.

Epstein, Lee, and Jack Knight. 1998. *The Choices Justices Make*. Washington, D.C.: CQ Press.

_________. 2000. "Toward a Strategic Revolution in Judicial Politics: A Look Back, A Look Ahead." *Political Research Quarterly*. Vol. 53, No. 3. (Sept.)

Epstein, Richard A. 1985. *Takings: Private Property and the Power of Eminent Domain*. Cambridge: Harvard University Press.

_________. 1993. "*Lucas v. South Carolina Coastal Council*: A Tangled Web of Expectations." *Stanford Law Review*, 45: 1369.

_________. 2005. "Can Your Town Take Your Home? Richard A. Epstein and J. Peter Byrne Debate." *Legal Affairs*, Feb. 21.

_________. 2005. "Takings, Commons, and Associations: Why the Telecommunications Act of 1996 Misfired." *Yale Journal on Regulation*, 22: 315.

Fennell, Lee Anne. 2004. "Common Interest Tragedies." *Northwestern University Law Review*, 98: 907.

Fischel, William A. 1995. *Regulatory Takings: Law, Economics, and Politics*. Cambridge: Harvard University Press.

Frank, Jerome. 1963. *Law and the Modern Mind.* Garden City: Doubleday Anchor Books.

Fuller, Chris. 1994. "Legal Anthropology, Legal Pluralism and Legal Thought." *Anthropology Today*. Vol. 10, No. 3, June.

Geertz, Clifford. 1983. *Local Knowledge: Further Essays in Interpretive Anthropology*. New York: Basic Books, Inc.

Gillman, Howard. 1993. *The Constitution Besieged.* Durham: Duke University Press.

_________. 1999. "The Court as an Idea, Not a Building (or a Game): Interpretive Institutionalism and the Analysis of Supreme Court Decision-Making." *Supreme Court Decision-Making.* Chicago: University of Chicago Press.

Gillman, Howard, and Cornell W. Clayton. 1999. "Beyond Judicial Attitudes: Institutional Approaches to Supreme Court Decision-Making." *Supreme Court Decision-Making.* Chicago: University of Chicago Press.

Glendon, Mary Ann. 1991. *Rights Talk: The Impoverishment of Political Discourse*. New York: The Free Press.

Goble, Dale D., and Eric T. Freyfogle. 2002. *Wildlife Law*. New York: Foundation Press.

Guillet, David. 1998. "Rethinking Legal Pluralism: Local Law and State Law in the Evolution of Water Property Rights in Northwestern Spain." *Comparative Studies in Society and History*, Vol. 40, No. 1 (Jan.).

Gujarati, Damodar N. 1995. *Basic Econometrics*, 3rd ed. New York: McGraw-Hill, Inc.

Haffner, Julia C. 1997. "*Suitum v. Tahoe Regional Planning Agency*: The United States Supreme Court Revisits Ripeness in Regulatory Takings Context." *Tulane Environmental Law Journal*, 11: 129.

Haffner, Paul F. 1993. "Regulatory Takings—A New Categorical Rule." *University of Cincinnati Law Review*, 61: 1035.

Haltom, William, and Michael McCann. 2004. *Distorting the Law: Politics, Media, and the Litigation Crisis*. Chicago: University of Chicago Press.

Hardin, Garrett. 1968. "The Tragedy of the Commons." *Science* 162:1243-1248.

Harrington, Christine B. and Z. Umut Turem. 2006. "Accounting for Accountability in Neoliberal Regimes," in *Public Accountability: Designs, Dilemmas and Experiences*. MW Dowdle, ed. New York: Cambridge University Press.

Hart, H.L.A. 1994. *The Concept of Law*. 2nd ed. New York: Oxford University Press.

Hiley, David R., James F. Bohman, and Richard Shusterman, eds. 1991. *The Interpretive Turn*. Ithaca: Cornell University Press.

Hitchcock, Michael B. 1998. "*Suitum v. Tahoe Regional Planning Agency*: Applying the Takings Ripeness Rule to Land Use Regulations and Transferable Development Rights." *Golden Gate University Law Review*, 28: 87.

Hof, William M. 2002. "Trying to Halt the Procedural Merry-Go-Round: The Ripeness of Regulatory Takings Claims After *Palazzolo v. Rhode Island*." *St. Louis Law Journal*, 46: 833.

Hudgins, Edward. 2005. "Your Castle No More," *Washington Times*, June 27 at A20.

Hunt, Alan. 1993. *Explorations in Law and Society: Toward a Constitutive Theory of Law*. New York: Routledge, Inc.

Innes, Robert, et al. 1998. *Takings, Compensation and Endangered Species Protection on Private Lands*, 12 J.Econ. Persp. 35.

Jacobs, Harvey M., and Brian W. Ohm. 1995. "Statutory Takings Legislation: The National Context, the Wisconsin and Minnesota Proposals." *Wisconsin Environmental Law Journal*, 2: 173.

Johnson, Jenny. 2006. "Environmentalists fight to save 'species over people' law that infuriates land developers." *Financial Times*, April 21.

Johnson, Lise. 2004. "After Tahoe-Sierra, One Thing is Clearer: There is Still a Fundamental Lack of Clarity." *Arizona Law Review*, 46: 353.

Kagan, Robert A. 2004. "American Courts and the Policy Dialogue: The Role of Adversarial Legalism." *Making Policy, Making Law: An Interbranch Perspective*. Mark C. Miller and Jeb Barnes, eds. Washington, D.C.: Georgetown University Press.

Kellert, Stephen R. 1996. *The Value of Life: Biological Diversity and Human Society*, Washington, D.C.: Island Press.

Kendall, Douglas T., and Charles P. Lord. 1998. "The Takings Project: A Critical Analysis and Assessment of the Progress So Far." *Boston College Environmental Affairs Law Review*, 25: 509.

Kennedy, Duncan. 1976. "Form and Substance in Private Law Adjudication." *Harvard Law Review*, 89: 1685.

Kmiec, Douglas W., and Katherine Kmiec Turner. 2005. "Property Lost: The Takings Clause in the 2004 Term." *Preview of U.S. Supreme Court Cases*, 8: 471.

Kornhauser, Lewis A. 2005. "Economic Rationality in the Analysis of Legal Rules and Institutions." *Philosophy of Law and Legal Theory*. Martin P. Golding & William A. Edmundson, eds. Malden: Blackwell Publishing.

Kostyack, John. 2001. "*NWF v. Babbitt*: Victory for Smart Growth and Imperiled Wildlife," *Environmental Law Report*, 31: 10712.

Kronman, Anthony T. 1993. *The Lost Lawyer: Failing Ideals of the Legal Profession*. Cambridge: The Belknap Press of Harvard University Press.

Kupiec, John A. 2008. "Returning to Principles of 'Fairness and Justice': The Role of Investment-Backed Expectations in Total Regulatory Taking Claims." *Boston College Law Review*, 49: 865.

"Land Use and Endangered Species Insurance." 2005. *California Insurance Law & Litigation Alert*, November 30.

Lazarus, Richard J. 1993. "Putting the Correct 'Spin' on *Lucas*." *Stanford Law Review*, 45: 1411.

Maltzman, Forrest, et al. 1999. "Strategy and Judicial Choice: New Institutional Approaches to Supreme Court Decision-Making." *Supreme Court Decision-Making*. Chicago: University of Chicago Press.

Marzulla, Roger J., and Nancie G. Marzulla. 1991. "Regulatory Takings in the United States Claims Court: Adjusting the Burdens That in Fairness and Equity Ought to be Borne by Society as a Whole." *Catholic University Law Review*, 40, 549.

McCann, Michael W. 1994. *Rights at Work: Pay Equity Reform and the Politics of Legal Mobilization.* Chicago: University of Chicago Press.

McCay, Bonnie J. 1998. *Oyster Wars and the Public Trust: Property, Law, and Ecology in New Jersey History.* Tucson: University of Arizona Press.

_________. 2002. "Emergence of Institutions for the Commons: Contexts, Situations, and Events." *The Drama of the Commons.* Ostrom, Elinor, et al., eds. Washington, D.C.: National Academy Press.

Melnick, R. Shep. 1983. *Regulation and the Courts: The Case of the Clean Air Act.* Washington, D.C.: The Brookings Institution.

_________. 2004. "Courts and Agencies." *Making Policy, Making Law: An Interbranch Perspective.* Mark C. Miller and Jeb Barnes, eds. Washington, D.C.: Georgetown University Press.

Meltz, Robert. 2007. "Takings Law Today: A Primer for the Perplexed." *Ecology Law Quarterly*, 34: 307.

Merry, Sally Engle. 1988. "Legal Pluralism." *Law and Society Review*, 22:5.

Michelman, Frank. 1967. "Property, Utility, and Fairness: Comments on the Ethical Foundations of 'Just Compensation' Law." *Harvard Law Review*, 80: 1165.

Mihaly, Marc B. 2007. "Living in the Past: The *Kelo* Court and Public-Private Economic Redevelopment." *Ecology Law Quarterly*, 34: 1.

Mixon, John, and Justin Waggoner. 1998. "The Role of Variances in Determining Ripeness in Takings Claims Under Zoning Ordinances and Subdivision Regulations of Texas Municipalities." *St. Mary's Law Journal*, 29: 765.

Mohr, Lawrence B. 1976. "Organizations, Decisions, and Courts." *Law and Society Review*. 10: 621-642.

Montesquieu, Charles de Secondat, Baron de. 2002. *The Spirit of Laws*. Amherst: Prometheus Books.

Moore, Erin P. 1993. "Gender, Power, and Legal Pluralism: Rajasthan, India." *American Ethnologist*, Vol. 20, No. 3. (Aug.).

Moore, Sally Falk. 2005. "Certainties Undone: Fifty Turbulent Years of Legal Anthropology, 1949-1999," Huxley Memorial Lecture, *Journal of the Royal Anthropological Institute* 7(1) (2001). Cited from excerpts in Moore, Sally Falk, ed. *Law and Anthropology*. Malden: Blackwell Publishing.

__________, ed. 2005. *Law and Anthropology*. Malden: Blackwell Publishing Ltd.

Murphy, Walter F. 1970. *Elements of Judicial Strategy*. Chicago: University of Chicago Press.

Nakamura, Robert T., and Thomas W. Church. 2003. *Taming Regulation: Superfund and the Challenges of Regulatory Reform*. Washington, D.C.: Brookings Institution Press.

Nedelsky, Jennifer. 1990. *Private Property and the Limits of American Constitutionalism: The Madisonian Framework and Its Legacy*. Chicago: University of Chicago Press.

"N.H. Town Votes on Justice Souter's House," Associated Press, March 14, 2006.

Nichol, Gene R., Jr. 1987. "Ripeness and the Constitution." *University of Chicago Law Review*, 54: 153.

Nyden, Paul. 1987. "Collapsing Mine Land Still Takes Toll in Homes." *The Charleston Gazette*. Jan. 11. p. 1B.

O'Connor, Karen. 1992. "The Effects of the Thomas Appointment to the Supreme Court." *PS: Political Science and Politics*. Vol. 25, No. 3.

Odendahl, Teresa and Aileen M. Shaw. 2002. "Interviewing Elites," in *Handbook of Interview Research: Context and Method*. J.F. Gubrium and J.A. Holstein, eds. Thousand Oaks: Sage Publications.

Office of the Property Rights Ombudsman. State of Utah. http://propertyrights.utah.gov.

O'Leary, Rosemary. 2006. "Environmental Policy in the Courts." *Environmental Policy: New Directions for the Twenty-First Century*, 6th ed. Norman J. Vig and Michael E. Kraft, eds. Washington, D.C.: CQ Press.

Ostrom, Elinor. 1990. *Governing the Commons: The Evolution of Institutions for Collective Action*. New York: Cambridge University Press.

Pandolfi, Terri. 1989. "Putting the Cart Before the Horse: Just Compensation for Regulatory Takings in *First English Evangelical Lutheran Church v. County of Los Angeles*." *Brooklyn Law Review*, 54: 1413.

Parenteau, Patrick A. 2002. "Unreasonable Expectations: Why Palazzolo Has No Right to Turn a Silk Purse Into a Sow's Ear," *Boston College Environmental Affairs Law Review*, 30: 101.

Pashukanis, Evgeny B. 2002. *The General Theory of Law and Marxism*. New Brunswick: Transaction Publishers.

Perry, H.W., Jr. 1991. *Deciding to Decide*. Cambridge: Harvard University Press.

Peterson, Andrea L. 1989. *The Takings Clause: In Search of Underlying Principles, Part I—A Critique of Current Takings Clause Doctrine, California Law Review*, 77: 1301.

Peterson, Shannon. 2002. *Acting for Endangered Species: The Statutory Ark*. Lawrence: University of Kansas Press.

Plater, Zygmunt J.B., et al. 1998. *Environmental Law and Policy: Nature, Law, and Society*. 2nd ed. St. Paul: West Publishing Co.

Posner, Richard A. 1986. *Economic Analysis of Law*, 3rd ed. Boston: Little, Brown and Company.

Power, Garrett. 2009. "Regulatory Takings: A Chronicle of the Construction of a Constitutional Concept." *BYU Journal of Public Law*, 23: 221.

Protos, Jill Dickey. 1993. "*Lucas v. South Carolina Coastal Council*: A Tremor on the Regulatory Takings Richter Scale." *Case Western Reserve Law Review*, 43: 651.

Rasband, James, James Salzman, and Mark Squillace. 2004. *Natural Resources Law and Policy*. New York: Foundation Press.

Ratner, Steven R. 2008. "Regulatory Takings in Institutional Context: Beyond the Fear of Fragmented International Law." *The American Journal of International Law*. Vol. 102, No. 3 (July). pp. 475-528.

Rohde, David W., and Harold J. Spaeth. 1976. *Supreme Court Decision Making*. San Francisco: W. H. Freeman Press.

Rose, Carol M. 1996. "Propter Honoris Respectum: Property as the Keystone Right?" *Notre Dame Law Review*, 71: 329.

__________. 2002. "Common Property, Regulatory Property, and Environmental Protection: Comparing Community-Based Management to Tradable Environmental Allowances." *The Drama of the Commons*. Ostrom, Elinor, et al., eds. Washington, D.C.: National Academy Press.

Rosenberg, Gerald N. 1991. *The Hollow Hope: Can Courts Bring About Social Change?* Chicago: University of Chicago Press.

Rossi, Jim. 2005. *Regulatory Bargaining and Public Law*. New York: Cambridge University Press.

Sabath, Mark E. 2004. "The Perils of the Property Rights Initiative: Taking Stock of Nevada County's Measure D." *Harvard Environmental Law Review*, 28: 249.

Saunders, Debra J. 2005. "Your Home Could Be Pfizer's Castle." *San Francisco Chronicle*, June 30. B9.

Sax, Joseph L. 1964. "Takings and the Police Power." *Yale Law Journal*, 74: 36.

_________. 1996. "Takings Legislation: Where it Stands and What is Next." *Ecology Law Quarterly*, 23: 509.

_________. 1999. *Playing Darts with a Rembrandt: Public and Private Rights in Cultural Treasures*. Ann Arbor: University of Michigan Press.

_________. 2005. "Why America has a Property Rights Movement." *University of Illinois Law Review*, 2005: 513.

Scheberle, Denise. 2004. *Federalism and Environmental Policy: Trust and the Politics of Implementation*, 2nd ed. Washington, D.C.: Georgetown University Press.

Scheingold, Stuart A. 1974. *The Politics of Rights: Lawyers, Public Policy and Political Change.* New Haven: Yale University Press.

Schorr, David B. 2005. "Appropriation as Agrarianism: Distributive Justice in the Creation of Property Rights." *Ecology Law Quarterly*, 32: 3.

Schultz, D. 2010. "Courts Matter: The Supreme Court, Social Change, and the Mobilization of Property Rights Interests," in *Property Rights and Neo-Liberalism: Cultural Demands and Legal Actions*. Ashgate Publishing. Forthcoming.

Segal, Jeffrey A., and Harold J. Spaeth. 1993. *The Supreme Court and the Attitudinal Model.* New York: Cambridge University Press.

Seidman, I.E. 1991. *Interviewing as Qualitative Research: A Guide for Researchers in Education and the Social Sciences*. New York: Teachers College Press.

Singer, Joseph William. 2000. *Entitlement: The Paradoxes of Property*. New Haven: Yale University Press.

Smith, Matthew B. 1994. "Defining Property in the Post-Lucas World." *University of Illinois Law Review*, 1994: 443.

Smith, Rogers M. 1988. "Political Jurisprudence, The 'New Institutionalism,' and the Future of Public Law." *The American Political Science Review*, Vol. 82, No. 1.

Somit, Albert, and Joseph Tanenhaus. 1967. *The Development of Political Science*. Boston: Allyn and Bacon.

Sparrow, Malcolm K. 2000. *The Regulatory Craft: Controlling Risks, Solving Problems, and Managing Compliance*. Washington, D.C.: Brookings Institution Press.

Statement of Craig Manson, Assistant Secretary of the Interior for Fish, Wildlife and Parks. http://www.fws.gov/midwest/wolf/esa-status/manson_stm_dec05.htm. Dec. 16, 2005.

Sterk, Stewart E. 2004. "The Federalist Dimension of Regulatory Takings Jurisprudence." *Yale Law Journal*, 114: 203.

Strachan, Gordon C., and Adam Strachan. 2002. "The Ripeness Doctrine in Regulatory Takings Litigation." *Journal of Land Resources and Environmental Law*, 22: 19.

Sunkin, Maurice. 2004. "Conceptual Issues in Researching the Impact of Judicial Review on Government Bureaucracies." *Judicial Review and Bureaucratic Impact: International and Interdisciplinary Perspectives*. Marc Hertogh and Simon Halliday, eds. New York: Cambridge University Press.

Teske, Paul. 1991. "Interests and Institutions in State Regulation." *American Journal of Political Science*. Vol. 35, No. 1. (Feb.).

Thompson, Barton H. 2000. "Tragically Difficult: The Obstacles to Governing the Commons." 30 *Environmental Law*, 30: 241.

Townsend, R., and J.A. Wilson. 1987. "An Economic View of the Commons." *The Question of the Commons*. Bonnie J. McCay and J.M. Acheson, eds. Tucson: University of Arizona Press.

Treanor, William Michael. 1995. "The Original Understanding of the Takings Clause and the Political Process." *Columbia Law Review*, 95: 782.

Trigaux, Robert. 2005. "Your Home Could be Up for Grabs," *St. Petersburg Times*, June 24, at D1.

Unger, Roberto Mangabeira. 1976. *Law in Modern Society: Toward a Criticism of Social Theory*. New York: The Free Press.

_________. 1983. *The Critical Legal Studies Movement.* Cambridge: Harvard University Press.

United States Fish and Wildlife Service. Conservation Plans and Agreements Database.

Van Loh, Sara D. 2004. "The Latest and Greatest Commerce Clause Challenges to the Endangered Species Act: *Rancho Viejo* and *GDF Realty*," *Ecology Law Quarterly*, 31: 459.

CASES AND LAWS

Abbott Laboratories v. Gardner, 387 U.S. 136 (1967)

Agins v. Tiburon, 24 Cal. 3d 266 (1979)

Agins v. Tiburon, 447 U.S. 255 (1980)

Aloisi v. United States, 85 Fed. Cl. 84 (2008)

Apollo Fuels, Inc. v. United States, 54 Fed. Cl. 717 (2002)

Apollo Fuels, Inc. v. United States, 381 F.3d 1338 (2004)

Armstrong v. United States, 364 U.S. 40, 49 (1960)

Babbitt v. Sweet Home Chapter of Community for a Great Oregon, 515 U.S. 687 (1995)

Benchmark Resources Corporation v. United States, 74 Fed. Cl. 458 (2006).

Berman v. Parker, 348 U.S. 26 (1954)

Boise Cascade Corp. v. United States, 296 F.3d 1339 (2002)

Brief of the Natural Heritage Institute & the Environmental Law Foundation as Amici Curiae Supporting Defendants at 31, *Tulare Lake*, 49 Fed. Cl. 313 (No. 98-101L)

Cane Tennessee, Inc. & Colten, Inc. v. United States, 54 Fed. Cl. 100, 106-108 (2002)

Cane Tennessee, Inc. & Colten, Inc. v. United States, 57 Fed. Cl. 115 (2003)

Casitas Municipal Water District v. United States, 543 F.3d 1276 (2008)

Catron County Board of Commissioners v. U.S. Fish and Wildlife Service, 75 F.3d 1429 (1996)

Center for Biological Diversity v. Norton, 254 F.3d 833 (2001)

Chancellor Manor v. United States, 331 F.3d 891 (2003)

Christy v. Hodel, 857 F.2d 1324 (1988)

Coffin v. Left Hand Ditch Co., 6 Colo. 443 (1882)

Concrete Pipe and Products of California v. Construction Laborers Pension Trust for Southern California, 508 U.S. 602 (1993)
Connecticut General Statute § 8-186
Curtin v. Benson, 222 U.S. 78 (1911)
Decision. Petition to Designate Certain Lands in the Rock Creek Watershed, Tennessee as Unsuitable for Surface Coal Mining Operations. Jed D. Christensen, Director, Office of Surface Mining Reclamation and Enforcement. March 24, 1987. 50 Fed. Reg. 10174, March 30, 1987.
Defenders of Wildlife v. Babbitt, 130 F.Supp.2d 121 (2001)
Defenders of Wildlife v. Norton, 258 F.3d 1136 (2001)
Del Monte Dunes v. Monterey, 920 F.2d 1496 (1990)
Dolan v. City of Tigard, 512 U.S. 374, 390 (1994)
Eastern Minerals International, Inc. v. United States, 36 Fed. Cl. 541 (1996)
Endangered Species Act, 16 U.S.C. § 1531 (1973)
Fallbrook Irrigation Dist. v. Bradley, 164 U.S. 112 (1896)
First English Lutheran Church v. Los Angeles County, 482 U.S. 304 (1987)
Florida Rock Industries v. United States, 45 Fed. Cl. 21 (1999)
Friends of Endangered Species v. Jantzen, 760 F.2d 976 (1985)
GDF Realty Investments, Ltd. v. Norton, 236 F.3d 622 (5th Cir. 2003)
Geer v. Connecticut, 161 U.S. 519 (1896)
Gibbs v. Babbitt, 214 F.3d 483 (4th Cir. 2000)
Hawai'i Housing Authority v. Midkiff, 467 U.S. 229 (1984)
Hodel v. Virginia Surface Mining & Reclamation Ass'n, 452 U.S. 264 (1981)
Iowa Coal Mining Co. v. Monroe County, 494 N.W.2d 664 (Iowa S.C. 1993)
Kaiser Aetna v. U.S., 444 U.S. 164 (1979)
Kelo v. City of New London, 545 U.S. 469 (2005)
Keystone Bituminous Coal Assn. v. DeBenedictus, 480 U.S. 470 (1987)
Klamath Irrigation District v. United States, 67 Fed. Cl. 504 (2005)
Lingle v. Chevron, U.S.A., 125 S.Ct. 2074 (2005)
Loggerhead Turtle v. County Council of Volusia County, Florida, 120 F.Supp.2d 1005 (2000)
Lopez, United States v., 514 U.S. 549 (1995)
Loretto v. Teleprompter Manhattan CATV Corp., 458 U.S. 419 (1982)

Lucas v. South Carolina Coastal Council, 505 U.S. 1003 (1992)
M&J Coal Company v. United States, 30 Fed. Cl. 360 (1994)
M&J Coal Company v. United States, 47 F.3d 1148 (1995)
MacDonald, Sommer & Frates v. Yolo County, 477 U.S. 340 (1986)
Machipongo Land and Coal Co., Inc. v. Commonwealth, 719 A.2d 19 (Pa. Cmwlth. 1998)
Machipongo Land and Coal Co., Inc. v. Commonwealth, 799 A.2d 751, 760 (Pa. S.C. 2002)
Martin v. Waddell, 41 U.S. 367 (1842)
McCready v. Virginia, 94 U.S. 391 (1877)
Morris v. United States, 392 F.3d 1372 (2004)
Mountain States Legal Foundation v. Hodel, 799 F.2d 1423 (1986).
Mugler v. Kansas, 123 U.S. 623 (1887)
National Ass'n of Home Builders v. Babbitt, 130 F.3d 1041 (D.C. Cir. 1997)
National Wildlife Federation v. Babbitt, 128 F.Supp.2d 1274 (2000)
Natural Resources Commission v. AMAX, 638 N.E.2d 418 (Ind. S.C. 1994)
Nebraska v. Rural Electrification Admin., 12 Env't Rep. Cas (BNA) 1156 (1978)
New Mexico Cattle Growers Association v. U.S. Fish and Wildlife Service, 248 F.3d 1277 (2001)
Nollan v. California Coastal Comm'n, 483 U.S. 825 (1987)
Palazzolo v. Rhode Island, 533 U.S. 606, 627 (2001)
Penn Central Transportation Co. v. New York City, 438 U.S. 104 (1978)
Pennell v. City of San Jose, 485 U.S. 1 (1988)
Pennsylvania Coal v. Mahon, 260 U.S. 393 (1922)
Poletown Neighborhood Council v. City of Detroit, 410 Mich. 616 (1981)
Presault v. Interstate Commerce Commission, 494 U.S. 1 (1990)
Rancho Viejo v. Norton, 323 F.3d 1062 (D.C. Cir. 2003)
Rith Energy, Inc. v. United States, 44 Fed. Cl. 108 (1999)
Rith Energy, Inc. v. United States, 247 F.3d 1355 (2001)
Riverside Bayview Homes, United States v., 474 U.S. 121 (1985)
R.T.G. v. Ohio, 98 Ohio St. 3d 1 (Oh S.C. 2002)
Ruckelshaus v. Monsanto Co., 467 U.S. 986 (1984)
San Diego Gas & Electric Company v. San Diego, 450 U.S. 621 (1981)

Schooner Harbor Ventures v. United States, 569 F.3d 1359 (2009)
Seiber v. United States, 53 Fed. Cl. 570 (2002)
Sierra Club v. Babbitt, 15 F.Supp.2d 1274 (1998)
Solid Waste Agency of Northern Cook County v. Army Corps of Engineers, 531 U.S. 159 (2001)
St. Louis v. Stern, 3 Mo. App 48, 53 (1876)
Suitum v. Tahoe Regional Planning Agency, 520 U.S. 725 (1997)
Surface Mining Control and Reclamation Act, 30 U.S.C. § 1201 (1977)
Tahoe-Sierra Preservation Council v. Tahoe Regional Planning Agency, 535 U.S. 302 (2002)
The Stearns Co., Ltd. v. United States, 53 Fed. Cl. 446 (2002)
The Stearns Company, Ltd. v. United States, 396 F.3d 1354 (2005)
Thomas v. Peterson, 753 F.2d 754 (1985)
Tulare Lake Basin Water District v. United States, 49 Fed. Cl. 313 (2001)
TVA v. Hill, 437 U.S. 153 (1978)
Ward v. Harding, 860 S.W.2d 280 (Ky S.C. 1993)
Whitney Benefits, Inc. v. United States, 18 Cl. Ct. 394 (1989)
Whitney Benefits, Inc. v. United States, 926 F.2d 1169 (1991)
Williamson County Planning Comm'n v. Hamilton Bank, 473 U.S. 172 (1985)
Wyatt v. United States, 271 F.3d 1090 (2001)

Index

CPSIA information can be obtained at www.ICGtesting.com
Printed in the USA
BVOW030413110713

325118BV00003B/10/P

9 781593 324001